THE DETERMINANTS OF ARAB
ECONOMIC DEVELOPMENT

THE DETERMINANTS OF ARAB ECONOMIC DEVELOPMENT

Yusif A. Sayigh

ST MARTIN'S PRESS   NEW YORK

Copyright © 1978 Yusif A. Sayigh

All rights reserved. For information write:
St. Martin's Press, Inc., 175 Fifth Avenue, New York, N.Y. 10010
Printed in Great Britain
Library of Congress Catalog Card Number: 77-3846
First published in the United States of America in 1978

Library of Congress Cataloging in Publication Data

Sayigh, Yusif.
    The Determinants of Arab economic development.

    1. Arab countries – Economic policy. 2. Arab countries – Economic
conditions. 3. Economic development. I. Title.
HC498.S28   338.9'00917'4927   77-3846
ISBN 0-312-19583-4

Printed and bound in Great Britain by Biddles Ltd, Guildford, Surrey

Contents

Acknowledgements

I would like to record my enormous debt to the Kuwait Fund for Arab Economic Development which gave me a generous grant to enable me to take long leave from the American University of Beirut, on whose faculty I served at the time, in order to undertake the research, travel, and writing called for by the two volumes of this study, and to finance the research and secretarial assistance required.* While my debt to the Board of Directors of the Fund is heavy, it is particularly so to Mr. Abdul-Latif Al-Hamad, the Director-General of the Fund, for his appreciation of the importance of the study and his sympathetic understanding when the study took much longer to complete than originally planned.

It is to be stressed, in this connection, that the views and judgements made, and there are many, are mine. The Management of the Fund is not to blame for any of these. On the contrary, it is to be thanked for allowing me the freedom to express my views. I trust I have not abused of this privilege, but have used it responsibly, and hope that the Fund will not in any way have reason to regret either the award of the grant, or the liberty it accorded me in expressing myself, whether in the survey or analysis undertaken, in the judgements made, or in the conclusions reached.

The manuscript was read by some of the economists serving on the staff of the Fund. As a result, I have benefited from a number of comments and suggestions made. While expressing my gratitude to those who took the trouble to read the manuscript, I would like to extend my apologies for not accepting all the comments and suggestions offered. It may be an author's failing to resort to his own judgement in the final analysis, but this is at the same time a privilege that he enjoys.

It is my pleasure likewise to thank the very large number of persons in the twelve countries covered — about 350 in all — whom I interviewed for the study in the course of my field work, and who gave me the benefit of their wisdom and experience, and the many who supplied me with published reports, studies, and statistics of relevance to my research. To all of these, who must remain unnamed, I extend my gratitude and appreciation. I hope they will feel that I have made proper use of the help they accorded me, and that the study reflects their opinions correctly and responsibly.

Finally, I would like to record my warm thanks to Mrs Sana' Najjar Izzeddin who alone typed and re-typed the very long manuscript, and organised the many tables, always with cheer, precision, and perfect cooperativeness. Without her the task would have been much more demanding and less manageable.

Beirut, 31st January, 1977   Y.A.S.

*A companion volume to the present one appears simultaneously under the title *The Economies of the Arab World*.

1 Development and its Determinants: some Conceptual and Methodological Issues

The present volume is designed to provide scope for the identification of the major determinants, or the prime movers, of development in the Arab world, and for the exploration of the manner and reach of their operation.[1] To provide a frame of reference and a measuring rod for this objective, an examination of the concept of development is first undertaken. There would be no clear purpose to the enquiry if *the* development whose determinants were to be explored was not first defined, even if operationally. Finally, this volume serves as a sort of crystal ball (albeit one using analysis as a basis) in the final chapter, through which an assessment of the potential for development of each country, and of the Arab region as a whole, is attempted.

More specifically, the present chapter is meant to provide focus for five lines of vision. It is, *first*, to serve as intellectual base for the study as a whole, in its two volumes, but more particularly for the present volume. As such, it sets out to explain the nature of development and to provide some precision in the differentiation between this concept on the one hand, and growth, industrialisation and modernisation on the other hand. While so doing, it will suggest the scope of these concepts and steer thought away from a simplistic attitude to them by identifying and interrelating the various aspects of the concepts in the economic as well as the non-economic realms.

Indeed, while emphasis is on the final analytical-cum-operational purpose of the whole enquiry, the reader's awareness is at the same time heightened of the social, cultural, and even philosophical issues that are related to or intertwined with development. Furthermore, as an intellectual base for the two volumes, and more so for the present volume, the chapter provides perspective within the depth of which the institutions, the forces, the determinants and the mechanisms of development can be better understood, designed or manipulated — always within the context of the Arab world. And finally, it is hoped that through the intellectual interaction attempted in the chapter, it will become possible to differentiate between development as a state, and as a process. The differentiation is significant if only because it reveals the difference between a descriptive, static and an analytical, dynamic approach to development.

It might be objected that this first purpose of the present chapter, namely, to be an intellectual base for the study as a whole, ought to have been served by the Introduction, which formed the first chapter of Volume I, the companion volume. This argument gains strength from the fact that the record of the twelve countries covered in the study (and of the region as a whole) with respect to development achieved could not be set down and evaluated without 'development' having first been defined. This is true. But, to circumvent the objection, we set out in the Introduction to provide a provisional, operational definition of development which may not have been rigorous but hopefully was adequate, and we also differentiated development from associated concepts sufficiently for the purpose of Volume I. In any case, the reader who wanted a deeper analysis of the concept was invited in the Introduction to turn to the present chapter before proceeding with the rest of Volume I.

In the *second* place, the present chapter sets out to help the reader appreciate the diversity that characterises contemporary thinking about development and the multiplicity of avenues that can lead to development. In other words, the three main contemporary models, or interpretive systems, of development are compared with regard to specific measuring rods, but essentially with regard to the one underlying criterion of their effectiveness and credibility as engines (or at least frameworks) of development.

Beyond this point, the chapter becomes a little more specific and area-oriented, though it continues to present a conceptual framework and intellectual base for the whole study. Thus, in the *third* place, the chapter identifies the major determinants of development in the Arab context, and it identifies and examines a set of the most important institutions and forces through which some of the determinants operate in the Arab region.

The *fourth* line of vision for which the chapter provides focus is the attempt to arrange the determinants and institutions and forces into some order of causality, that is, as a system which could conceivably explain development (or failure of development to occur). This last purpose is served with flexibility, inasmuch as the process of development may take a different path in one country as against another, and the operation of the determinants may well vary in intensity and timing from one country to another. Nevertheless, as many propositions applicable to the whole region as possible are formulated.

The *fifth* and final object that the chapter sets out to serve is to identify the major issues of development in the Arab world. Not all or even most of these are peculiar to the region, since the Third World as a whole shares more or less the same experience with respect to the leading issues and option-problems in development. Yet it is useful to underline these issues, options or controversies, and in so doing indicate their relevance to the course of development and the developmental performance of the Arab countries and the region as a whole.

1. CLARIFYING CONCEPTIONS: DEVELOPMENT VERSUS GROWTH, INDUSTRIALISATION AND MODERNISATION

In the early fifties, when the literature on development was still a trickle and not the torrent it now is, the terms 'growth' and 'development' were on the whole used interchangeably. Attempts to differentiate between the two were rare,[2] although a distinction had already been made before World War One by Schumpeter.[3] It is now accepted that the concept of growth should be restricted to the characterisation of change in national product (or national product per head) in real terms, within the 'given' institutions and non-economic factors relevant to growth — within the 'circular flow', to use Schumpeter's terms. However, development is taken to mean growth of a magnitude or speed, of a content and comprehensiveness, and in directions that could not have taken place without important changes having occurred, or occurring, in socio-cultural, political and technological institutions, structures and forces — in addition to significant changes in the economic sphere proper.

This understanding of development immediately reveals the breadth of the concept and the richness of the content of development, which embraces economic as well as non-economic change in society. Such richness becomes all the more obvious as the analyst identifies and examines in greater detail the various socio-cultural, political and technological forces and institutions of relevance. These will be found to be many in number, complex in structure, baffling in operation, and above all extremely elusive and mysterious in the timing, nature and logic of their interrelation and interaction.

This writer is not fully satisfied with this kind of definition — comprehensive and far-reaching as it is — and insists that development means more than substantial economic growth associated with (or preceded by, or predicated on) a noticeable change in certain significant non-economic variables.[4] In addition to all this, a number of conditions or characterisations must be satisfied before development can be said to take place. *First*, the growth should be the outcome of the performance largely of the society itself, not of foreign islands of capital, entrepreneurship and technology, that is, of a major foreign industry or activity such as tin-mining, large plantations, or a petroleum sector virtually totally managed by a foreign concessionary company. Even if the activity of these alien economic 'islands' were to result in a very high income per head of the population, the economy would still be classified as underdeveloped if the economic performance of the population at large were poor and produced a low income in the non-tin, non-plantation or non-oil sectors. The characterisation of the economy as developed could only be made if the *national* economy itself had reached, or was heading towards, an improved level of action and productivity, and this level could then account for the high national product per head.

A closely related *second* condition is that 'the political and social environment should be able to provide the economy with many of the ideas, knowledge, attitudes, and institutions essential to efficient functioning'.[5] *Thirdly*, the preceding two conditions must make possible a *sustained* improved rate of growth. Thus, the 'technological and other change should continue in considerable measure, in order to enable the economy to sustain the rise in the rate of growth, or to sustain the rate itself if it has reached a high level.'[6] Otherwise, short-lived windfalls that reflect themselves for a brief duration in steeply rising national product *per capita* would be mistaken for real development.

In the *fourth* place, the rising income should not merely mean a concrete improvement per head, in the mechanistic sense of a higher arithmetic mean, but it should also be associated with a more equitable distribution of income. Thus, the marked increases in productivity and production (that reflect an improved performance) must be accompanied or shortly followed by a large measure of distributive justice, in such a manner that those who make a major contribution to the increase in the national product should share in the fruits of their mental and manual effort.

In this context, development should be oriented to the needs of the masses. This condition is critical. It is made all the more necessary in the light of the mechanistic, statistical approach to development, whereby cardinal global objectives are almost everywhere set for development strategies as well as plans and policies. These objectives are usually presented as reference points against which performance is measured, with the paradoxical results frequently encountered where very commendable rates of growth are reported and praised but where the mass of the people feel the blessing of the 'development' only marginally. In the context of this paradox even the casual observer often sees enormous buildings, shining new factories, colossal airports and impressive sports stadiums alongside poor peasants and miserably equipped urban dwellers pitifully in need of the basic amenities of life, to say nothing of the equally objectionable paradox of immense personal riches alongside the abyss of mass poverty. In brief, this contrast is the outcome of satisfaction with mechanistic, statistical development which neglects, and remains silent about, the real human beings in the urban slums and destitute countryside.

Concern for distributive justice does not arise solely from compassionate, humanistic motives; it is also based on hard-headed realism. For, unless the mass of the people who make the major contribution to production obtain an equitable share of the product in return, production will suffer in the long run. The socio-political conditions of the eighteenth and nineteenth centuries where labour could be forced to work hard and be grossly underpaid are much less palatable today.

The *fifth* condition insists that the improved performance, in the words used in the Introduction in Volume I,

> be accompanied by wide economic participation by the population, and that the social and political decisions involved in the design of development strategies and policies and in the allocation and use of development resources must be themselves also accompanied by wide social and political participation by the population.

Indeed, it is this writer's conviction that deep socio-economic transformation of developmental dimensions cannot occur without commensurate political transformation, and, specifically, without a high degree of popular and institutional participation. This must be embodied in the dialogue preceding socio-economic decisions and in their ultimate formulation, implementation and re-evaluation, as in the final distribution of the widespread benefit from these decisions.

It is essential at this point to emphasise what has probably become evident by implication: that though this writer's understanding of the issue involves a large measure of subjectivity, in fact the conditions that have social content are justifiable in terms of objective economic ends. Another word is due with respect to the normative tone of the discussion. The approach adopted here introduces values openly, instead of surreptitiously or, what is worse, ignoring them altogether as being 'not the subject matter of economics'. It would not be improper to repeat what was stated in the first chapter of Volume I, that the examination of the underdevelopment and development of societies and real human beings cannot remain a value-free matter in a world of poverty, disease, misery, social injustice and economic insecurity. Nevertheless, the correction of these social and economic ailments, which is motivated by social and humanistic concern, should be undertaken through well-grounded, sound economic policies, ones which can pass the rigorous tests of 'good economics'.

In the *sixth* place, development in the context of Third World countries, particularly those characterised by a heavy population pressure on resources and by a large volume of unemployment and underemployment like much of the Arab world, ought to aim at absorbing much of the under-use of manpower. Raising the level of employment must be treated as a very high priority in the formulation of development strategies and plans, and in the laying down of investment criteria. The point must be underlined owing to the facile attitude in most developing countries towards the choice of technology. Often the guiding principle is the adoption of the most advanced, labour-saving techniques and machines. At times this reaches the absurd point of opting for automation while there are hundreds of thousands of unemployed, able-bodied men milling around city streets or lazing in the sun in the countryside.

What makes the contrast more painful is the under-utilisation of women in the labour supply, and frequently even the failure to count them in this supply. Under the circumstances, and because of social, welfare considerations, it is of prime urgency and importance to treat the vast increase in employment as a condition of high priority if development is to be meaningful for the masses. And no development is worth the name if it is not truly and substantively need-oriented and mass-oriented.

The *seventh* and final condition is that emphasis should be placed on self-reliance in the drive for development. This should reflect itself in several ways: in the attempt to mobilise as much of the investment resources domestically as possible; in the adaptation of technology and the various factor mixes in production to local endowments and needs; in the ingathering of 'drained' high-level manpower; in the formulation of development strategies, plans and policies in the light of national and regional conditions and priorities, instead of the uncritical adoption of alien development models or the undiscriminating belief in the universality of some stage sequence simply because it suits the history of the West or satisfactorily describes its experience; in the caution taken lest the 'transfer of technology' also embody a projection of control by the advanced over the developing countries, inasmuch as the possession of advanced technology confers cultural and political power; and in the effort to rid the various countries of the oppresive state of dependence in which they have lived for centuries. This dependence on Western colonial powers has taken technological, economic and cultural, as well as political, form and substance. To insist that Third World countries should free themselves of this dependence is not to eulogise isolationism and autarky, or to preach against international co-operation: it is instead to emphasise co-operation, but to qualify the co-operation by saying that it ought to be based on mutual respect for the rights and interests of the parties concerned, that it should not involve exploitation of the poor and underdeveloped by the rich and advanced, and that it should be accompanied by a drastic effort, to the extent possible, to achieve self-help and self-reliance, on the principle that development can only be profound and durable if it is based on the mobilisation of national resources and energy before outside aid is sought.

It is no doubt obvious to anybody who is familiar with the post-war literature on development that the characterisation of development, and the conditions which, in this writer's view, have to be satisfied for it to be taking place, rarely appear in this fashion in the literature. With few exceptions, notably some of the writings of Joseph J. Spengler, W.W. Rostow, Gunnar Myrdal, Everett E. Hagen, and Irma Adelman and Cynthia Taft Morris,[7] development continues to be seen through a very narrow focus or, where awareness is shown of the need to enlarge the focus to include non-economic factors and manifestations, these are only passingly referred to or merely assumed. But even in some of the cases excepted, the introduction of non-economic consideration remains partial.

These introductory statements are not meant to claim originality for the ideas suggested here, though perhaps it is correct to maintain that our approach is different from the mainstream or even the less orthodox approaches with which the interested reader is familiar. Instead, the main purpose is to underline our insistence on the need for the enlargement of the angle of vision if development is to be understood in its true dimensions. Looked at from such an angle, development emerges as a truly revolutionary process, one which liberates society from many economic, technological and socio-political shackles. This is so both because the factors which bring development about involve the occurrence of drastic change which can be called revolutionary both in its quality and its degree, and because the state of the economy *and* society as a result of this process of change would be notably different from the state preceding the change. The wide reach, depth and significance of the developmental change merit the use of the qualifying adjective 'revolutionary', but they also indicate how difficult and time-consuming the process of development truly is. In part this explains why it is intriguing to explore the determinants which bring about development, and to try to understand the working and interaction of the various determinants, and whether or not all this unfolds inside some system, and if so, how. However, these latter questions will occupy us further down in the chapter.

So far an attempt has been made to differentiate between growth and development. No more will be said about growth, but we will have occasion to refer again to development in several other contexts. For the time being, we will try to distinguish development first from industrialisation, and later from modernisation.

In the late forties and early fifties, a number of works appeared which used the terms 'industrialisation' and 'development' almost interchangeably. In most instances, no explicit statement was made that the two were identical, but this was often implied. The confusion of the two concepts was somewhat understandable, given the strength of feeling that industrialisation was both the key for and the symbol of development, and given the strength of the drive for industrialisation by countries seeking fast development *and* the identification in the minds of political leaders between growth and development. Lastly, industrialisation was the economic symbol of fulfilled independence, a necessary supplement to political independence and maturity.

The identification of the one process with the other is unwarranted, both conceptually and empirically. For development is conceptually much wider than industrialisation, and the forces making for the latter are not necessarily as far-reaching as those making for the former. Furthermore, while industrialisation admittedly occupies a central position in the process and state of development, it cannot be considered the whole process or state. This is true even if we think of industrialisation as tending towards industrialism, in the sense in which Clark Kerr *et al.* use the term in their book *Industrialism and Industrial Man*, to mean a state towards which industrialisation tends to lead where economic rationality, organisation, government-management-labour relations and advanced production technology reach a peak in their historical evolution. Furthermore, empirically, development can be identified without industry being the major sector in the economy; some instances exist in support of this point, such as Denmark and New Zealand. And it can be seen in practice that a large measure of industrialisation could be achieved without development in the sense in which it has been defined above having materialised.

The subtle relationship between industrialisation and development, part convergence, part divergence, ought to be clearly seen and appreciated. This is particularly urgent in view of the facile tendency in development and planning agencies to emphasise speedy industrialisation at the expense of development of the agricultural sector, even though the latter is the unavoidable underpinning for all development and societal structure in most of the developing countries of the world, and even though a mechanistic and simplistic overemphasis of industrialisation might subvert the very foundations that support the building of a healthy and viable industrial sector.

Clear differentiation has another justification. Often speedy industrialisation is viewed as closely related to the socio-economic system prevailing in society. Thus it is often assumed that only in a system where the public sector plays a major economic role and where government exercises a large measure of decision-making in the economy — a measure which cannot be satisfied without public ownership of a large slice of the means of production and without control of a sizeable portion of investment — only in such a system can speedy industrialisation take place. This assertion, though not totally untenable, is essentially based on the assumption that industrialisation requires a certain quality and volume of non-mercantile entrepreneurship which cannot be forthcoming unless the public sector is vested with a substantial proportion of the entrepreneurial function. Again, this justifies the clarification of the distinction between industrialisation and development, both on conceptual and empirical grounds.

A final point to be made in this context is that often the pace of industrialisation is accelerated, and industry comes to occupy a significant place in the sectoral structure of the economy, without much change having taken place, or taking place simultaneously in non-industrial sectors and the other aspects of society's life. This relates to cases where industrialisation is mainly an act of importing factories and industrial processes, and to the operation of this new industrial capability almost in isolation from parallel and far-reaching changes in the rest of the economy, in its institutions, and in social attitudes. This can happen inside the framework of an alien sector or subsector, as well as indigenously.

In either case, but particularly in the former, the industrialisation witnessed would be far from development. And, it ought to be added, although the various sectors interact and influence each other through various and many channels of communication or linkage, both conceivably and practically the linkage may be slow and weak, with the result that the advances made in industrialisation may well leave the rest of the economy lagging behind. Finally, as a qualification to these assertions, it must be remembered that once the process of industrialisation becomes far-reaching and indigenous, and once it is associated with the appropriate changes in attitudes, in government-management-labour structures, and in the understanding of economic cause-effect relationships, and once science and technology have advanced enough to contribute to industrial processes and to machine design, then industrialisation and development must be converging on each other and duality must be diminishing significantly.

The third differentiation to make is probably the most difficult: that between modernisation and development. A discussion of the subtleties of this differentiation will have to take us into a somewhat detailed examination of the form and substantive content of modernisation. The subtlety and elusiveness of the distinction lie mostly in what we view as the fact of the fundamental similarity between the two processes. We cannot conceive of development, defined as broadly as it has been in this chapter, except as incorporating the dynamic forces and the changes that are usually associated with modernisation. Both involve transformation in the scale of values, in socio-cultural and political institutions and forces, in technology and attitude to technological change, that to separate the Siamese twins would require a degree of semantic surgery not commonly possessed or practised.

And yet there are grounds on which the distinction between the two concepts must be attempted. It is probably true that the main difference between them lies in the emphasis on the social content of development which we stated as a condition earlier on. To this must be added a non-substantive difference: that between the social scientists examining and appraising both concepts, and their respective training and predilections.

Regarding the first point, modernisation suffers from 'guilt by association'. The fact that most Western writers describing or analysing modernisation have treated it as a process which is mostly associated and identified with structural, economic and technological changes, and with changes relating to certain attitudes (for instance to time, rationality, and the like), has created the impression that the process is largely value-free, or, more correctly, is laden with values which do not, by themselves, necessarily emphasise humanistic considerations and notions of social justice. Thus, the term is used in the sense that it involves no normative orientation, except the overall one that modernisation is desirable. As a result, many radical social thinkers have acquired resistance to 'modernisation', particularly inasmuch as it has come to be understood as a way of life and of doing things by 'superior', *Western* societies which other societies are urged to emulate. Development, on the other hand, must aim at the pursuit of one's own course and the rejection of imported moulds of thought and models of organisation and operation. This is all the more so, the more self-reliant a society wants to be, and the more concerned it is with the real needs of its masses and their cultural fulfilment. Furthermore, the values imputed to modernisation are not of the same category as those which this writer has set as conditions for development, in insisting that the latter *must* have a social content expressed in concern for the destitute, the ignorant, the economically insecure, and the victims of social injustice. Modernisation *per se,* at least as generally identified and understood, has no such concern.

The second point of difference relates more to the concept-*user* rather than the end-concept used. A sociologist, and a social thinker in general, would probably think and talk in terms of modernisation; a conventional economist would think of development in terms of growth; only a somewhat heretical economist, or one who has been exposed to the ideas world of social thinkers in general would think of development in the terms which have been set down earlier. Naturally, such an economist ends by finding himself not accepted by the sociologists, who consider him insufficiently trained in their field and not sensitised enough to it. He probably also finds himself disowned by many economists, especially those whose medium of expression is highly mathematical, and probably accused of disobeying the rules of the game in introducing value judgements and normative injunctions — if not altogether condemned as a badly trained economist justifying his philistinism by escape into non-economic sanctuaries. But, it is hoped, the economist who feels sharp concern for the real human beings and their socio-economic problems, and who therefore gives development a personal dimension, is at peace with himself and with the subjects of his serious concern, if not with many of his fellow economists.

Owing to the importance of the concept of modernisation in the modern world, and to its closeness to that of development, it would not be irrelevant at this point to ask what, then, is modernisation, and what are its form and substance?[8] The answer attempted is both general, and particular to the Arab world, inasmuch as modernisation has come to mean Westernisation.

Modernisation can be seen in ten types of institution or organisation: the school, the city, the medium of mass communication, the factory, the bank, the corporation, the small (nuclear) family, the representative political organ both at the local level and the national level, the plan and the income tax. These ten institutions do not all exist in each of the Arab countries, but enough of them are developing almost everywhere to justify the conviction that modernisation is taking place, at least outwardly, to begin with.

None of the ten manifestations of modernisation is a totally new phenomenon, if we are willing to stretch our terms. Schools and cities are thousands of years old; the workshop and the craftsmen did in the past, though on a smaller scale and at a less complex level, what the factory does today; the newspaper or radio of today had its forerunner in ancient times in the messenger and the *munadi* (the town-crier); financial houses performing banking functions of a sort have been with us for centuries; the small nuclear family was not unknown in past centuries when the members of the extended family could not get along together or inheritance customs did not necessitate the large family as a unit of production or a mechanism of social insurance; representative politics goes as far back as the ancient Greeks; planning was not unknown to the Pharaohs if we do not mind considering the biblical story of Joseph and Pharaoh and their stocking of food supplies in the seven good years for the seven lean years as a fourteen-year plan; and the income tax — progression of rates apart — has for ancestors the Judaic tithe and the Islamic *zakat.*

Steeped in Arab and Mediterranean history and tradition as the ten manifestations may be, none of them had the functions, the scope and the complexity that it has today. Their modern characteristics have come to be considered essentially Western. The manifestations of the past did not occur side by side, nor did they carry the implications that they do today. To equate the ancient institutions with their modern counterparts or projections is like equating a horse carriage with a jumbo jet, or a carrier-pigeon with a satellite.

We need not dwell in any length upon the manifestations of modernity or their significance. But a few words about each will indicate in what sense they are differentiated from their ancient counterparts. The school has become the place of learning by thinking and cognition and experiment, rather than being mostly a place of teaching by assertion; it has furthermore blossomed horizontally into universal education and vertically into the university with its diversified and highly complex curriculum, a curriculum where science has precedence over theology. The city is no more the habitat of large numbers of people gathered together for security reasons, hiding behind a river or a high wall, or nestled in the lap of a protective mountain; it has instead become a metropolis that flourishes the more open it is, which draws in large numbers of rural inhabitants because it promises, and often provides, much more opportunity and fascination and income and entertainment than the village could ever dare to hope for. The breadth and the resources of the modern bank and the modern corporation, and the scale of their operations, compared with the banking house and the partnership in Aleppo, Alexandria, Baghdad or Mecca centuries ago, are eloquent enough to require no further elaboration.

The modern factory differs dramatically from the artisan's workshop, not only in the size of the labour force employed, the scale of operations, the range of products, and the speed of production, but also in technology. Industrial establishments are outstanding embodiments of modern technology in its revolutionary dimensions: in its machines, precision, complexity and performance. Furthermore, industry embodies the transition to industrial mentality, rationality and calculation, work discipline, and man's power over his environment and its resources.

Likewise, the dramatic emergence of the media of mass communication: the newspaper, the book, the radio, the transistor, the film — along with the development of the communication industry in its many branches — is a revolution in its own right. The implications of this revolution for the socio-cultural, economic and political life of society are enormous in the Arab world, particularly for modernisation. This revolution has permitted widespread mass participation and sharing in ideas and knowledge, in patterns of behaviour, and in expectations. It has also shortened the processes of emulation and adaptation — in the technical as in the social and political realms, in the arts as in public health. The means of communication have also raised the level of 'attitudinal social mobility'. This mobility brings closer the general tendencies and outlooks of various population groups.

The break-up of the large extended family and the decline of the father's authority is part of the change in functions of the family. The latter is much less today a productive unit or a mechanism for social insurance, in view of the emergence of other forms of organisation to take up these functions: the firm, the social insurance scheme in the private sector, and national social insurance.

There is little to report, however, with regard to the development of representative political organs, where probably the slowest progress relatively speaking has been made, and this progress has been far from uniform among the region's countries. Two trends pulling in opposite directions can be discerned. On the one hand, there is heightened political awareness thanks, *inter alia,* to economic, educational and scientific advances and the revolution in media and communications; the contemporary Arab is much more intimately aware of political events and issues and less prone to declaring political matters none of his business. All this constitutes a form of increased *indirect* participation. On the other hand, direct participation has proceeded slowly if by this we mean participation by the citizens in the decision-making process through some form of elective representation. The balance is positive, since the net result of the two trends is increased capability to participate. This will probably bring about strong pressure for direct participation and ultimately provide the opportunity and institutions for such participation, although the pace of these developments will be far from uniform in the region.

The significance of planning cannot be overestimated, if by planning we mean the wise husbandry of scarce skilled human and material resources for the sake of certain societal objectives, and if we remember that there is no Arab country that does not suffer from certain critical scarcities. Underlying the concept of planning is a changed philosophy: resources are now believed to belong to society, and welfare is society's business and no more a private business. The fact that every Arab country either has a plan or is in the process of formulating one is at least in part a reflection of the conviction of the new philosophy. The further fact that some countries may draw plans only to shelve them later proves rather than denies the point. It remains to be added that the recourse to planning is one aspect of the increased belief in the methodical control and organisation of society's activities and the heightened concern for its needs. This concern encompasses both the production of goods and services and their distribution.

Lastly, income tax. By this manifestation of modernisation we mean not the tax in itself as a fiscal measure but the attitude underlying progressive taxation — an attitude based on the conviction, shared by governments and most educated and responsible members of society — that it is now the right and the duty of the state to have increased resources for social and other basic services and for effective improvement in the level of living of the population, as it is the right of the people to expect the services and the improvements, and their duty not to run away from the tax collector. That many influential and rich citizens do escape assessment and payment does not invalidate the assertion regarding enlightened attitudes towards progressive taxation.

It should be added that none of these manifestations of modernisation is free of drawbacks, any more than the manifestations of development are. If it is right to say that development involves socio-cultural, economic and technological revolutions, it is equally right that development can and usually does suffer counter-revolutions, to borrow the notion from Gerschenkron.[9] Thus, education has often expanded fast at the expense of quality, with little emphasis on intellectual curiosity and discovery and excessive emphasis on diplomas and degrees, and it has often allowed rewards to the educated so rich that the link between effort and reward has been blurred. The pressure of numbers has distorted the teacher-student ratios and forced educational institutions to rely heavily on lectures to excessively large numbers of students. Furthermore, laboratory and library facilities frequently lag behind the expansion in student enrolment.

Urbanisation has often meant more promise in the cities than actual fulfilment and it has meant a widening of the gap between the village and the city. Several social and cultural problems have resulted from demographic movements and overcrowding. These include the mushrooming of urban slums, the *bidonvilles*, which are a harsh verdict on modern society. It is worth noting that the new urban conglomerations have brought into being new popular, simplified cultural styles and expressions. The development constitutes cultural democracy in bringing culture closer to the masses — both as producers and consumers. Although this threatens cultural deepening and sophistication, it provides scope for creativity and originality in the realm of cultural contribution.

Factory organisation has frequently missed the basic point of industrialism and has neither attended satisfactorily to the social needs of workers nor served as a focal point for the spread of technological innovation. The extended family has broken up without its functions being adequately taken up elsewhere and without the patriarch's authority being fully replaced. Planning has often been rash or ill-conceived or ostentatious, or has been guided by glamour rather than usefulness, and has been based on pseudo-statistics rather than solid facts, with disastrous effects.

These few illustrations are enough to indicate that the forms of modernisation have come by not without distress and waste and even moral damage — to which can be added the serious consideration that cultural fulfilment and dearly held values may have suffered in the transformation. Furthermore, a case can be made for the pleasures of traditional life, for the proportion of people that do not want their ways and mode of life and environment to be torn apart or radically and indiscriminately changed, for the charm of the quaint. However, be that as it may, it seems fairly certain that the majority in most Arab countries desire the change and seek it, each in his way, and that decision-makers in society, in bringing transformation about, do not violate the will of the majority in a flagrant way, notwithstanding the strains and stresses accompanying the transformation. Regret must be expressed that a very inadequate effort is being made in the Arab world — indeed, in the Third World at large — to minimise the strains and the dislocations, the slums and the anxieties.

An attempt has been made to bring out the difference between modernisation as understood and written about by those sociologists and economists who refer to it approvingly, and development as the present writer has qualified it. It is certainly not fair to contend that the mainstream body of Western thinking has merited the full harsh judgement made earlier on when 'modernisation' was being contrasted with 'development'. Indeed, there is awareness among many writers that it is wrong to assume automatically that modernisation (or Westernisation, or Europeanisation) is useful and valuable, and worthy of universal application. Equally, most writers would disagree with the notion that it should only refer to those changes accompanying industrialisation and material progress. And probably none would maintain that the agonies caused by it are minimal and negligible. However, it is to the general tone of the mainstream literature that we are referring when making critical comments, since this tone is not only generally approving but invocational as well. Some works do not even stop to question the profound and painful implications of modernisation for the societies for which it is prescribed.[10] A few closing comments will be in order here to underline the misgivings we have in this respect.

In identifying modernisation with Westernisation or Europeanisation, the Arab who is critical of the concept cannot but link this concept (and the process itself) with Western colonialism and imperialism, and their contemporary variants. As such, modernisation can be seen to have carried and to still carry with it painful associations. For one thing, there have been many instances of coercive modernisation; even a thing which can be said to be 'good' in itself becomes abhorrent if forced by a colonial agent. Furthermore, the colonialists — partly in self-deception, partly in outright deception and hypocrisy — have often claimed to be the carriers of a *mission civilisatrice*. The irony of this claim never passed unnoticed by the Arabs under foreign domination. This is particularly so as consciousness grew of the peripheral or marginal status forced on the colonised by the colonisers who occupied the 'centre' of the world politico-economic system. As the children of the former were being educated and socialised, in the narrow and individual sense of the term, to fit into a subjugated society, so were Arab societies socialised in order to fit into the Western conception of the international system, its 'rules of the game' and division of labour, as designed and played by the Western industrial community of nations.

Needless to say, the more traditional the group or sub-group, and the more sensitive, the more deeply it was hurt by the disruption that modernisation caused. This disruption reached into all aspects of life. The most frustrating aspect in this context, and the area where the most painful helplessness was felt, was with respect to the overpowering capability to coerce and to destroy which the modern world possessed, exemplified at its highest in the war machine which so twisted the economic, social and political life of the Arab world as to make it totally serve the interests of the West.

It is no wonder therefore that modernisation frightened many Arabs and made them suspicious of the more innocuous — even the beneficial — aspects of transformation. In this context, it is surprising that many Western writers and orientalists who analysed the confrontation beween Islam and the modern world, or the Islamic rejection trends and movements, could not see the backdrop to the reaction of the Islamic world at large, and the Arab world in particular.

2. AVENUES TO DEVELOPMENT

There is no one road to development, nor do all roads lead to it. Over the past two centuries, thinkers, policy-makers and businessmen have put their faith in one road or another, depending on their ideological convictions, personal predilections, the historical experience available to them and influencing their stance, or the system within which they live and by whose ideas and performance they are conditioned.

It is not intended in this chapter to list and examine the various avenues to development that exist or have existed (in the sense of theories explaining development, or socio-economic systems serving as frameworks for it), nor to defend the merits of any one of these. Nevertheless, it is necessary to indicate awareness of the multiplicity of avenues, and to suggest the implications of the choice of one as against another. The connection between this limited option taken and the present study arises from the necessity of making explicit the choice of determinants made for the purposes of this enquiry, as well as the causes for the expectation that these determinants will be operative in bringing about development.

Yet there is another, probably more compelling, reason why the whole issue of the presentation of 'theories of development' has been largely avoided here. This is the doubt that hangs over the very existence of such contemporary theories. There is general agreement that the classical school of economics presented us in the late eighteenth and the early nineteenth centuries with a long-term analysis of growth which could be considered a theory of development, and that this analysis incorporated certain non-economic factors of growth, such as population and technology. It is also true that the Marxist school presented us with a more rigorous analysis of long-term growth, which also incorporated non-economic factors, and that these factors covered a wider range than those in the classical analysis. The Marxist analysis included not only technology and population in its matrix, but also socio-political organisation and motivation.[11]

However, the literature does not contain theories of more recent vintage. The marginalists were not essentially concerned with long-term growth; the stagnationists were even obsessed with the opposite of growth, that is, long-term stagnation; Schumpeter, who is hailed as a great contributor to the theory of development, in fact presented us only with a partial explanation, since he emphasised the one factor of entrepreneurship and, although he was greatly concerned with the questions of capitalism and socialism, the central place in his concern remained the role of entrepreneurship in different contexts.[12] The list of partial theories is long. It includes writers who can be classified as belonging to the neo-classical school of thought, who in fact were mainly concerned with short-term growth considerations, as well as Keynes and post-Keynesian theorists, whose concern was not with long-term development any more than that of the earlier or the later neo-classical writers.

Partial theories, or partial analyses, can also be encountered in some attempts at the explanation of the rise of capitalism, such as those of Max Weber in *The Protestant Ethic and the Spirit of Capitalism,* Werner Sombart,[13] or R. H. Tawney in *Religion and the Rise of Capitalism* — to name only a few of the earlier writers. More recent writers who saw development from a narrow angle, thus emphasising one aspect or factor in their analysis, include Rosenstein-Rodan, Hirschman, Nurkse and Hoselitz[14] — again to name only a few. In these and the numerous instances of like inclination, the writers try to observe, interpret or anticipate development via one major factor or determinant. This factor can be economic in nature, or non-economic, as the references to Weber and Tawney suggest. Two illustrations of the latter category that deserve separate citation are David C. McClelland and Everett E. Hagen. The first, a psychologist, has made a major contribution to the explanation of development via the operation of a motivational factor which he designated as 'Need-for-Achievement', while the second, an economist, has accepted the primacy of this factor and built his whole system of explanation around it.[15]

Essentially, all these explanations contain instances of partial analysis. This analysis either takes into account the operation of one factor (or one cluster of factors) to the virtual exclusion of others, or else, as in the case of the question of balanced-versus-unbalanced growth, does not dwell on the identity of the factors in operation, but on the manner in which factors operate. In the latter case, for instance, the controversy centred mostly around the lumpiness as against the even spread of capital investment.

Considering the wide focus of this study, in the sense that a broad array of factors is examined for its impact on development, we are interested in general theories or general explanations of development. This is to say that the explanation of development is sought via the interplay of a large number of determinants which fall in the economic, socio-cultural and political-administrative fields. For this reason, the writings of J. J. Spengler, W. W. Rostow and Irma Adelman and Cynthia T. Morris[16] are of special significance for us.

We will have occasion to refer again to the contributions of these writers in the section to follow, when we come to consider the determinants of development. For the time being, we are merely concerned with their approach to the subject. This approach covers a wide avenue in all three instances. But, whereas Spengler lists a number of factors of development which ride across the frontiers of all the social disciplines, he does not attempt to relate these to each other in a system, either conceptually or operationally. [17] On the other hand, Rostow in *The Stages of Economic Growth* attempts something which is much more ambitious. He not only sets out to relate economic to social and political forces in the 'workings of societies', as he states in the Preface, but offers his book as 'A Non-Communist Manifesto', as the subtitle itself claims. This work in effect is presented in such a manner as to suggest that it contains a theory of development, that is, an organised system of thought which is not only capable of explaining the past, but also has predictive powers. Furthermore, it is also relevant that many of the readers both in advanced industrial, and in underdeveloped countries, have taken it to present a theory of growth or development.

Many economists and economic historians have criticised Rostow's *Stages*. Some have disagreed with its concepts, some others with its methodology, yet others with its substance and its facts, and many with its conclusions.[18] Though we do not intend to examine the 'theory' and the criticisms levelled at it, we must none the less register scepticism with respect to the legitimacy of the claim that the *Stages* presents us with a universal theory endowed with powers of interpretation and of prediction. On the other hand, in fairness, the admission must be made that a social theory can hardly claim to meet the specifications and conditions that a theory in the natural sciences is supposed to meet. The explanatory power of Rostow's *Stages*, as well as its schema, presents us with a helpful guideline for the understanding of the development of economies. If the whole notion of stages is erroneous and cannot be substantiated, or if the frontiers of the stages are wrongly drawn, or yet if the concept of the Rostovian take-off which is central to the 'theory' is inappropriate, this should not mean that the whole approach should be jettisoned. A differentiation can still be made between a systematised approach to the explanation of growth (and development), and a theory, rigorously defined. Rostow's *Stages* may well fall short of being a theory in the sense in which Simon Kuznets expects a theory of development to emerge,[19] but the schema deserves a great deal of credit for its interpretive value. This is so all the more once the reader is ready not to take the stages too literally in terms of content and demarcation lines, and to accept the overlap between them.

The approach that Irma Adelman and Cynthia Morris follow in explaining development is quantitative. Their joint research started in the early sixties, and their first joint piece of writing appeared in 1965. This was followed by a few joint essays and a book, *Society, Politics, and Economic Development*.[20] As the title of the book suggests, a large number of variables in the economic, social, cultural and political realms were selected and their impact on development (narrowly defined as change in GNP *per capita*), as well as the interdependence among the whole array of variables was measured. The various economic, social and political factors were scrutinised separately, then as clusters, for their influence on GNP. The method used was factor analysis. The results of the calculations suggested the directions and the size of the effect of each of the independent variables on development. The study concluded with a number of broad inferences deriving from the tendency of certain economic, social and political variables to cluster together. This in turn suggested some sequence in the unfolding of the effect of the groups of factors, in the sense that one cluster would operate before another at a certain level of development, while the order would be different at another level.

This study has the widest coverage among studies of similar kind, both in the sense that it deals with more underdeveloped countries, and with more factors or variables. We will have occasion in the section to come to refer at greater length to this study, since this writer is indebted to it for some ideas and it exerted an attraction with respect to the methodology used. Although in the end the methodology was not adopted in the present study, the Adelman-Morris research and model provide a reference group of determinants (or variables) of great usefulness for comparison purposes. The findings and conclusions are also of immense interest, since they largely confirm some of the present writer's hypotheses and findings with respect to the operation of the major clusters of factors or determinants of development in the Arab world. The agreement, and the divergence, will become clearer as we proceed.

Although the examination of development and the forces behind it in this study proceeds along pragmatic more than ideological lines, an attempt is made to fit development into a body of ideas, if not an ideology in the rigorous sense of the term.[21] These ideas, broadly stated, have been presented earlier on in the differentiation between development and growth. Development thus defined cannot be totally dissociated from the model or framework within which it unfolds. The reader might wish to know what model has been selected as providing the most appropriate *ambiance* for development, or at least what model is implied.

It ought to be explained right away that what is at issue here is not a characterisation of econometric models of development, that is, growth models as referred to in technical economic parlance. The term 'model' is used in the sense of *institutional* framework and a framework of ideas, within which different economies function. More specifically, the term is used to describe the system or web of relations, both socio-political and economic, characterising the factors of production and the activity of production, in so far as ownership of the means of production, investment, determination of output and economic decisions in general are concerned; in so far as the different rationales or philosophies underlying the web of relations are concerned; in so far as the criteria of efficiency are concerned; and, finally, in so far as the distributive system and pattern and the final objectives of economic activity are concerned.

Such usage of the term model makes it almost synonymous with the term 'economic system'. Indeed, essentially what is being asked in an investigation of the contemporary models of development is the type and nature of socio-economic systems within which development can take place.

To follow the Weberian approach, we can say there are basically two 'ideal type' models or systems, the private free enterprise (capitalist) system, and the socialist system. However, reality only approximates ideal types, and in practice systems in operation (as against systems in sophomore-level textbooks) are 'real types' which overlap at the edges, though they remain different at the core. They also produce combinations.

This is probably an important point, for it can provide explanation for the claims made that a private enterprise system, like that of the United States, is 'approaching' the socialist system of the Soviet Union. Claims of this type appear particularly as a result of the divorce between capital ownership and management in the big 'capitalist' corporation, the increasing control exercised by government, the greater resort to central planning, and the egalitarian measures taken with regard to the distribution of wealth and income in a capitalist society. On the other side, the claims appear as a result of the growing awareness of the importance of personal incentives in the 'socialist' society, the introduction of the concept of 'profit' into the evaluative process of economic efficiency, and the growing decentralisation of the decision-making process.

These and similar manifestations of overlap are genuine developments that have not failed to draw the attention of careful observers of the capitalist and the socialist systems. However, essentially at heart the two systems are still very different: in structure of relations between economic factors and forces, in method of operation and locus of decision, in motives and incentives, in objectives, and in social framework and values generally.

The overlap between the two systems has produced a third, derivative model: the mixed system, or the system of joint enterprise. This last model deserves careful examination, since it seems to be destined to play a much larger role, especially in Third World countries. Its mixed parentage cannot, or does not always enable the observer to determine the true identity of one of the parents. Thus, to the extent that the mixed system partakes of major characteristics attributable to or derived from the private enterprise (capitalist) system, there is little room — if any — for confusion. To carry the analogy of 'parenthood' a little further, the identity of a mother is always easy to establish; it is the identity of a father that rouses doubts in certain instances. Likewise, what ought to be established, and what is not always easy to establish, is whether the fact that in a mixed system there are certain sectors that are publicly owned, and that certain methods and mechanisms of resource allocation such as central planning are used — whether these considerations justify the claim that the second parent is socialism.

If it is, we are face to face with an interesting phenomenon which calls for careful investigation and would raise fundamental questions and lead to far-reaching conclusions. The questions and the conclusions would be both conceptual and practical, but they centre around the possibility of coexistence *within the same society* of socialism and capitalism.

If, however, investigation does not support the claim that the second parent is socialism, but *étatisme* or national socialism or state capitalism — the nomenclature depending on the investigator's taste — then this ought to be established and its implications understood. Conceptually at least, there is quite a difference in philosophical foundations, values, objectives and methods between socialism and national socialism, as the latter came to be identified in the European experience between the two wars. The main relevance of such questioning for the present study lies in the effectiveness and the credibility of the specific system or model in existence as framework and engine of development. The issue is not merely conceptual and theoretical. As we saw in Volume I of this study, it has been a real and live issue for many countries. The controversy has raged and still rages, as to whether Egypt, Syria, Iraq or Algeria have really established socialism as their leaders claim, or whether it is indeed state capitalism that has been instituted.

3. THE MAJOR DETERMINANTS OF DEVELOPMENT

The notion of 'determination' in the context of development is rather elusive, because it is difficult to establish a formal cause-effect relationship between a determinant and development. In this connection, Hoselitz says,

> The main problem in the theory of economic growth which arises as a consequence of relating social-structural and cultural factors to economic variables is to determine the mechanisms by which the social structure of an underdeveloped country becomes altered and takes on the features which characterize an economically advanced country.[22]

Some of the criticism directed against Rostow's concept of the 'take-off' arises precisely from this source of disagreement, namely the time, and the cause-effect relationships between determinants and development. As it has been put by some critics, the socio-cultural and political factors which make their appearance in one stage and lead to the unfolding of the next stage are themselves frequently the manifestation that development is actually taking place, rather than a pre-condition for development. Once these factors or conditions have appeared, then development is in fact occurring. (Jerome B. Wiesner once put this whole matter in a concise and picturesque way in so far as education is concerned. He said, 'A good education system may be the flower of economic development, but it is also the seed.'[23])

Another aspect of the problem here is timing: thus, do the determinants operate first and bring development about thereafter, or is the relationship almost simultaneous? And, more significantly, is it not legitimate to say that the emergence or satisfaction of many of the determinants (like education, acceptance of technological change, development of financing institutions, emergence of a modernising middle class, etc.) is *in itself* an indication of the unfolding of the process of development, to the point where 'determinant' and 'determined' become mistaken for each other, or where the two occur simultaneously as different facets of the same process? And, since the dependent variable in the present context (namely, development) in turn influences the nature, direction and intensity of the independent variables themselves through a relationship of interaction and interdependence, is there not the danger that any separation between the two categories is likely to become artificial and misleading, once the process of development has been set in motion?

These, and other conceptual and methodological problems arise in a rigorously formal examination of determination and determinants. But perhaps one of the most nagging questions that confuse the researcher is the determination of the point of cut-off in an enquiry like the present one. Thus, how far back in the chain of causality is the investigation to go? For it is not sufficient to say that education is a major determinant, when decisions with respect to the spread and quality and content of education are absolutely crucial for the course and speed that development will take, and it is therefore essential to know what kind of government (and of private educational institutions) take those decisions which indeed make of education an effective determinant. And so on with other determinants like modern technology, the availability of investment capital, or the existence of an energetic middle class. To pursue such probing and questioning would ultimately lead all the way back to 'original determination'. But then one would reach one or at most a few basic determinants which would be the fount of all subsequent action and thus would confuse the cause-effect relationship between independent and dependent variables, as among the independent variables themselves as a group. This return to the roots, or to prime movers, is like the identification of one basic, original sin which is the mother of all subsidiary sin. But, in this capacity, original sin would make it difficult to discover the responsibility of subsequent sins.

McClelland and Hagen, in their deep dive to find the original force behind development, came up with one answer: motivation through the 'need-for-achievement'. Every human endeavour relating to growth and development was related or referred back to this 'n-ach', as the 'need-for-achievement' is designated in the professional jargon. This is a satisfying conclusion, since it is general enough and therefore versatile enough to provide room for almost all other subsidiary determinants. One can thus accommodate the existence of an energetic middle class within the generous confines of the McClelland-Hagen conclusion, as well as the acceptance of technological change, the developmental orientation of political leadership, or education. But, because of being so versatile, 'n-ach' becomes too telescopic in focus and therefore insufficiently useful as an analytical and interpretive instrument.

On the other hand, the Adelman-Morris approach which used a very large number of factors or indicators — 41 to be exact — tends to over-diffuse the 'responsibility' by spreading it thinly. Evidently, Adelman and Morris found that these 41 variables had different degrees of significance and impact, and their methodology was appropriate for such a number of variables. (The present writer, who has not used factorial analysis, has relied on direct observation, interviews, the literature on the various variables in the countries covered, and, finally, analysis with all these other means in hand, using a much smaller number of factors.)

It was not an easy decision to determine the degree of concentration in the selection and acceptance of determinants. The range being very wide, any of several sets could be selected, beginning with one central, fundamental determinant like motivation (need-achievement), and ending with several dozen determinants, all of which, it could be argued cogently, were of proven relevance to development. For a few years the present writer experimented in graduate seminars with the identification of independent variables influencing the course and pace of development. At one time, the seminar group identified more than seventy of these variables. But it was established, after sufficient scrutiny, that although these variables were all 'independent' and relevant, there were indeed many degrees of independence and relevance. Furthermore, in insisting on the identification of *determinants* the present writer necessarily narrowed the range of possibility, since the term itself suggests a specially *forceful* type of independent variable – a prime mover, so to speak.

Obviously, there is no easily determinable number of determinants, as a review of a few leading illustrations in the literature indicates. Thus Rostow in *The Process of Economic Growth* lists six basic 'human motives' or 'human propensities' of importance to economic development:[24]

1. The propensity to develop fundamental science (physical and social).
2. The propensity to apply science to economic ends.
3. The propensity to accept innovations.
4. The propensity to seek material advance.
5. The propensity to consume.
6. The propensity to have children.

On the other hand, Spengler listed 20 'determinants of the level of *per capita* net product, 19 of which are specifically identified' and one which is a residual category.[25] (See Appendix A for Spengler's list.)

Spengler is aware of the interrelationships among these determinants, and of the differences between the degrees of relevance and potency of each of them. He says in this respect:

Each determinant, when ... defined, will be found to be related to some other determinant or determinants; and the whole group will be discovered to constitute a network of more or less interdependent elements. No one of these elements will be found always to act as a prime mover that initiates change and compels other elements to adjust thereto.[26]

This writer attaches great importance to Spengler's thought. This is both because many of the determinants he identifies are of significance as prime movers in the drive for development, and his observations and conclusions are to a large extent relevant and applicable to the Arab context which defines this study. While he insists that 'a high rate of economic growth can be realized in societies with differing cultures provided that the regnant value systems stress material ends and technical progress', Spengler also insists that within any one country 'a high rate of economic growth presupposes compatibility between the economic and the non-economic components of a cultural system.' These and other considerations lead him to doubt the possibility of formulating a general theory of development, both because of differences between countries (states, societies, civilisations, etc. in his words), and of changes over time in one or more of these units. Thus he says: ' ... it is probable that a final and unchanging principle of societal growth can never be formulated, that the empirical principles which are formulated will have to be recast periodically if they are to remain useful.' One sees the affinity between him and Kuznets when he sums up by stating that at present no satisfactory theory of societal growth exists. In Kuznet's view, what the student of development now witnesses is no more than the probing for a theory of growth.[27] We record the convergence of the positions of the two distinguished writers here because we find solace in them in the context of this study. The hypothesis which was adopted for the study with respect to the determinants of development in the Arab world, and the conclusions with which the study ends, have both benefited from their broad agreement with the general trend of the analytical conclusions of Spengler and Kuznets. (It ought to be pointed out, however, that Kuznets has not devoted much space in his extensive writings to the question of non-economic determinants, although he is fully aware of their significance. They remain largely implicit in his writings, whereas Spengler has stated them explicitly.)

The third illustration of an attempt to draw a list of determinants comes from the study and book of Adelman and Morris. (They refer to indicators, indices or variables in their study.[28] See Appendix B for a list of the variables selected by them.)

In preparing for this study, the present writer benefited mostly from Spengler's list of determinants, Adelman and Morris's latest list,[29] from interaction with the graduate students in the writer's seminar on 'The Framework of Development', and from a long period of research, field-work and assessment.[30] All these intellectual inputs were brought to bear on his experience with and extensive observation of the twelve Arab countries covered in the study. When the study was designed, twelve clusters of determinants were identified as most operative in the Arab context. Subsequently, when the final design of the study was made, and especially after the first pilot interviews were undertaken, the list was somewhat shortened and simplified. This was not essentially on grounds of expediency, but because of the growing realisation that the search for *prime movers* necessitated some curtailment, and that efficient and effective interviewing, like the survey of the scanty literature on most of the items in the list, necessitated simplification. Although the final list will be presented before this section ends, it will probably be useful to record the initial list made in the first attempt to design the study. The presentation both of the original and the final lists can also show the evolution of the writer's thinking on the subject. (The original twelve clusters appear in Appendix C.)

The field-work and preliminary interviewing confirmed the writer's earlier misgivings with regard to the practicality of identifying all these factors and examining how they operate and how effective they are in promoting development. As more thought was put into the matter during the phase of work preceding field-trips and interviewing, it became evident that the approach needed to be redirected. Thus, more emphasis was to be placed on the prime movers, particularly on the forces operating and taking or influencing decisions of developmental impact, while many of the components of the determinants in the preceding list were to be described and assessed in the country chapters of Volume I, rather than examined in detail and depth as determinants in the present volume. This was less a matter of expediency and time-saving than one of methodological necessity.

As a result of the rethinking undertaken, and of the first pilot, experimental interviews, another more feasible list of determinants was selected. This was the one used finally for the interviewing conducted, and for the search in the literature. This list follows:

1. Economic determinants
   a. Resource and performance base (with special reference to petroleum and gas).
   b. Economic structure, especially with regard to dualism.
   c. Industrialisation: base and process.
   d. Agrarian reform and agricultural development.

   e. Capital availability (internal and external).
   f. Physical infrastructure.
   g. Manpower: size, quality, training, compatibility of supply and demand.
   h. Entrepreneurship and management: locus, spread, quality.
   i. Arab economic co-operation and complementarity.

2. Political and administrative determinants
   a. Development orientation and commitment of leadership (indicators, policies, party and government platforms).
   b. Planning and plans.
   c. The civil service: attitudes; recruitment, training and upgrading; loyalties; professionalism; bureaucratisation; allocation of authority.
   d. Political stability; national homogeneity.
   e. Role of the public sector (indicators, including economic institutions, area of decision-making, nationalisations, social welfare, budgeting, extent and seriousness of planning).
   f. Degree of participation by the population.

3. Socio-cultural determinants
   a. Education: level; spread; content and philosophy; methodology (including extent of experimentation, research and intellectual exploration); relevance to development.
   b. Acceptance of technological change: areas and indicators (sophistication of production and distribution methods and of business, research, organisation, etc.).
   c. Agents of change: military and party élites; political leadership, the middle class; minority (deviant) groups.
   d. Motivation and incentives; development-oriented social tension.
   e. Social mobility; family and system of authority; traditionalism *v.* modernisation in attitudes; place of status symbols.

The grouping of the determinants was easy to undertake, except in two or three cases. One of these is entrepreneurship, which has socio-cultural, as well as economic, aspects. But it was considered more warranted to place it among the economic determinants. A second case is planning, which could equally justifiably have been included in the first category. Its inclusion among political and administrative determinants is justified on the grounds that the emphasis on planning is more closely related to the decision-makers' attitude to the control and allocation of resources and the objectives behind this attitude than to the actual mechanism of allocation. Yet a third case is Arab economic co-operation and complementarity. This is more of a political (and, deeper down, a socio-psychological) than an economic factor. One might add 'the agents of change' to the list of political determinants, particularly in so far as the political leadership or the military and party élites are concerned. However, the exact classification is not of great significance, since almost all the determinants interact and are interdependent. Under the circumstances, some overlap is permissible.[31]

Presenting a list of the determinants finally selected is not enough for the purposes of this chapter: there is further need for explaining what is meant and intended by each of the determinants, and how it is thought to operate and influence development. However, the question of the right place for such an explanation was debated at length by the writer. It was felt that to fit it at this point would be rather cumbersome, as this would result in a long discussion of widely different determinants, involving abstraction and untied to specific situations and contexts. Alternatively, to postpone this discussion till the next chapter would enable us to explain and expand on each of the determinants when its turn came up for examination. This would have the dual advantage of splitting the discussion and making it less clustered, and of tying it to the specific and concrete context, in each case, of the determinant put to the test at the time. In the end, the latter alternative was adopted.

The writer also paused at length to think about and select a methodology for the study. He was greatly tempted at the start to use the same methodology as that used by Adelman and Morris. Their empirical approach consisted of factor analysis whose

> primary purpose . . . is to reduce the original number of explanatory variables to a smaller number of independent factors in terms of which the whole set of variables can be understood . . . The technique of factor analysis shares certain characteristics with both non-quantitative comparative studies and statistical regression analyses.[32]

This approach necessitated the scoring of every one of the 74 countries covered in the Adelman-Morris study for each of the 41 variables or indicators selected,[33] prior to the processing of the data within the requirements of the statistical model designed. The results of the correlation matrix for social, political and economic indicators permitted the ranking of the countries (which had been divided into three categories on the basis of the level of *per capita* income) for the three groups of indicators. And finally, as a result of the rotation of the clusters of indicators or factors (which the technique of factor analysis makes possible), certain very broad conclusions and generalisations were made with respect to each of the three categories of countries. (We will have occasion to refer to these conclusions when we come to our own conclusions in the next two chapters.)

The Adelman-Morris study in its entirety calls for admiration. The technique chosen enabled the two economists to handle a very large body of material for a vast number of countries within the confines of a medium-sized book. The presentation is neat and clear. However, strong as the temptation to emulate their technique was, it was none the less resisted for two reasons. The first is this writer's inability to handle, and his general shying away from, sophisticated statistical and mathematical techniques and models. To this must be added the fear that the rigour and elegance of these often hide the fact that they inhibit flexibility in analytical exploration and forbid the introduction of nuances and qualifications that are necessarily inseparable from enquiries into human and societal behaviour. This is all the more true in the case of the discussion of development and its determinants. The second reason for the decision not to follow in the footsteps of Adelman and Morris relates to the approach itself. The basic and most significant step in it is the scoring, which was undertaken on the basis of the opinions of many experts who are knowledgeable about the many countries and the many indicators involved, but who, nevertheless, undertook the scoring at a great distance from the 'theatre of operations'. The present writer felt that to apply a numerical score to a country with respect to such questions as the character of basic social organisation, or the degree of improvement between two dates in financial institutions, in manpower, in the tax system, or in the techniques of agriculture — to name only a few illustrations — would be to apply concreteness where it did not belong. Understandably, some criteria or measurement devices were formulated by the authors and referred to the experts. Nevertheless, a nagging fear remained that the scoring was too arbitrary and artificial to provide comfort.

The present writer preferred to rely on his intimate knowledge of the twelve countries covered and his renewed observations, in addition to the 350 interview he personally conducted and the literature he examined, to enable him to pass judgement — admittedly often qualitative and highly qualified — on the state and operation of the various determinants. This approach seemed to provide more confidence than the apparently more reassuring numerical scoring. It was felt that, after all, we were dealing with some elusive concepts and institutions, with delicate and often unpredictable human reactions, and with a process in which many economic, socio-cultural and political-administrative forces were intertwined that any concreteness in assessment or judgement would necessarily be *misplaced* concreteness. Furthermore, along with the examination of the determinants went another of institutions and forces of relevance to development, which again required qualitative analytical rather than statistical or mathematical evaluation. This is primarily because institutions and forces, being the transmission lines via which the power generated in the realm of ideas, values and generally intangible determinants can reach the field of development and its mechanisms properly speaking, are near-impossible to quantify.

4. INTERWEAVING OF THE DETERMINANTS

It is necessary that some conceptual order be finally put into the array of determinants, institutions and forces, in such a way that the 'system of thought' thus produced may be capable of explaining the performance of the Arab economies and of helping to gauge the outlook for development in the near future.

The capability to explain and to predict is usually attributed to systematic theory. We do not pretend that the conduct of the study has led, nor did we initially believe it would lead, to the elaboration of a theory of development capable of explaining the development process — even if only in the Arab world. Abler and hardier writers have shied away from such endeavour or from the claim that it was possible at all — given the 'state of the arts'. We presumed, however, that the approach adopted in the design of the study, and the coverage, would lead to meaningful conclusions and generalisations with regard to development in the Arab region, and as a minimum would allow us to divide the Arab countries into two or three categories on the basis of the operation of the determinants in their development, and the outlook for development in their economies and societies. It is hoped that the two chapters to follow, with which the book ends, will warrant these expectations.

This last point with respect to the possible division of the region's countries into a few categories has special significance. Empirical research, particularly that of Adelman and Morris, has revealed that the socio-cultural, political-administrative and economic clusters of determinants operate with varying degrees of intensity and at different stages of development between one group of countries and another, depending on the initial level of development of the group concerned, and on the response to the determinants. Thus, at the lowest level, it has been established by Adelman and Morris,[34] it is the socio-cultural determinants that are most relevant and the satisfaction of which appears to be the *sine qua non* for the unfolding of the process of development. They also found that only when the socio-cultural conditions had been satisfied did the political determinants begin to be noticeably operative. And only when the political conditions had been satisfied, in countries at a relatively higher level of development than those in the group before, could the purely economic determinants begin to operate.

These findings have been treated as propositions for the purposes of this study. They have proved very useful both as starting points for an examination of the course of development in the Arab world, and as reference conclusions to measure those of the present study against. This role of conclusions-cum-propositions has been shared by a slightly different formulation by Galbraith.[35]

This latter writer proposes that developing countries can be grouped into three main categories: (a) those which need a socio-economic revolution before they can begin to move in the direction of development, such revolution involving agrarian reform and other areas of radical change (a stage which is comparable to that needing far-reaching socio-cultural change in the Adelman-Morris formulation); (b) those countries where the revolution or its objective has materialised that now need a 'development platform', or an infrastructure, which stable dynamic government can establish; and (c) those countries which have had their revolution and their platform, where purely economic endowments (capital, entrepreneurship, and so on) can now operate effectively.

A question which remained active during the present study was: how true is the Adelman-Morris formulation, or the Galbraith variation, in the context of the Arab world? And, more specifically, how true is it within the differentiated framework of the capitalist (private enterprise), the socialist, or the mixed system? For, although the study was not designed in order to test these formulations but had its own autonomous foundations and questions to answer, it was thought useful to keep the lessons of other studies in mind and to identify any affinity or divergence between the findings of this study and those of other studies of relevance.

As we did not design the study in accordance with the model of any special ideology or doctrine, we started with a great degree of flexibility and openness to what the enquiry had to offer by way of important suggestions. Yet the slate was not at all blank: it had on it a certain conceptualisation of development and its content, and of the need for an interdisciplinary approach to development. The concept and content, and the approach, helped us select the determinants thought to be strongly operative. The selection in itself was an implied proposition with respect to the forces that were thought to loom large behind development. However, we kept an open mind as to how these forces operate in interaction to bring about development, allowing ourselves to be guided by the observations and insights which the enquiry provided. Although this approach could not possibly claim to produce a formal theory of development, it was believed capable of leading to a better understanding of the nature and aspects of development in the Arab world, how it has proceeded in the thirty-odd years since the end of World War Two, and what its prospects and outlook are in the years to come.[36]

5. MAJOR ISSUES IN DEVELOPMENT

Many issues — major and minor — arise in the conceptualisation, design and planning, and promotion and materialisation of development. No standard work on development fails to discuss the more obvious of these issues, or at least to refer to them. Most of the literature, particularly works of the textbook type, focuses on the problems and issues relating to the basic 'factors of production', essentially resource shortages and under-utilisation, labour scarcity in the categories of skill needed for economic modernisation, the serious limitation of domestic savings and of investment capital, the shortage of managerial and entrepreneurial resources, and the primitiveness and inefficiency of organisation.[37]

Were these to be the problems and issues meant here, there would hardly be an excuse for devoting a section of this chapter to the subject. Indeed, it is because of the desire to underline certain special problems, issues and misgivings relating to development, and more particularly to development in the Arab context, that space is allowed to the question at the close of the present chapter. More specifically, what is to be emphasised is, first, those issues that do not receive adequate consideration in the standard works whose focus is usually restricted to the economic aspects of development, and, secondly, those issues of particular concern and relevance for the Arab region.

1. The first cluster of issues relates to the content and philosophy of development. Much of the substance of the issues that belong here has already been referred to in the first section of this chapter, when the content of development was examined and differentiated from that of growth. We need only recapitulate the more important points, which are:

(a) The danger of holding a mechanistic view of development, one which focuses on the overall rate of growth without sufficient concern for the actual needs of the masses and the actual pattern of distribution of income and wealth;

(b) The danger of a fragmented, disconnected approach to development, whereby some aspects of society's life and well-being receive attention and many others are neglected; and

(c) The danger of permitting the coexistence of a schizophrenic view of development, whereby much emphasis is placed on growth and industrialisation, along with disrespect, or non-concern for the human being and his dignity at the social and political levels.

2. The second cluster relates to the motive force behind development:

(a) Will society's faith in the 'Invisible Hand' continue, that is, in the operation of the system of private enterprise based essentially on the expectation that self-interest among the producers and the consumers will bring about maximum satisfaction to all, or will this faith be based on an expanded economic role for the state, planning, and some socialist measures?

(b) To what extent is participation by the adult population in political life (and therefore in political and economic decision-making) possible?

(c) To the extent that a new political and socio-economic structure is created as an outcome (or a pre-condition) of development, is there not the danger that the 'new class' of rulers might become in turn exploitative, though in a different fashion from the old class? And how will society guard against this danger?

3. A third major issue centres around the question of the distribution of national product: how will society establish that happy balance between concern for, and requisites of, increased production (including increased investment and therefore necessarily increased savings), and concern for a more equitable distribution? And how is distributive justice to be applied among regions, sectors and groups, without seriously violating the criteria of economic efficiency?

4. Education, which is of paramount economic and social significance, raises some serious questions itself.

(a) There is, to begin with, the clash between the pressures to provide universal education, that is, to spread education horizontally, and those to provide better education and training to certain strategic categories of youth whose developmental function is considered critical. These groups include engineers, foremen, economists, physicians, administrators and executives, craftsmen and skilled workers, and the like.

(b) In addition to this issue of spread versus quality, there is the equally important issue of ensuring that education should have a social dimension, that it should not largely constitute an avenue of enrichment for certain select categories of highly trained men and women, which stand out as isolated islands in a sea of poverty and near-illiteracy.

(c) Finally, there is the issue of the choice of framework for educational efforts, particularly where professional institutes, universities, and large undertakings of research and technological experimentation are concerned. The question here is: to what extent will these efforts remain restricted to the national state, and to what extent will they become a regional undertaking aiming at the achieving of economies of scale, better distribution of manpower in the Arab region, and a better allocation of the scarce resource of high-level manpower?

5. Next, the choice and transfer of technology create certain problems and raise issues of significance.

(a) With regard to the choice of technology, the problem is no different from anywhere else, involving such questions as capital intensity, automation, and whether the choice can be global or be the subject matter of global policy, or whether in the final analysis it has to be made establishment by establishment, industry by industry.

(b) The second issue, namely the transfer of technology, is of relevance to the Third World countries, but of special urgency to the Arab countries, and more so to the large oil exporters among them. Thinking and policy must centre around the elaboration of the best means to speed the technological advancement of the region, thus shifting from the importation wholesale of modern techniques and machines, first to the adaptation of these to local requirements, then ultimately to innovation. This involves much greater stress than there is today on scientific education, experimentation and research. Indeed, it involves a revolutionary change in the philosophy, content and methodology of education, as well as the necessary financial and manpower outlays called for by the change. The question of transfer of technology also raises a social and political question: the danger that the advanced industrial countries will exert undue influence and power in the recipient countries as a result of their possession of the advanced technology, and that the industrial countries will retard the indigenous development of technological and scientific capability in the Arab countries. (In referring to the advanced countries we also include their transnational corporations which wield immense power in the field of technological development and transfer.)[38] How is the Arab world at the same time to effect 'the transfer of technology', and guard against exploitation and a warped development of its scientific and technological capability?

6. The role of the resource base (including natural resources and man-made resources) also raises a number of questions. One standard question is how to apportion the resources

that the GNP puts into the economy between consumption and saving/investment, or how to attend to the needs of this generation as against those of the next generation? However, we would like to emphasise two other questions that do not usually form part of the economist's concern in this respect.

(a) How can investment be accelerated without excessive dependence on foreign donations and loans which necessarily have adverse political and socio-cultural implications, or, what is the happy balance between insulation and slow investment on the one hand, and dangerous exposure to the pressures and interests of donors and creditors on the other hand? The fundamental issue of self-reliance arises here. Each country, and the region as a whole to the extent that there is regional thinking, planning and policy formulation, ought to seek self-reliance without autarky or insulation and to establish harmony between the opposite pulls of these two poles. It will probably be found that the surest way of achieving this harmony will be through the maximum mobilisation of domestic efforts and resources, and the search for international co-operation with confidence, self-respect and awareness that the strong are usually not saint-like in their economic relations with the weak and that therefore the forging of relations with the industrial countries ought to be undertaken with circumspection.

(b) The second issue in this cluster relates to the need for the devotion of certain sizeable resources to defence, though the Arab world is in great need of resources for development. The conflict between defence and development is real, if we are to limit it to the obvious fact that they both claim a large share in the region's limited resources, particularly those of the 'confrontation countries', namely Syria, Jordan and Egypt.

However, it would be idle to speculate on the benefits that would accrue to development if defence were to claim much more modest resources, as the region continues to be in a state of war with Israel and to feel that Arab security is threatened by Israel's military might. Under the circumstances, defence must be rationalised as the fence and guardian of developmental gains, as much as development is to be additionally rationalised as the solid base for defence. The pattern of resource allocation between the two remains a matter of delicate balance that has to be worked out carefully; optimally, the character and technology of defence ought to be so chosen and designed that maximum security can be obtained from each unit of military outlay, and that development must be so designed as to serve both as a solid base for defence and a source of welfare for the population.

7. Three issues will be singled out with respect to the cluster of population and manpower.

(a) The fast increase in population which accompanies the early phases of development, and which makes a slight improvement in the rate of economic growth of little effect as it gets devoured by the rate of population increase. Gerschenkron has referred to this problem in suggesting that frequently the Malthusian counter-revolution defeats or threatens the developmental revolution.[39] The issue here is two-sided: how to influence family planning to control the fast rate of increase and thus reduce the proportion of the dependent in the population, and how to raise the general economic performance of the population so that the numerical increase will stop being a burden and turn into an asset.

(b) The second issue is that of unemployment and underemployment, whose treatment does not receive all the attention, effort and resources that it deserves in the Arab world, in spite of the enormity of the problem. Often this problem is intensified through the wrong investment and choice of technology policies, and through an inappropriate apportioning of emphasis between traditional education aiming at the production of clerks, and vocational and professional training aiming at and capable of providing useful operators for the economy, whose absorption in gainful employment is much easier than that of general clerks.

(c) There is finally the problem of the 'brain drain', which is of special significance for the Arab world.[40] Two questions arise here, namely the handicap to development that this drain constitutes, and the loss to society, since the high-level manpower which is lost must have cost the Arab countries substantial financial resources and valuable years during the training process.

8. Government and the civil service constitute another cluster of issues that merit consideration. We will state two of these issues briefly here:

(a) The first is the vastly expanded functions of the government administration, especially owing to the undertaking of many economic tasks by the public sector (including ownership of substantial productive assets, planning, and execution of development works), without parallel expansion in the capability of this administration. Related to this issue is that of slow professionalisation in the civil service, though good beginnings have been marked in several countries in the region.

(b) The second relates to the heavy emphasis in a few of the Arab countries on party membership and loyalty for appointment and promotion in the civil service. Where one party controls the reins of power, this insistence on party affiliation is understandable. But the price ought also to be realised, since party membership need not be synonymous with efficiency and eligibility. (Often the reverse is true.) The reconciliation of the contradiction involved is of great urgency in the countries concerned. (In several other Arab countries the problem takes another form. Appointment and promotion, and the extent of authority, often depend outwardly on entrance examinations and tests, but in reality on some degree of nepotism and the trading of influence and favours among politicians and religious leaders.)

9. Finally, a significant cluster of issues arises in connection with Arab regional development, and co-operation and complementarity among the region's countries. The major premiss underlying these issues is that such co-operation and complementarity are beneficial and essential for the region viewed as one unit, and for the national states within it. Flowing from this premiss are the following issues or questions:

(a) What are the modalities best suited to co-operation and complementarity, and how can they be implemented and translated into institutions, policies, measures and reality in general within the continued attachment to the sovereignty of the individual national states?

(b) How can special interests be accommodated within the framework of co-operation and complementarity so that they may not stand in opposition or turn into subversive vested interests? Such accommodation will require, *inter alia,* compensatory measures for establishments and interests that suffer from a greater exposure to competition under conditions of complementarity or co-operation, or else it will call for a relocation of capital in sectors and activities that are likely to benefit from the new structures of co-operation.

(c) How can manpower and capital be encouraged to move more freely and substantially in order to achieve an optimal distribution over the region? How can the impediments to such mobility, which are political and socio-psychological as well as economic and institutional in nature, be overcome?

(d) How can truly regional projects be promoted (in distinction from projects in any one country in the financing of which several countries participate) in such a manner that the circuit of economic life in the region is intensified, and mutual and common interests are strengthened, as a solid step towards economic unity, and further towards that political unity to which many Arabs aspire? (The regional approach to education, science and technology, and research have already received mention under an earlier point.)

(e) Finally, and most importantly, how can the major resource of the region, hydrocarbons, be put in the service of the region's development (via country and joint projects alike), in such a manner that the region will achieve all aspects of development: economic, technological, social and political? How can the flow of resources from the large oil exporters to the Arab capital-importing countries be intensified in spite of the hesitations of the surplus oil countries? What modalities must be invented, or, if in existence, expanded, for the institutionalisation and intensification of development aid to Arab (and other Third World) countries, via individual projects, programmes, and whole sectors? In brief, how can oil truly become a powerful determinant and engine of development through a truer sense of Arab co-operation, a clearer and more earnest vision of development, and more effective and far-reaching policies?

To make an inventory of such major issues as those just briefly presented is more to pose central conceptual questions than to answer them. The enormity, ramifications and implications of these issues and questions place them beyond the scope of this chapter for full discussion. However, we have touched on or dealt with several of them as we moved along Volume I, especially in its last chapter. More attention will be directed to a few more in the remaining chapters. However, the main purpose in making the inventory is to bring about greater sensitisation and awareness of these and like basic issues, an oversight of which would be tantamount to a gross misunderstanding of development and its real purposes and value.

APPENDIX A: SPENGLER'S LIST

1. Age composition of the population.
2. Biological composition of the population.
3. Health composition of the population.
4. Material equipment (i.e. resources, productive machinery, etc.) per worker.
5. State of the industrial arts.

6. State of the educational, scientific and related cultural equipment of the population.
7. Make-up of the prevailing value-system: in particular, the values of the socio-economic leaders and the values which significantly affect economic creativity and the disposition of man to put forth economically productive effort.
8. Dominant character of the politico-economic system: is it free enterprise, mixed, social democratic, or totalitarian in character?
9. Effectiveness and stability of the rules, institutions and legal arrangements designed to preserve economic, political and civil order.
10. Degree of co-operation and amity obtaining between the groups and classes composing the population.
11. Degree to which the population's pattern of consumption is adjusted to its pattern of resource-equipment.
12. Flexibility of the institutional structure and physical apparatus of the economy.
13. Relative amount of vertical and horizontal mobility characteristic of the population.
14. Internal geographical distribution of economic activities.
15. Exchange relations obtaining between the economy under study and other economies.
16. Degree of specialisation and division of labour in effect.
17. Scale of economic organisation and activity prevalent.
18. Relative amount of complete, partial and disguised unemployment present.
19. Distribution of the power to make and execute entrepreneurial decisions.
20. Residual factors which, though not significant at present, may become significant.

APPENDIX B: ADELMAN AND MORRIS'S LIST

1. Rate of growth of real *per capita* GNP: 1950/1–1963/4 (this is strictly speaking the dependent variable in the study, but the variables are all listed as interdependent, in conformity with factor analysis principles).
2. Size of the traditional agricultural sector.
3. Extent of dualism.
4. Degree of modernisation of outlook.
5. Importance of the indigenous middle class.
6. Extent of social mobility.
7. Extent of literacy.
8. Extent of mass communication.
9. Degree of social tension.
10. Degree of national integration and sense of national unity.
11. Degree of cultural and ethnic homogeneity.
12. Crude fertility rate.
13. Degree of administrative efficiency.
14. Extent of centralisation of political power.
15. Strength of democratic institutions.
16. Degree of freedom of political opposition and press.
17. Predominant basis of the political party system.
18. Degree of competitiveness of political parties.
19. Extent of political stability.
20. Extent of leadership commitment to economic development.
21. Strength of the labour movement.
22. Political strength of the traditional élite.

23. Political strength of the military.
24. Level of effectiveness of the tax system.
25. Level of adequacy of physical overhead capital.
26. Level of modernisation of industry.
27. Level of effectiveness of financial institutions.
28. Level of modernisation of techniques in agriculture.
29. Gross investment rate.
30. Degree of improvement in the tax system since 1950.
31. Change in degree of industrialisation since 1950.
32. Degree of improvement in financial institutions since 1950.
33. Degree of improvement in agricultural productivity since 1950.
34. Degree of improvement in physical overhead capital since 1950.
35. Rate of improvement in human resources.
36. Structure of foreign trade.
37. Abundance of natural resources.
38. Character of agricultural organisation.
39. Extent of urbanisation.
40. *Per capita* GNP in 1961.
41. Character of basic social organisation.

APPENDIX C: SAYIGH'S EARLY LIST

1. Education and training:
   (a) extent and level;
   (b) quality, content and methodology;
   (c) relevance to economic life;
   (d) formal and on-the-job training;
   (e) policies and implications.

2. Socio-cultural determinants:
   (a) social structure;
   (b) social mobility;
   (c) the middle class; deviant groups; traditional *v.* modernising élites;
   (d) loyalties and values;
   (e) system of authority;
   (f) degree of urbanisation;
   (g) emancipation of women;
   (h) religious values of economic relevance.

3. Modernisation:
   (a) mass media indicators;
   (b) economic and other indicators (especially modern institutions);
   (c) openness to the influence of more advanced countries;
   (d) acceptance of technological change (factors and indicators);
   (e) social tension in transitionalism.

4. Political determinants:
   (a) development-mindedness of political leadership;

(b) transmission of popular development consciousness;

(c) locus of economic decision-making (type of system prevailing);

(d) political stability and predictability;

(e) national integration and sense of identity.

5. Public administration determinants:

(a) motivation of public administration (system of appointment, rewards and penalties; delegation of authority, scope for initiative; internal control; and the civil servant's attitude to his function);

(b) efficiency of administration (centralisation, bureaucratisation and efficiency; degree of professionalism; emphasis on problem-solving; non-politicisation).

6. Entrepreneurship and innovation:

(a) locus of entrepreneurship;

(b) quality of entrepreneurship;

(c) sources of entrepreneurship;

(d) incentives and motivation of entrepreneurship;

(e) rejuvenation of the entrepreneurial spirit;

(f) ecology of entrepreneurship (social valuation; governmental relations with the economic community; institutions and legislation of relevance to economic activity).

7. Economic base:

(a) natural resources (special emphasis on petroleum and gas);

(b) infrastructure;

(c) manpower (health, education and training);

(d) level of performance of the economy (the respective shares of agriculture and of industry; structure and the degree of dualism; national product per head, and the pattern of income distribution);

(e) finance (institutions; tax system; consumption and saving habits and magnitudes).

8. Absorptive capacity for capital investment:

(a) manpower availability (of critical categories);

(b) adequacy of supporting infrastructure and factors;

(c) diffusion of knowledge of economic opportunities;

(d) size of market;

(e) design of projects and feasibility studies;

(f) system of investment priorities;

(g) past performance.

9. Rural organisation and reform:

(a) ownership pattern and tenure relationships;

(b) agrarian reform: objectives, content, effectiveness;

(c) technology (extension services, co-operatives, irrigation and drainage, grading-packing-marketing, research, mechanisation);

(d) credit facilities;

(e) organisation and management;

(f) extent of improvement in distribution of wealth and income.

10. Planning and plans:
    (a) socialisation of means of production (social-economic system as framework);
    (b) attitude to planning;
    (c) nature and extent of planning;
    (d) method of formulation of plans (degree of participation by the public, by the outlying districts, and by private sector groups);
    (e) execution and follow-up of plans, and adjustments in the light of experience;
    (f) relationship of planning and budgeting;
    (g) effectiveness of planning in achieving its objectives.

11. Intra-Arab economic co-operation and complementarity:
    (a) trade, the movement of persons and capital;
    (b) trade, payments, and other regional agreements;
    (c) Arab League and Council of Arab Economic Unity efforts in co-operation and complementarity;
    (d) Arab aid agencies;
    (e) Economic Unity Agreement and Arab Common Market;
    (f) joint Arab ventures;
    (g) joint petroleum policies and activities;
    (h) forces for and against co-operation and complementarity.

12. International factors: trade and aid:
    (a) international trade (size, directions, composition, policies);
    (b) the trend of the terms of trade;
    (c) balance of payments position;
    (d) foreign aid and capital flows (bilateral, multilateral, private);
    (e) technical assistance.

NOTES

1. Sections 1 to 4 of this chapter draw heavily on a paper prepared by this writer late in 1972 upon the request of the Director of the Graduate Programme in Development Administration at the American University of Beirut. The GPDA was to use the paper as a framework and guideline to the faculty involved in a basic course on development. The paper was entitled 'Nature, Concepts, and Aspects of Development in the Middle East'.

2. One of the early post-war signs of awareness of the difference was shown by James Baster in 'Recent Literature on the Economic Development of Backward Areas', *Quarterly Journal of Economics,* December 1954, pp. 585-602.

3. Joseph A. Schumpeter, *The Theory of Economic Development* (Cambridge, Mass., 1949, originally published in German in 1909), Ch. II, Section I.

4. See, for instance, my *Entrepreneurship and Development: Private, Public, and Joint Enterprise in Underdeveloped Countries* (doctoral dissertation at the Johns Hopkins University, 1957; unpublished); 'Toward a Theory of Entrepreneurship for the Arab East', in *Explorations in Entrepreneurial History* (Research Center in Entrepreneurial History, Harvard University),

Vol. X, Nos. 3-4, April 1958; and 'Development: The Visible or the Invisible Hand?', in *World Politics* (Princeton University), Vol. XIII, No. 4, July 1961.

5. Yusif Sayigh, *Entrepreneurs of Lebanon: The Role of the Business Leader in a Developing Economy* (Cambridge, Mass., 1962), p. 15. Ch. 2 of this book attempts in its first few pages to bring into relief the distinction between growth and development.

6. Ibid.

7. This is by no means an exhaustive list, especially if we include those writers who have emphasised non-economic factors of, or impediments to, development. (For some illustrations of this latter group, see references in Adamantios Pepelasis, Leon Mears and Irma Adelman, *Economic Development: Analysis and Case Studies* (New York, 1964), Part I, Ch. 6; and Bernard Okun and Richard W. Richardson (eds.), *Studies in Economic Development* (New York, 1961), especially Part Seven, Chs. 28-34 and references in these chapters.

The authors listed have made their contributions in the following writings in particular: (a) Joseph J. Spengler, 'Theories of Socio-Economic Growth', in National Bureau of Economic Research, *Problems in*

the *Study of Economic Growth* (New York, 1959);
(b) W. W. Rostow in *The Process of Economic Growth* (New York, 1952), and *The Stages of Economic Growth* (Cambridge, UK, 1960); (c) Gunnar Myrdal, *The Asian Drama: An Inquiry into the Poverty of Nations* (Penguin Books, 1968), 3 vols.; *The Challenge of World Poverty: A World Anti-Poverty Programme in Outline* (Penguin Books, 1971); *Economic Theory and Underdeveloped Regions* (London, 1963); and *The Political Element in the Development of Economic Theory* (London, 1953). In most of his writings Myrdal reveals his sensitivity to the moral issues involved in, or associated with, poverty and development, and the non-economic aspects of development; (d) Everett E. Hagen, *On the Theory of Social Change: How Economic Growth Begins* (Homewood, Ill., 1962); and (e) Irma Adelman and Cynthia Taft Morris, *Society, Politics, and Economic Development: A Quantitative Approach* (Baltimore, 1967). The contrast can be seen in most textbooks or general expositions, such as those of S. Kuznets, N. S. Buchanan and H. S. Ellis, W. A. Lewis, P. T. Bauer and B. S. Yamey, G. M. Meier and R. E. Baldwin, C. P. Kindleberger and B. Higgins. These writers, and many like them, concentrate on economic aspects and factors.

8. The following discussion of modernisation draws heavily on part of a seminar paper by the writer given on 27 March 1966, at a seminar on 'Economists and Economics in the Arab World' held by the Economic Research Institute of the American University of Beirut. However, the writer has become distinctly disenchanted with modernisation – as the text suggests – for its lack of 'warmth', its amoral tone as compared with development, and the implied superiority of the 'modernity' that is to be emulated.

9. Alexander Gerschenkron, *Economic Backwardness in Historical Perspective* (Cambridge, Mass., 1962), pp. 27-8.

10. See, for instance: (a) Frederick H. Harbison, Joan Maruhnic and Jane R. Resnick, *Quantitative Analyses of Modernization and Development* (Princeton, N. J., 1970); (b) Myron Weiner (ed.), *Modernization: The Dynamics of Growth* (New York, 1966), where, in 25 essays, only passing references are made to the strains and agonies, the disruptions and even unsavoury connotations of modernisation; (c) C. E. Black, *The Dynamics of Modernization: A Study in Comparative History* (New York, 1966); however, this book is sensitive to the agonies and disruptions associated with or arising from modernisation; (d) Daniel Lerner, *The Passing of Traditional Society: Modernizing the Middle East* (New York, 1958); (e) Robert N. Bellah, *Religion and Progress in Modern Asia* (New York, 1965); (f) J. H. Thompson and R. D. Reischauer, *Modernization of the Arab World* (Princeton, N. J., 1966); and (g) William R. Polk and Richard L. Chambers (eds.), *Beginnings of Modernization in the Middle East: The Nineteenth Century* (Chicago, 1968). In addition, several works deal with modernisation in the Third World though not necessarily with clear focus; they suffer from the same overall shortcoming: (a) Walter Z. Laqueur (ed.), *The Middle East in Transition* (London, 1958); (b) Manfred Halpern, *The Politics of Social Change* (Princeton, 1963); (c) Morroe Berger, *The Arab World Today* (New York, 1964); (d) William R. Polk (ed.),

The Developmental Revolution: North Africa, The Middle East and South Asia (Washington, D. C., 1963); (e) Paul Y. Hammond and Sidney S. Alexander (eds.), *Political Dynamics in the Middle East* (New York, 1972); (f) Sydney Nettleton Fisher (ed.), *Social Forces in the Middle East* (Ithaca, N. Y., 1955); (g) David E. Apter, *The Politics of Modernization* (Chicago, 1965); (h) D. A. Rustow, *Politics of Westernization in the Near East* (Princeton, 1956); and (i) Bert F. Hoselitz and Wilbert E. Moore (eds.), *Industrialization and Society* (The Hague, 1963). The basic criticism about nearly all these works is that, even when they show awareness of the conflict between the old and the new, or the traditional and the modern, or of the cultural, social and psychological costs of modernisation, they fail to suggest what safeguards can be established in order for modernisation to have built-in concern for the masses and protection for the poor and the weak (be they individuals, groups or nation-states) versus the rich and the strong.

11. Paul Baran stands out as a modern neo-Marxist whose contribution is worthy of serious examination. See for instance, Paul Baran, *The Political Economy of Backwardness* (New York, 1957).

12. Joseph A. Schumpeter's principal works dealing with or relating to development are: (a) *The Theory of Economic Development*, translated by R. Opie (Cambridge, Mass., 1934); (b) *Business Cycles* (New York, 1939); (c) *Capitalism, Socialism, and Democracy* (second edition, New York, 1947); and (d) *Imperialism and Social Classes*, translated by H. Norden (New York, 1951).

13. For a crisp presentation of Sombart's views on the factors behind the rise of capitalism, see his essay in *The Encyclopedia of the Social Sciences*, under 'Capitalism'.

14. See: (a) P. N. Rosemstein-Rodan, 'Notes on the Theory of the Big Push', in H. S. Ellis and H. C. Wallich (eds.), *Economic Development for Latin America* (New York, 1961); (b) A. O. Hirschman, *The Strategy of Economic Development* (New Haven, Conn., 1958); (c) Ragnar Nurkse, *Problems of Capital Formation in Underdeveloped Countries* (New York, 1953); and (d) B. F. Hoselitz, *Sociological Aspects of Economic Growth* (New York, 1960). For a large sample of writings on non-economic factors in development, see Bernard Okun and Richard W. Richardson, *Studies in Economic Development: A Book of Readings* (New York, 1961), especially Part Seven: Values and Institutions; and Ralph Braibanti and Joseph J. Spengler (eds.), *Tradition, Values, and Socio-Economic Development* (Durham, N. C., 1961), all nine essays, but particularly the first six. The well-known journal *Economic Development and Cultural Change* must be accorded great credit for making immense contributions over the years to a better understanding of non-economic factors in development.

15. David C. McClelland, *The Achieving Society* (Princeton, N. J., 1961); and Everett E. Hagen, *On the Theory of Social Change* (Homewood, Ill., 1962).

16. See: (a) J. J. Spengler, 'Economic Factors in Economic Development', in *American Economic Review*, Vol. XLVII, No. 2, May 1957, *Papers and Proceedings*, pp. 42-56; (b) J. J. Spengler, 'Theories of Socio-Economic Growth', in *Problems in the Study of Economic Growth*

(New York, 1959); (c) W. W. Rostow, *The Process of Economic Growth* (New York, 1952; second edition, Oxford, 1960); (d) W. W. Rostow, *The Stages of Economic Growth* (Cambridge, 1960); (e) Irma Adelman and Cynthia Taft Morris, 'A Factor Analysis of the Interrelationship between Social and Political Variables and Per Capita Gross National Product', *Quarterly Journal of Economics*, Vol. 79, November 1965; (f) Adelman and Morris, *Society, Politics, and Economic Development: A Quantitative Approach* (Baltimore, 1967); (g) Adelman and Morris, 'Performance Criteria for Evaluating Economic Development', *Quarterly Journal of Economics*, Vol. 82, May 1968, which is of some relevance; and (h) Adelman and Morris, 'An Econometric Model of Development', *American Economic Review*, Vol. 58, December 1968.

17. The same is true of A. K. Cairncross in his book, *Factors in Economic Development* (London, 1962), and of Rostow in *The Process of Economic Growth*.

18. The Conference of the International Economic Association of 1960 was devoted to an examination of Rostow's 'take-off'. The papers submitted were afterwards reproduced in the Proceedings of the Conference under the title *The Economics of Take-Off Into Sustained Growth* (London, 1963). The heaviest questioning and criticism came from Simon Kuznets and Alexander Gerschenkron.

19. Kuznets does not believe that we are yet in possession of a theory of development. See the first essay in his book, *Economic Growth and Structure: Selected Essays* (London, 1965), entitled 'Toward A Theory of Economic Growth'. It is to be noted that Kuznets, like Rostow, uses the term 'growth' to mean 'development' in fact – as the context suggests.

20. See note 16 above, items (e) to (h).

21. The term 'ideology' is used with reverence, or pejoratively, depending on the position where the judge stands. We are using the term very much in the sense in which Apter (op. cit., p. 270) defined it. He says: 'Ideology . . . can be defined as the explicit and derivative articulation of political norms.' To this we add that the articulation must be organised into a system of thought which has internal solidarity. For a broad spectrum of views in social theory touching on or relevant to ideology, see Robin Blackburn (ed.), *Ideology in Social Science: Readings in Critical Social Theory* (Fontana/Collins, England, 1972). See also Karl Mannheim's *Ideology and Utopia: An Introduction to the Sociology of Knowledge* (London, 1960 edition) for a profound analysis of the distortions which arise as a result both of the uncritical espousing of ideologies and the fanatical attack on them. For a discussion of the place of ideology in the modern industrial world, see Daniel Bell, *The End of Ideology* (Glencoe, Ill., 1960).

22. Hoselitz, op. cit., p. 42.

23. I am indebted to a former graduate student for this quotation. But, alas, the source is lost to me.

24. W. W. Rostow, *The Process . . .*, Ch. 1, pp. 13-14.

25. J. J. Spengler, 'Theories of Socio-Economic Growth', in National Bureau of Economic Research, *Problems in the Study of Economic Growth* (New York, 1959), pp. 52-3.

26. This and subsequent quotations are from different pages in the same essay by Spengler.

27. In 'Toward a Theory of Economic Growth', Kuznets, op. cit.

28. Adelman and Morris, *Society, Politics, and Economic Development*, p. 279.

29. For a much shorter but better-focused list by the same authors, see their article in *AER* referred to in note 16 above, item (h).

30. A few other writers have used the term 'determinants' in the present context, but without making enough contribution to justify separate reference here. See, for instance, Adamantios Pepelasis, Leon Mears and Irma Adelman, *Economic Development: Analysis and Case Studies* (New York, 1961), Part I, 'Determinants of Economic Development'.

31. Before leaving the subject of choice of determinants, it will be relevant to indicate that there have been several attempts to make a selection of indicators of economic, social and/or political development. Some are merely enumerative and descriptive; some analytical. See, for instance: (a) Frederick H. Harbison, Joan Maruhnic and Jane R. Resnick, op. cit.; (b) Bruce M. Russett, Hayward R. Alker, Jr., Karl W. Deutsch and Harold D. Lasswell, *World Handbook of Political and Social Indicators* (New Haven, 1964); and (c) Arthur Banks and Robert Textor, *A Cross-Polity Survey* (Cambridge, Mass., 1964).

32. Ibid., p. 131. For a full presentation and discussion of the technique of analysis, see Ch. III of Adelman and Morris, *Society, Politics, and Economic Development*.

33. As the authors state (p. 131), in factor analysis 'all variables are dependent and independent in turn. Thus, by contrast with regression analysis, which is a study of dependence, factor analysis is a study of mutual interdependence.'

34. Adelman and Morris, *Society, Politics, and Economic Development* Chs. IV-VIII. (In their subsequent *AER* article, they came up with more refined findings. See note 16 above, item (h)).

35. This formulation was made by John Kenneth Galbraith in a speech at the conference of the Society for International Development, in New York, March 1965 (mimeographed). For an earlier formulation (which is not as succinct) see Galbraith's *Economic Development in Perspective* (Cambridge, Mass., 1962), Ch. I.

36. The methodology used by me fits into what is ' . . . sometimes inelegantly referred to as "fishing", that is, going to the data without a clearly formulated hypothesis and letting the data themselves suggest relationships . . .' 'Yet,' the quotation continues, 'the activity should not be disdained, particularly if it takes the form of a constant dialogue between theory and data . . .' (Bruce M. Russett *et al.*, op. cit., p. 2.) It is here submitted that the net has come up with a catch of fish, and to this extent the methodology has been justified.

37. This statement finds evidence in the standard books on development theory and policy (such as those of Meier and Baldwin, Kindleberger, Higgins, and the readings collections of Okun and Richardson, and of Agarwala and Singh – all of which are too well known to require detailed bibliographical annotation). It also can be supported more concretely by a perusal of Gerald M. Meier's *Leading Issues in Development Economics:*

Selected Materials and Commentary (New York, 1964), as this work draws on the writings of many economists.

For examples of writings where greater awareness is manifested of the concerns underlying this section on 'Major Issues', see Gunnar Myrdal's *Economic Theory and Underdeveloped Regions* (London, 1957); *Asian Drama* (Penguin Books, 1968), Vols. I, II and III; and *The Challenge of World Poverty* (Penguin Books, 1970). See also The Society for International Development, *International Development 1969,* Proceedings of the Eleventh World Conference (Madras, India, 1970).

38. See The Dag Hammarskjöld Foundation, *What Now? The 1975 Dag Hammarskjöld Report* (Upsala, 1975), especially pp. 93-4.

39. Gerschenkron, op. cit., p. 28.

40. A. B. Zahlan is probably the Arab who has directed most thought to the matter. See 'The Brain Drain', in *Middle East Studies Association Bulletin,* Vol. 6, No. 3, October 1972, pp. 1-16.

2 The Determinants in Operation

This chapter serves as testing ground for the propositions, whether explicit or implicit, made in the last chapter. Essentially, these centre around or relate to the determinants considered highly relevant and selected for examination in this study, and the manner in which they act on development, whether singly or in combination, and in what sequence or within what system of relationships. In this latter respect, the propositions were far from explicit: indeed, they were tentative, the methodology adopted being one which was to permit the search and groping for generalisations from the body of data to be amassed, on the basis of a number of general ideas and positions set forth earlier.

The economic, political-administrative and socio-cultural determinants are examined in the three sections that follow. Two determinants of special significance, the oil and gas resources and Arab co-operation and complementarity, which would ordinarily have fallen inside the economic category, have been singled out for separate treatment and are discussed together in the fourth section.

The examination of determinants is essentially conducted through the large number of interviews undertaken. But the interviews are supplemented, qualified, or otherwise influenced by the relevant literature and the writer's long familiarity with the region under study. As the discussion moves along, the devices, measuring rods or notions utilised in testing the effectiveness of the various determinants will be indicated. However, as pointed out in the last chapter, the methodology used is not one which permits or requires quantitative measurement, except in a few cases in the category of economic determinants.

The arrangement into categories is itself a matter of convenience and is by no means rigorous; the categories are not mutually exclusive, and some items could equally well fit into a category different from the one in which they have been placed. This was considered forgivable. The alternatives would have been to establish a separate category for cases of overlap, or to group all determinants together. But, since many of the determinants have bearing on more than one field, and the whole approach is interdisciplinary in any case, it was felt that the arrangement adopted was legitimate.

Another observation with regard to the discussion in this chapter relates to the order of the sections. The sequence adopted is not necessarily an indication of the time sequence, the priorities, or the pattern of causality according to which the determinants operate and their impact is felt. Both the sequence and the pattern will be explored as we move along. Likewise, the manner in which the determinants act and interact among themselves will receive attention in the last part of the chapter. Some concluding remarks will also be made there with respect to the system or framework within which the development process has been unfolding, and how this framework can be adjusted to speed the process and enrich the content of development.

1. ECONOMIC DETERMINANTS

The library research and field-work relating to economic determinants aimed at exploring the significance of ten of these. Eight will be discussed in this section, while the first and the last items in the list as set out in the last chapter (the oil and gas resources, and Arab economic co-operation and complementarity, respectively) which have been taken out of this category, will be allowed a section to themselves.

Standard introductory textbooks of economics group the factors of production into four headings: land (including water and subsoil natural resources), labour, man-made capital and entrepreneurship. These four factors form the core of the present category, with four other items added: economic structure, industrialisation, agrarian reform and physical infrastructure. Each of the items will be introduced and discussed in turn. This procedure will be followed in the other sections as well.

1. The resource and performance base of any economy is obviously of great significance for its growth.[1] The natural resources available themselves promote or inhibit the diversification and productive performance of the economy — depending on their abundance, value, accessibility and marketability. However, the resource base is not something fixed and final, or in itself independent. It is, instead, a function of the capital and technology available to the country, the studies and surveys undertaken to determine the quantity and quality of the resources, the markets accessible to them, the country's capability to process them, and the seriousness in the efforts made to develop them.

The Arab countries surveyed here vary widely with respect to their resource base.[2] In some instances, as in Lebanon, this is mainly restricted to land, water, beautiful scenery and a climate suitable to varied agricultural production and tourist activities. At the other extreme, as in Iraq, the resource base includes, in addition to abundant land and water and beautiful scenery in parts of the country, rich reserves of petroleum, gas, sulphur and phosphates, as well as a few other minerals. Until petroleum was discovered and exploited commercially, the desert parts of the Arab world, particularly in the Arabian Peninsula and Libya, were considered very poorly endowed. Petroleum has revolutionised the endowment situation. In general, it can be said that each of the countries under survey has some natural resource that is commercially exploitable, or otherwise usable for the production of some important marketable product. This is true of the oil and gas where they abound, as of land and water, or of the phosphates in Morocco, Tunisia, Jordan, Iraq and Syria — apart from the scenery and climate of several of the countries which enable them to market important tourist services.

However, nowhere but in the five major oil-producing countries are the natural resources of enough significance to form a solid base for development. Yet even there, a major qualification is called for. This is that until 1973 the oil resource formed a *financial* base for development, by providing the revenues capable of being translated into capital goods, education programmes and other investment-related expenses. Only very recently did oil begin to become a 'leading sector' in the fuller sense of the term, activating other sectors and promoting industries and activities upstream and downstream through integration or the operation of backward and forward linkages. The non-oil resources, even the more important among them, have served neither function to a considerable extent; that is, they have neither provided a large volume of financial resources, nor provided the impetus for the accelerated development of the rest of the economy.

The question of scale and quality apart, the impact of the resources on growth and development is closely and causally tied to the quality and determination of the political management of the economy. Thus, even in the case of oil, it was only in the late sixties and early seventies that the Arab governments decided to insist on a more satisfactory return for their oil exports. It is true that the energy situation in the world then helped them in their decision, but their determination was a necessary condition for the improvement in their relative position *vis-à-vis* the oil companies and the large consumers.

In addition to the question of determination, there is that of the organisation of the industry concerned. Thus, such matters as the speed and efficiency of the exploitation of the natural resources available, their processing and marketing, and the bargaining capability of the agency in control – all these factors influence the extent to which the resources generate income for the country. In this respect, the Arab countries have registered some significant steps towards efficient and effective organisation, administration, control and operation. The bureaux or authorities that control the phosphates mines in Morocco, Tunisia, Jordan or Syria; the national oil companies in all the oil-producing countries (but with varying degrees of success, crowned by the outstanding example of SONATRACH of Algeria), the cotton boards of Egypt, Sudan and Syria (with the notable example of the Gezira scheme of Sudan) – all are manifestations of the realisation of the role of the controlling agencies and the relevance of these agencies to the optimisation of the exploitation of resources.

Finally, the optimal exploitation (and by this we mean not just the mining or extraction of the resource, but also its processing, industrialisation, marketing and distribution, as well as the determination of volume produced and price demanded) to a certain extent depends on the performance base of the economy. This relates to the efficiency of manpower and of institutions, to their problem-solving capabilities, and in the final analysis to the level of national product *per capita* and the proportion of it used for investment purposes.

The relationship between the resource base and the performance base is of great significance. A satisfactory performance base can go far in compensating for a feeble resource base. The case of Lebanon is instructive. Here the performance of the private sector has been high in purely economic terms, while the resources are modest. Yet the economy has succeeded in extracting notable returns from these resources. The case of Iraq until the mid- or late sixties provides us with the opposite illustration: a well-endowed resource base producing returns far from commensurate with the resources, because of the unsatisfactory performance base and the poor political management of the economy. Sudan too falls in this latter category where, with the exception of the Gezira Scheme, the performance base was far from adequate for the enormous resource base of the country. In this case, one encounters a huge excess of water available over storage facilities, and a similar excess of cultivable over cultivated land. The idleness of resources is attributable to inadequate infrastructure, insufficient investment capital, shortage of skilled manpower plus weak motivation, low level of versatility between crops requiring different techniques, frequent change of government, and diversion of resources to 'pacification of the South' for many years. We have gone into some detail here in order to underline the point that resources by themselves tell us very little about the prospects of development.

It is not necessary to classify all the Arab countries according to this typology; suffice it to point to this important relationship between the resource base and the performance base, and to add that the political management of the economy, and the organisation and control mechanisms applicable to the resources constitute factors as important in the assessment of the role of the resources in development as the abundance and quality of the reserves available.[3] To sum up, for the twelve countries and the major resources under examination, the assessment brings out varied conclusions. By and large, much of the resource base has been explored and is under exploitation, but in larger part the underground resources are still sold in their crude form. Processing and industrialisation are still at an early stage of development, and much more time will have to pass before more advanced forms of utilisation will predominate. With the growing realisation of the significance of such advanced utilisation, and of the improvement in the organisation and control mechanisms and the political management of resources, these latter will acquire a distinctly increasing economic role as a factor in development. If we were to end with one sentence, we would say that the resources available constitute opportunities for development, which meet with serious constraints on the one side, and with efforts to overcome or loosen the constraints on the other side. The outcome determines how effective resources are as a factor in economic development.

If we turn to the land and water resources, we find that these are still far from being a major, active factor in development. The region is still a large importer of foodstuffs. The agrarian reform measures undertaken, which will come under discussion further down, are related to the question presently examined. It is sufficient at this point to emphasise the need for much greater development in the rural sector at large (water and land utilisation, rural education, extension services, and the like), if this sector is to provide a strong base for development. But the whole question will later come under closer scrutiny.

2. The economic structure, especially with respect to the degree of dualism in existence, has been selected for examination as a determinant. This refers to the sectoral distribution of the economy, its market organisation (the degree of monopolistic and oligopolistic predominance), and the extent of dualism in the sense in which Boeke used the term (that is, where modern foreign-dominated, and very archaic indigenous, industries or sectors exist and operate side by side without the first influencing the second much).[4] It was thought initially that a structure characterised by a rather large contribution by manufacturing industry and the existence of modern organisations or institutions such as banks and corporations would be capable of providing an impetus for development. Where dualism exists, and it does (or did until recently) to a certain extent in most developing countries, the issue is different.

Dualism can be said to promote growth through the 'example effect' which the modern, foreign-owned or -controlled sector or industry exerts on the backward, indigenous sectors or industries. Alternatively, it can be said to inhibit the fast growth and modernisation of the other sectors, partly because the foreign interests would want the discrepancy between the modern and the traditional sectors to continue in order for them to get cheap labour and materials from the depressed sectors, and to extend the phase of dependency by the depressed on the modern sectors. Furthermore, the example effect does not operate where the gap in technology, capital availability, labour skills and organisation is very wide.

To go back to structure. When we set out to examine this aspect of the Arab economies, we found that by and large manufacturing industry, with a few exceptions, contributed a small share to the national product.[5] Furthermore, modernisation in basic production, distribution and financing institutions was limited, though proceeding noticeably in most countries. However, market structures varied as the economic systems varied from country to country. In those economies where private enterprise was still accorded a prominent place, as in Lebanon, Saudi Arabia, Kuwait, Jordan and Morocco, there were strong monopolistic and oligopolistic set-ups, in effect if not overtly and explicitly. In these other countries where socialism (or state capitalism) was the predominant form of organisation, the state was found to be or to behave as a monopolist in effect, though official condemnation of monopolies was loud. But in either case, early on in the enquiry we realised that the structure was not a determinant of significance. It was essentially a reflection of the state and level of modernisation and development at any one time, more of a result than a cause of development. The degree of relevance of structure was seen to be very small, in the context in which factors are examined as determinants.

The situation was found to be quite different with respect to dualism. It was felt that dualism was more of an inhibiting than a promotive factor. And this was truer, the larger the extent of dualism. Invariably, traces of the 'example effect' were found, where the demonstration value of the modern sector or industry had been effective in urging some entrepreneurial elements to establish business linked somehow to the needs of the modern sector and to a certain extent emulating the simpler aspects of its technology or organisation. (The predominant examples of such promotive impact were around Aramco in Saudi Arabia, but were hard to find elsewhere.[6]) By and large, as the modern industry or sector (whether oil, a plantation or a railway) has remained separate, aloof and insulated, the leavening effect of its existence and operations has remained minimal. To sum up, it can be said that the promotive value of the modern sector, where it can be seen, has arisen precisely from the attempt by this sector, or by the government on being sensitised to the modern sector's insulation and separateness, to establish greater interaction with the non-modern sectors — that is, to counteract the dualism and its implications. Thus dualism can be said to be a negative factor, while the measures to reverse dualism or reduce its extent have been a promotive factor. Evidence of these conclusions can be found most clearly in the Maghreb economies, where the modern sector had enjoyed political-social, as well as economic, privilege and power, and in the oil economies where the concessionary oil companies had enjoyed extensive privileges, and had found shelter behind concession agreements and the fact that the Western countries to which they belonged exercised veiled if not overt power. It is only where these powerful, foreign-dominated sectors have come under national control that they began to have a promotive effect.

3. The industrial base and the industrialisation process were examined as the third economic determinant.[7] The country chapters in Volume I have shown the relative size of the industrial sector in each of the economies, and indicated that this size is small — hovering around 10 per cent of national product, except for Egypt, Lebanon and Algeria, where it averages about 20 per cent. (The proportion of the labour force in industrial activities is close to that of the sector's contribution to GNP. Likewise, its share in exports is very small on the average.) But there is more to the base than mere relative size in GNP or labour structure. The degree of modernity is of special importance here, involving newness in the products manufactured, sophistication in the technology used, efficiency in industrial organisation, recourse to research and innovation, and development of the structure of management-labour relations in such a way as to be capable of coping with modern industrial problems and requirements.

These aspects of the industrial *base* are all of significance for an assessment of the degree of modernisation and efficiency of the industrial sector. However, they are essentially determined by development, rather than a determinant of it, even though once they become more pronounced, they contribute to the speeding of modernisation and of economic development — in other words, they fit into a pattern of 'determined-determinant-determined . . .', and so on. This brings us to the *process* of industrialisation.

The distinction between base and process is of relevance to our enquiry. Thus, the base itself can be considered static within a relatively short period of time, and to that extent its promotive power will be modest; as already indicated, it will be limited to influencing later phases of industrialisation, rather than being a prime mover. On the other hand, the industrialisation process is a dynamic force. This is truer, the faster the process, and the deeper it goes. By depth we mean the inculcation of industrial attitudes and frames of mind, the prevalence of industrial entrepreneurship, the acceptance of industrial values such as factory discipline and labour commitment, rationality, a greater belief in economic cause-effect relationships and in man's power to control and shape his environment, the development of the innovative faculties in the industrial manpower, and the growing significance of capital goods industries in the structure of industry.

Here again, the unfolding of the process in the sense in which we understand it is as much the outcome and manifestation of modernisation and development as the industrial base was stated to be. But with one important difference. This lies in the content of the process, and in the power of the various manifestations to influence the speed and course of economic development. As these manifestations reflect deeper changes in the *ambiance* of the industrial sector and in its institutions and the attitudes related to it, they will have a larger role to play as determinants than the mere relative size of the sector, or the newness of the machines imported.

Field-work and library research have shown great unevenness in the industrial base among the countries surveyed, but more so in the process of industrialisation.[8] Perusal of the literature on hand, and scrutiny of the observations made in interviews with government authorities, officers of chambers of industry, labour leaders, university professors, journalists and businessmen have shown that many of the more profound aspects of transformation are yet to come. What is witnessed is more an outward, mechanistic expansion in industrial investment and activity, than a deep and far-reaching process of industrialisation. Algeria and to a lesser extent Egypt and Lebanon are to be excepted from parts of this judgement, but elsewhere the process is still slow and of modest volume. This is true even in such countries as Saudi Arabia, where huge investments are being made in industry. Iraq, on the other hand, seems to be moving in the same direction as Algeria, with increasing attention to the intangible aspects of industrialisation such as research attitudes, and the like.

What reduces the actual potency of the industrialisation process as a determinant of economic development still further is the shortcomings in industrial policies and institutions in most of the countries under survey. Thus, policies often oscillate between hesitation and wobbliness on the one hand, and rashness on the other; the underpinning of studies and industrial strategies is weak; frequent inconsistency arises between the speedy and far-reaching industrialisation desired, and the economic, financial and fiscal, and educational and manpower policies formulated; and probably above all, industrial policies are laid on a purely local basis (that is, they are tailored to the size of the national state), instead of taking the opportunities in the Arab region as a whole into account. The mutual disregard among countries of what the others are doing in this respect and what industries they are developing and with what capacity, necessarily leads to waste, adoption of a small scale of operations, and a slowing down of the pace of industrialisation.

Complaints about defective policies, or even the absence of policy in the true sense of the term in certain instances, were made almost everywhere. However, it is interesting that in those countries where policy formulation and the quality of industrial policy were somewhat more advanced, the complaint was stronger and more articulated than elsewhere. This is probably because where awareness is greater of what sound policy should be, is also where ambitions stir for yet better policy. One area where the failings of policy deserve special mention is the delimitation of the terrain left to private enterprise, in distinction from that set for the public sector. This is particularly relevant to the countries claiming to have a socialist system. As this delimitation is both unclear and subject to erratic shifts, investment is inhibited and potentially energetic industrial entrepreneurship is underutilised and wasted.[9]

The slow development of appropriate institutions is another factor in the limitation of the effectiveness of the industrialisation process as a factor in development. Every country surveyed has a ministry or a department of industry, and an industrial bank or some other specialised financing agency;[10] some have special centres for the promotion of industry, and many undertake the promotion through the ministries or departments in charge of industrial affairs. But in the overwhelming number of cases these institutions fall short of the needs. Financial resources for investment are inadequate even in some large oil countries; research and experimentation are extremely poor, unimaginative and haphazard; promotion is superficial; and the supply of entrepreneurial ideas is limited. It is particularly suggestive of the inadequacy of the institutions set for research and promotion that their own authorities consistently complained of the poor quality and limited reach of the work of their institutions.

Another complaint centred around the lack of seriousness of policy-makers in their attitude to and dealings with these institutions. Often there was no continuous link between the policy-makers and their presumed 'research and think tanks' in the field of industrial development. The shortcomings in the areas of policy and institutions combined reflect themselves in further depriving the process of industrialisation of some of its important components and in slowing it down, thus resulting in slowing down economic development itself.

It ought to be mentioned, finally, that expansion in the industrial sector has often been motivated by the desire to look modern and advanced, or to conform to some ideological model in which the industrial sector occupies a conspicuous place. As such motivation has shallow roots and does not reach deep down to that fundamental transformation which is called for by profound industrialisation, it tends to distort reality and to weaken the real drive for industrialisation. The situation is reminiscent of 'Gresham's Law', according to which bad money drives good money out of circulation. Here, too, the false or insufficiently deep motives for industrialisation drive the sound motives out of circulation.

Some specific illustrations can bring the generalisations we have made in this section into greater relief. Thus, with respect to policy, instances were encountered where the industrial bank of a certain country gave loans to new or existing industries while the Ministry of Finance refused to give customs exemptions to the same industries which were to be encouraged. Incorporation proceedings are almost invariably time-consuming, expensive and complicated. The profits tax on corporations in this same country is fixed at about 60 per cent on profits beyond about $35,000 but progressive below that level. Finally, confused policy can be seen in the instance when the Minister of Economy, in a speech with which he opened a conference of the General Union of Arab Chambers of Commerce, Industry, and Agriculture in his country, condemned the Arab bourgeoisie without consideration for the fact that he was addressing the flower of that bourgeoisie from the whole Arab region.

In yet another country, the industrial estate set up to promote the establishment of industry and provide it with external economies has its power plant under the jurisdiction of one ministry, while the estate's board falls under another ministry. And when the board displeased the ministry, it was dissolved and not replaced for many months. In the meantime, the director-general's authority was curtailed to the point that the administration performed none but the most routine activities. In this same country, it took seven years of 'active consideration' before an industrial bank was set up. However, in this instance, the result justified the long wait, since the bank was adequately provided with share and working capital, and succeeded in having a capable and dynamic president, with the necessary authority. (In another country, after an equally long wait, the industrial bank was formed but was allowed a very small capital although the country had much more resources than it could cope with domestically.) Again, though some measures were being taken to promote industry, both institutional and financial, several key policy-makers declared themselves to this writer as not quite sure that it was wise to undertake industrialisation.

In the countries from which illustrations have been drawn, as in several others (notably the Maghreb area), industrial entrepreneurship is in very short supply. The industrialists had in the vast majority of cases moved into industry from a background of trade or finance, and have carried with them the attitudes and outlooks appropriate to the sectors they had been in, not the one of their recent choice. Again, in these several countries, foreign entrepreneurship is welcome to enter into partnership with nationals, though the association may take different forms and pursue different formulas.

In Algeria and in Iraq in particular the choice of industry and its location are subjected to certain strategic, social and demographic criteria, apart from the obvious technical and economic criteria. Thus, in Algeria, the provision of employment, the achievement of better population and economic balance between provinces and between rural and urban centres, the avoidance of mammoth industrial centres although these can be defended on the grounds of scale and external economies — are considerations that receive due attention in deciding on the location of industrial plants.

Finally, in at least nine out of the twelve countries surveyed, it is declared policy to take co-ordination and complementarity among the Arab economies into account when examining the establishment of industry. But nowhere is there any evidence of actual change in the decision in the light of the logic of such co-ordination and complementarity. As a result, there is duplication, waste, unnecessary competitiveness, and of necessity the choice of a reduced capacity and therefore of higher unit cost than otherwise.

4. The fourth determinant to be examined is agrarian reform and agricultural development.[11] Not all the Arab countries under survey have had agrarian reform; where such reform has been instituted it has been examined in the country chapters of Volume I of this book. What we aim to do here is to look at agrarian reform in its capacity as a determinant of development. To this end, we will first identify the manner in which the reform can fulfil this function, then test it accordingly to see if it has actually fulfilled it, and if not, how it can do so. As far as possible, repetition of the presentation of the reform measures undertaken will be avoided. Finally, the role of agricultural development proper will be scrutinised for its contribution to overall economic development.

The basic criterion and test to be applied is the ability of agrarian reform to revolutionise the structure of relations in the rural sector and its performance. Reform is designed to raise the motivation of the mass of small landowners, agricultural workers and peasants in general; to raise the level of effort and commitment of the rural population as a result of the acquisition of a greater stake in improved performance; to raise the general level of the farmers' technical capability and organisation in the various aspects of agriculture (such as farming methods, grading and packing, marketing and co-operation); to expand credit facilities, simplify borrowing procedures, and ease collateral requirements; and to improve and widen rural services (such as education, piped water, electricity) in such a way as to make the countryside more attractive to live and work in. The end result is to make work more remunerative at the individual level, and to make the agricultural sector more productive and contributive to the national product and to society's well-being in general.

The various improvements have to reach a large proportion of the rural community, and have a lasting effect, if agrarian reform is to be a determining factor in development. Furthermore, it is not enough that this reform should mainly mean or result in a redistribution of income, important as this may be. It ought, additionally, to result in distinctly increased production and income. To this end, the organisation of production has to be examined and adjusted. Thus, if the limitation of the size of ownership as one aspect of agrarian reform were to result in fragmentation, the disappearance of large land holdings which formed efficient units of operation, and finally sub-optimal total production, then the advantages of small ownership and the expansion of the family-farm form of ownership ought to be combined with co-operative or collective operation. In this manner the productive units may become as large as efficient operation requires, while family ownership continues to exist and the average family holding continues to be small in area. Finally, the rural community itself has to have a say in the design of agrarian reform, as it is best informed of the shortcomings and ills of the system needing reform. This community must also participate in the implementation of reform measures. Participation, to which we allocate a great deal of significance in the process and content of development, will thus be achieved in the present context.

It was found in the country chapters above that serious and far-reaching agrarian reform measures were undertaken in only four of the twelve countries examined, namely Egypt, Syria, Iraq and Algeria. Minor and limited measures had also been undertaken in Sudan, Jordan, Tunisia, Libya and Morocco. In Libya but more so in Morocco, the dispossession of Italians and Frenchmen, respectively, of the land they had on the whole acquired illegally or through twisted, pseudo-legal means, was considered land reform. But in Libya certain supplementary measures have been undertaken. These aim at regional development, the provision of basic services such as water, technical advice and credit, within a framework of redistributive and corrective measures.

While some of the services have also been extended in Morocco, they have been less adequate, and they have not been aimed essentially at the poorer peasants and smaller land holdings. Indeed, in Morocco the privileged tended to become more privileged, since many of the services and investments, as in irrigation dams and networks, were designed to benefit the rich and powerful or at least ended in benefiting them. Kuwait, with no agricultural land to speak of, remains outside this account. Lebanon's efforts remain negligible. Saudi Arabia's reform measures are piecemeal, and are largely restricted to some land reclamation, resettlement of tribesmen, the provision of water for farming and the animal stock of tribesmen, and agricultural credit.

The criteria for the relevance of agrarian reform to development have been identified. It remains for us to see whether this reform has been instrumental in development. The testing will have to be undertaken for the two groups of countries: the eight which have limited and haphazard reform measures, and the four that have had far-reaching, integrated reform. We can dispose of the first group readily: the scale, content and reach of the reform measures have been so modest, limited and superficial that the measures have not been instrumental in promoting development. The library research, the perusal of relevant statistics and the interviews undertaken have uniformly failed to provide indicators to the contrary. Where agricultural production has expanded, in total or in the case of specific crops, this has occurred mainly through the extension of the areas cropped, the greater provision of irrigation water, or the use of improved seeds, more mechanisation, or more fertilisers — not through integrated agrarian reform. But even with these promotive measures accounted for, the impact has been weak. Thus, the widely acclaimed active dam-building policy of Morocco has served an area of 300,000–400,000 ha, much of which is reported to belong to rich and influential persons who own large tracts.[12] In Libya, agriculture has been neglected as contracting, government and construction have attracted many peasants away from the land. And Saudi Arabia's measures have been slow, modest, and of marginal influence.

The picture is mixed as far as the second group of countries is concerned, namely, Egypt, Syria, Iraq and Algeria. This is so in two respects: as between countries, and as between different aspects of agrarian reform. The three Mashreq countries are rather similar if viewed broadly. Egypt, Syria and Iraq instituted measures not dissimilar in any major respect. But these measures were implemented in different frameworks or against different settings, as we have had occasion to see.

In all three countries, emphasis proved in the final analysis to have been placed on two reform aspects: limitation of land ownership and improvement in tenancy terms, both of which had redistributive implications more than anything else. The ancillary services — extension, credit, promotion of co-operatives, grading and packing, marketing, and the setting up of community centres — were boosted, but have not taken significant dimensions. And in all three cases, but particularly in Syria and Iraq, the redistribution of the land expropriated from large landowners was very slow, which resulted in the freezing of the level of production, or even in its decline. Again, in all three countries but particularly in Syria and Iraq, very little has been achieved in the evolving of new modalities (such as co-operative or collective production, state farms, and the like) designed to counteract the damage of fragmentation arising from the reduction in the size of the unit of ownership. And finally, in all three countries but more so in Syria and Iraq, the management by agrarian reform authorities of the expropriated land has been inefficient and wasteful, with the result that land in substantial dimensions has remained idle and production has consequently suffered.

But perhaps more significantly, the three countries have registered little real improvement in the productivity, income and living conditions of the rural population. The tenants have experienced improvement in their circumstances, and this is probably the major achievement to record. But the mass of rural inhabitants have not felt enough social and economic improvement to justify the hopes initially pinned on agrarian reform.

Basically, this reform succeeded in breaking the structures that had stifled the countryside and introduced a revolutionary dimension of great promise into society. But the management of the reform failed to turn the promise into full reality. This is partly because the framework of ideas was insufficiently large to sustain the measures legislated and provide continued motivation for real reform, thus creating a situation where the legal framework rested on too insecure an ideas base; partly because the trained manpower needed for the far-reaching reform legislation was not available, and whatever manpower was available was insufficiently sensitised to the true content of reform, insufficiently radicalised, insufficiently motivated and excessively bureaucratised.

Furthermore, the reform was exaggeratedly centralised, from the design phase to final implementation. Participation by the rural community, the true instrument and the beneficiary of reform, was minimal. The whole operation remained largely in isolation from the overall development of the economy, and the notion of development itself remained mainly confined to its narrow economic dimensions. Under the circumstances, the social, cultural and political dimensions of agrarian reform were not adequately appreciated; indeed, even its economic dimension remained insufficiently appreciated, with the result that production itself suffered. Consequently, as a final verdict, one can say that agrarian reform, which was potentially a strong determinant of development, failed to fulfil much of the promise vested in it in Egypt, Syria and Iraq. However, now with the basic foundations laid, a clearer conceptualisation of the role and function of reform and a more efficient and consistent management would be capable together of removing the obstacles which block the action of agrarian reform as a potent determinant of development. Signs already exist of a favourable shift, mainly in Egypt beginning with 1972/3, but also in Iraq and Syria. There is more emphasis on raising production, and the under-utilisation of reform land has virtually disappeared.

The case of Algeria stands in contrast with that of the three Mashreq countries. Although Algeria's reform (or its agrarian revolution, as it is called there) has been launched very recently, in the early seventies, it has been designed, and is being implemented, quite differently. This reform is woven closely into the broad, overall view of comprehensive development as espoused by the political leadership of the country – the government and the party. The developmental fabric combines in an integrated fashion the economic, technological, social and political factors.

Specifically, a careful study of the conditions in existence (including the pattern of land ownership) was made, and the reform was designed to take care of this reality. The approach was to be pragmatic and flexible. The rural community was brought in at every phase, from design to the actual implementation of reform measures. This was achieved via the Assemblée Populaire Communale at the village level, on to the Governorate or District Assemblée, and finally to the national conference of representatives of the village APCs. The participation was real and widespread. Furthermore, it was up to each district and village to determine the *lot viable,* or the area deemed necessary for a family to operate and live on, and this approach was to lead to the determination of the ceiling ownership permissible, areas beyond which were to be expropriated.

The ancillary services, including housing and rural education, were energetically promoted, and the manpower needed for the delivery of these services was seriously trained. The local community was essentially mobilised to provide those elements of the manpower assigned to work in that community. The APC was not merely to undertake functions related to agrarian reform, but also to self-government in general, and, wherever possible, the execution of projects relating to the locality in the country's development plan. Politically, the APC was a representative body which provided training ground in grass-roots participatory democracy. Combined with *auto-gestion,* or the self-management of farms and plantations taken over from the *colons,* or passed on for exploitation by the government from state domain, agrarian reform measures constitute a major landmark in the development of rural society. While it is too early to examine the impact of the Algerian agricultural revolution on production proper, the indicators on hand suggest that this revolution will have marked positive results, on production, productivity, income and well-being combined – in addition to its beneficial social and political aspects.

In conclusion, it can be said that in Algeria more than in any other Arab country, agrarian reform already plays a marked role as a determinant of development, and promises to play an even larger role if the overall political and economic setting remains as suitable as it is. The impact of this determinant reaches beyond the economic into the social and political and participatory aspects of development. Thus, unlike most other Arab countries, the rural sector in Algeria does not lag seriously behind the urban sector and its related economic activities. Elsewhere the lag is very large, with the result that the harmony or social balance which development is supposed to bring about between the countryside and the urban centres has occurred only minimally. Furthermore, the Algerian example shows that in the countryside itself, the imbalance among landowners or among farmers is minimised, while even in the three Mashreq countries which have instituted agrarian reform, this imbalance is still large. Indeed, the imbalance has grown in Egypt to the point that protest by radical and socially conscious citizens has become loud and persistent.[13]

We must not leave this discussion without referring to Sudan's experience. Although Sudan did not institute agrarian reform, and it was the British colonial power that built up the Gezira scheme, this scheme has been of immense developmental impact. However, for such institutional arrangements to continue to be of strong impact, they have to be generalised to reach a large proportion of the cultivable land, supportive factors will have to come into play (particularly investible funds), and the reform measures must have to affect rural structure and motivation strongly.

So far we have dwelt on agrarian reform. Another component of the determinant under examination is agricultural development. Is this component properly speaking a determinant, and if so, how does it operate? And has it been instrumental in promoting overall economic development? These are the questions to which we will presently turn.

By agricultural development we mean the improvement of the equipment, techniques and methods of the sector, as well as the extension of the area under the plough, the reclamation of hitherto unutilised land, the harnessing and use of water resources for irrigation, and the application of research to agriculture. It will be seen that almost all these aspects of agricultural development are also encountered in agrarian reform. Yet the two are different, conceptually and in application. The difference lies essentially in the revolutionary aspect of agrarian reform, in the change in structures and institutions involved, and in the radical transformation in the power set-up related to land ownership. These institutional and structural changes involve something outside 'the circular flow', to borrow a concept from Schumpeter, in the sense that they constitute sharp and far-reaching departures from the existing pattern of relations, the state of the agricultural arts, and the socio-economic desiderata associated with agricultural activity.

With the definition and explanations indicated as starting-point, it seems legitimate to suggest two things: that agricultural development is more a result of overall economic development, or a process associated and simultaneous with development, than a determinant of it; and that only once agricultural development has proceeded some distance will it serve as a base for further overall development. Otherwise, to maintain that agricultural development helps bring about overall development would amount to circularity in reasoning, very much the same way that the contention that industrial development could bring about overall development was found earlier to involve circularity. But, as in that instance, agrarian reform, like its counterpart, the deep and far-reaching *process* of industrialisation, can be considered a potent determinant. The distinction derives from the different content of each of these components under discussion: agrarian reform and agricultural development. Specifically, the difference derives from attribution to reform of radical institutional and structural changes that drastically change the relations of production and the motivation of the whole rural sector, changes which are quite distinct from the content of agricultural development narrowly defined.[14]

These qualifications and distinctions notwithstanding, it can be said that if agricultural development could proceed far, thanks to the convergence of some favourable conditions and circumstances, and if as a result the production and export of agricultural produce were to expand considerably, then agricultural development could promote overall economic development via the financial resources made available by the expanded production and exports. (It is to be noticed that we have qualified overall development — as we had done before — with the term 'economic'. The qualification, wherever it occurs, is meant to remind the reader of the limited content of economic development, and of the necessity of having some additional important conditions satisfied for comprehensive development to occur.) Syria is a case in point where agricultural development in the post-war decade led to economic development through the intermediary of the greater financial resources made available for further investment. This observation cannot be made of any other country among those examined here, even though Egypt and Sudan have important agricultural sectors which form the backbone of the economy. Yet in neither country was there dramatic development in that sector in the post-war period. And, in the case of Sudan, no notable economic development has been recorded.

The discussion has so far been fragmented, centring first around agrarian reform, then around agricultural development. It ought, finally, to be pointed out that a fusion or concurrence of the two, or the implementation of agrarian reform of wide dimensions so as to include components of both processes will constitute a strong determinant of development. The impact of such revolutionary transformation in the rural sector will be widespread: it will reach into the socio-political and structural-institutional, as well as the purely economic, realms. Algeria, it seems convincingly evident, is well on the road to this comprehensive transformation, with Egypt, Iraq and Syria (and to a lesser extent Libya) moving in the same direction. There is also promise in the case of Sudan, which by late 1974 had embarked on the course of comprehensive planning for the integrated development of agriculture, thanks to the efforts and aid of the Arab Fund for Economic and Social Development, which had formed a team of experts to undertake the necessary studies for such integrated agricultural development, and which, upon the completion of these studies in 1975, obtained initial financing undertakings by certain oil-rich Arab states. Apart from the cases indicated, nowhere else in the Arab world has agrarian reform or agricultural development, where they can be said to have occurred, been of enough significance to merit being called a determinant of development. (Lebanon calls for a separate observation. Although the contribution of agriculture to GNP has declined over the years, this sector has grown considerably in absolute terms, and has made wide advances in qualitative terms. However, the growth registered in the economy as a whole has depended on or derived from agriculture only to a very limited extent.)

5. The fifth factor to examine is capital availability, both from internal and external sources.[15] That capital availability is an important factor is not in doubt; what is being questioned here is whether it is a determinant and a prime mover of development.

Prior to the autumn of 1973 and the steep rise in oil revenues, only Saudi Arabia, Kuwait and Libya, among the Arab oil producers covered in this study, had no reason to complain of shortage of investment capital. Even though important producers, Iraq and Algeria almost consistently felt the capital constraint sharply, as their ambitions went beyond the capital available. However, if these ambitions are matched against actual execution and performance, it will be found that the latter lagged behind, making the constraint in fact less real. The other countries, with the possible exception of Lebanon, suffered from the shortage of real savings and capital funds for investment. (It will readily be realised that what is meant here in the context of the external sector is funds that are translatable into foreign exchange and ultimately into capital goods imports and technical services.) The shortage was not merely in domestic capital, that is, in domestic savings, but also in the inflow of external capital.

Assessment of the availability of sufficient investment capital can lead to two widely different conclusions. The first, deriving from the narrow assessment which sets the availability against the proclaimed (or programmed) needs as recorded in development plans, indicates that capital is insufficient. It constitutes a major constraint on development. The second derives from a more comprehensive examination which takes account not merely of the availability of and proclaimed need for capital, but likewise of the capability of the country to use capital resources efficiently and effectively.[16] It is maintained in this latter context that during most of the post-war period, few worthy, well-studied and planned projects went without the necessary capital, if the general setting in which they were to be implemented was encouraging and promotive. For, it is further maintained, the worthiness of a project as revealed by technical and economic studies is a necessary but insufficient indicator of finance-worthiness. The latter is likewise influenced by the whole governmental system, the capability of the civil service, the relevant legal and institutional framework, and the availability of manpower with the skills required.

This second contention, to the extent that it is true, is truer of the last ten or twelve years in the Arab world, during which regional and foreign financial resources were more abundant than hitherto, and investment capital was less of a constraint. However, two seemingly contradictory observations of this latter period carry credence and weight. The first is that the region as a whole was capital-hungry, even if growth targets were kept modest (say 5 per cent per annum). The second observation is that a worthy and well-studied and planned project did not fail to be executed because of capital shortage.

The resolution of this seeming contradiction lies in the closer scrutiny of the second observation. Thus, no *one* worthy project missed the opportunity of financing, but if this contention were generalised to many projects or to a whole economy, and if it were to apply to the region as a whole, then serious capital shortage was certain to be seen and felt. To extend the contention from one project to the whole region would involve us in a massive fallacy of composition. Our own conclusion, based on a thorough examination of the capital resources for the region's countries, set against their needs or even against their development plans, is that before 1973 the resources fell far short of the needs and of the planned investment programmes. That actual execution of programmes and projects in turn fell distinctly short of the plans only qualifies the conclusion, in the sense that were the capability to execute the plans to be higher, the capital constraint would have become yet more strangulating.

This conclusion is very revealing with respect to the inhibiting effect of capital shortage. But the more relevant question for the purposes of our enquiry here is whether the widening of the capital resource bottleneck amounts to a positive determinant of development. Will an abundant supply of capital thus become a positive, operative determinant? Empirical evidence suggests that where capital resources have become abundant, economic development has been promoted, inasmuch as the capital constraint has been relaxed. But if capital sufficiency is a necessary condition for accelerated investment and the achievement of economic development, it is not a sufficient condition. Obviously, it has to be supplemented by a large number of other supportive, favourable factors in the spheres of government, manpower, seriousness of purpose, technological change, and so on. The conjuncture and convergence of all these factors for economic development to materialise is required in this instance no less than in other instances.

Our qualified conclusion with respect to the effectiveness of capital resources as a determinant of economic development has been stated in general terms. If the exploration were to be differentiated, it would reveal that the major oil-producing countries currently enjoy the benefit of this determinant, but that the other countries do not have the same advantage. This differentiation raises the question of regional capital flows, to which we will turn in section 4 below. For the present, we will merely say that owing to the very limited intra-regional flow of capital (that is, from the surplus oil countries to the capital-thirsty countries and to joint Arab projects and programmes), the region viewed as a unit is still short of investment capital. This capital can be a determinant of economic development, as the example of the oil countries reveals, but for the region it is still a potential determinant, one which has not yet been allowed full scope to operate. Nor have the supportive requirements — political, psychological, institutional and economic — been sufficiently developed.

6. The next determinant to examine is infrastructure. Infrastructure constitutes a platform, almost in the literal sense of the term, on which the building of directly productive projects and of programmes can be superimposed. It is quite possible, indeed customary, for a country to undertake physical infrastructural construction and project execution simultaneously. But for it to start with projects before some basic infrastructural requirements have been satisfied would be wasteful. The logical time sequence is to undertake infrastructural investment first, whether on a large, national, or on a local scale appropriate for one or a few projects, and then to turn to project development.

In the case of an economy which is extremely underdeveloped, this sequence is almost inevitable. The roads and other means of transport and communication, the electricity and water supply, the harnessing of water resources and building of irrigation works and facilities where they are called for constitute a *sine qua non* for further development. To do without these — to have private infrastructural facilities, like electricity generators, roads, and the like — would be unduly expensive and would put the establishments concerned at a competitive disadvantage. Furthermore, there would always be certain investments that no one businessman could or would undertake by himself. In any case, the private development of infrastructure would end by leading to the emergence of a multitude of small islands which might be self-sufficient with respect to some basic infrastructural services, but which could not communicate and interact because the same services and linkages do not exist in between the establishments. To argue the point is to show its absurdity.

What applies to physical infrastructure is equally true of non-economic infrastructure, such as law and order, education, and other services. Development is unthinkable without the rule of law and order and a minimal level of education, training, science and technology.[17] But, again like physical infrastructure, social and political infrastructure *in itself* does not bring development about; that is, it provides the basis or foundation, or the framework within which economic development can take place, but does not act as a direct determinant.

The Arab countries have since independence realised the important role of infrastructure, both physical and social, in promoting economic development. Their recognition of this role has manifested itself in the emphasis laid on investment in infrastructure. An examination of the pattern of public investments in the early post-war period, and of the structure of investment plans and programmes as they came to appear and as they stand even today thirty years after the end of World War Two, reveals the heavy emphasis on infrastructure, both physical and social. Even without the benefit of theoretical sophistication or of world-wide empirical studies, the *dirigeants* of the Arab countries have correctly assessed the broad priorities of their economies and societies.[18] Common sense is no mean asset!

However, realisation of the urgency and priority of infrastructural investment is not equivalent to the completion of such investment. Today, three decades after the end of World War Two, the Arab world is still in urgent need of much infrastructural work requiring immense investment. Merely to judge by the development plans in force today for the years 1975-80, the recognised need is in excess of $50 billion, and that is only for five years ahead. What the need is for the twenty more years before the century ends must run into scores of billions more, before infrastructural facilities and services can be considered adequate and satisfactory. It ought further to be recalled that expansion, renewal and innovation are endless in this respect, what with population increase, depreciation and obsolescence.

The Arab countries vary widely with respect to the degree to which they are equipped with infrastructural requirements. Where a country is well-equipped in one respect, as for instance Kuwait in electricity, water and roads, it can still be very under-equipped in some other respects, such as education and professional and vocational training. Egypt, which is well-equipped in the field of irrigation, in so far as water storage and networks are concerned, or in education in so far as the number of graduates is concerned, is pitifully starved for urban and inter-urban means of transportation, plant and equipment for public utilities, proper school buildings and laboratory and library facilities, telecommunications and health services — to name the more conspicuous shortages.

The three Maghreb countries formerly under French rule are to a far extent better supplied with physical infrastructure, but found themselves after independence woefully poor with respect to social infrastructure — only now are they beginning to catch up in this respect. Sudan is grossly under-equipped in both categories. Libya follows the pattern of its three neighbours to the west, though it is less well-equipped. Lebanon, Jordan, Syria and Iraq are moderately well-equipped, although each has large gaps. (Lebanon, for instance, has serious shortages in telecommunications, storage and port facilities.) Saudi Arabia is still short of most components of physical and social infrastructure. But all these countries, with the exception of Lebanon, have an appropriate setting or infrastructure with respect to law and order. That is to say, only in the case of Lebanon, and there in the past few years, have the authority of government, law and order deteriorated to the point that investment has been inhibited. Elsewhere, these requisites are satisfied. Where investment is not forthcoming or is shy, it is because of other inhibiting factors or of the absence of some essential supportive requisites.

There is yet another aspect of infrastructure which has to be considered. This is the construction and establishment of the physical and social infrastructural platform required for regional development. Several components form this platform, foremost among which are: intra-regional roads, railways, sea and air services, and telecommunications; the joint exploitation of rivers running in the territory of more than one country; the joint development of research, educational and training institutions, and the promotion of technological advances; and, where possible, the joint exploitation of water and gas resources for the generation of electric power, and the creation of multi-country power networks. (This list does not include the opportunity for many joint projects and programmes that are directly productive, such as the petro-chemical industry, the iron and steel industry, and the like. However, this whole area of Arab economic co-operation and complementarity will be treated separately further down in the chapter.)

In summing up, it can be said that physical and social infrastructures constitute basic promotive factors or determinants for development. Special mention must be made here of the great value for Saudi Arabia and Sudan, and for the southern regions of the four Maghreb countries, of better transport and communications. These services open up the distant regions to development, expose the inhabitants to outside influences, increase monetisation, facilitate marketing and promote agriculture and livestock-raising, and generally act as a strong agent of change. Taken together, the Arab countries — though in varying degrees — are still insufficiently equipped with infrastructural facilities and services. This is true both at the national, one-country level and the general, regional level.[19] Finally, though logically infrastructure must precede the appearance of projects that are directly productive, this does not mean that the latter must wait for infrastructure to reach an advanced stage of development and sophistication, nor that they can be proceeded with in disregard of infrastructure. The relationship is that of mutual support and interaction, with the infrastructural platform being extended and solidified, as projects are built. The former makes the latter easier to build, while the latter create pressure for the speeding-up of infrastructural development. But though there is mutuality, infrastructure remains a determinant of economic development in its own right.

7. Manpower is the seventh determinant to be examined.[20] Three aspects will be discussed: size, quality and compatibility between supply and demand. The three are interrelated, but they are set apart here to make the discussion easier.

What is meant by manpower is the effective labour force: the men and women who are capable of undertaking gainful employment on the basis of age and physical fitness, loosely defined. Viewed from this angle of minimal requirements, manpower becomes a determinant which is lacking nowhere in the world: every country seems to be adequately supplied with manpower for its immediate and foreseeable needs, if the supply is merely measured in quantitative terms.

Yet the size itself looks different, if certain qualifying observations are made. One of these is the health conditions of the population at large and of manpower more specifically. Another is the assumption of different levels of performance and economic activity which would influence the degree of adequacy of manpower resources. But to introduce these or similar questions would shift the discussion to the quality of manpower in the one instance, and to the compatibility between supply and demand in the other. Thus it would seem that the mere size of manpower resources is not very meaningful, since it does not constitute a constraint to development anywhere. In the Arab case these resources are particularly abundant, owing to the high rate of net increase in population which, as we saw earlier, is about 2.8−3 per cent per annum.

It is essentially the quality of manpower that is of profound relevance to our enquiry. This aspect can be viewed from different angles: education, training and skills, work commitment and the work ethic, mobilisation and commitment to the objectives of development arising from the sense of participation, and motivation in general. The last two angles of view will occupy us under separate headings in sections 2 and 3 below. We will restrict the present discussion therefore to the questions of education, training and commitment.

The acquisition by the labour force of a certain minimal level of education is essential for the mastery of the varied skills that a modernising economy requires. The proposition can safely be made that under such circumstances the labour force has to have completed elementary (or preparatory) education at least. At this first-cycle level, there is hardly any need for insistence on differentiated schooling or on the acquisition of special skills, as mastery of the 'three R's' is a basic essential useful to, and usable by, every member of society in every walk of life. Evidently, certain conditions or qualifications can and must be made with respect to the methodology of education in the primary cycle, but the content of the curriculum, though varying somewhat from one country to another, by and large generally satisfies certain minimal requirements. This is so although it may have a little excessive emphasis here or there on courses which do not form part of the core of elementary education as it relates directly to development.

It is beyond the primary cycle that wide differentiation begins, in the intermediary and secondary cycle if schoolchildren go into that cycle upon completion of the first, or in elementary and secondary vocational education if they transfer there after the elementary cycle. Close scrutiny of this phase of education is called for, for an assessment of its appropriateness to the developmental needs of the individual countries and of the region as a whole. The same is true of the third-cycle, or university-level education in its liberal arts, scientific, and professional sub-divisions.

Such a scrutiny will be attempted in section 3 below, when education is examined as a determinant of development. At the present moment, what is called for is an assessment of the educational capabilities of the manpower resources. Such an assessment shows that there is a marked difference between countries, between urban centres and rural areas, and between the young and the much older.

We have had occasion to measure student enrolment in each of the countries covered in this study as a proportion of the population that is of school age. The results showed that even in the countries with the highest proportion, this still fell very short of universal education at the elementary level, particularly where females are concerned, although fast strides have been made in the post-war decades. Furthermore, the drop-out rate between cycles was very high. It was further observed that the content of the second-cycle curricula in the academic stream was in general not readily useful and usable for vocational and professional training and work, but more for clerical work. (In this respect, Algeria, Tunisia and Iraq, and to a lesser extent Egypt, Jordan, Syria, and in very recent years Lebanon, have been reconsidering their curricula and making adjustments aimed at rendering them more appropriate for the demands of a modernising economy.)[21] Finally, at the third cycle, university and university-level education continue on the whole to use up the faculty and financial resources available more in horizontal, quantitative expansion than in qualitative improvement.

The shortcomings and weaknesses in the methodologies and contents of curricula in the various systems of education in the twelve countries examined have been referred to more than once, and will again be discussed within the focus of the present chapter. For the particular purposes of this section, we are interested in the relevance of education to manpower's role in development. This, evidently, is essentially an aspect of the examination of quality of education. It is also essentially closely related to the compatibility of supply and demand for skills which are at issue for development. In discussing the question of relevance we will therefore be discussing both quality and compatibility.

The question is not easy to tackle. In the first place, all education has built-in relevance to development, both because of the training it gives to the mind which proves useful in later life, and because education is an end in itself though also a means to life's work. In the second place, relevance can never be ascertained once and for all, assuming it could be measured. This is because the dynamic forces at work in development change the manpower needs of the economy continuously; therefore the manpower stock of any one moment — in its size and quality alike — satisfies the economy's needs in different degrees at different points of time. Specifically, it brings reduced satisfaction from one point to the next, as the economy becomes more advanced and sophisticated, and society becomes more modernised, with the combined result that altogether new skills are continuously being called for, and old, familiar skills suffer obsolescence and have to be improved or extended. Finally, there is the problem of measurement of the relevance of the skills possessed by manpower to development and the compatibility between the supply and demand for skills.

The supply of such skills is difficult to establish — both as stock at any one moment, namely people in the work pool, and as flow, namely persons in formal institutional training, i.e. 'in the pipeline', yet the supply remains much simpler to assess than the demand.[22] To establish the supply encounters the usual census problems of definition, categorisation and actual count. Apart from definitional questions, to establish the demand encounters the much more difficult problems of assessment of need by the many bodies in the private and public sectors, in a changing, dynamic situation where the nature and quality — and not only the number — of the skills in question are changing continuously.

Attempts have been made to surmount the difficulties involved, and more than one method of assessment has been suggested.[23] These methods relate to broad categories, such as the need for persons with secondary education, or with university education, say per 10,000 of the population, or relate to specific categories, such as engineers, physicians, electricians, and the like, broadly stated or broken down further into subgroups, such as electrical engineers, petroleum engineers, and so on.

Generally speaking, three main methods can be identified. The first takes the existing supply and the various ratios or coefficients that characterise it, and projects it mechanistically into the future, either as a constant proportion to the population (or population categories), or by adding some arbitrary rate of growth. The second sets as model or example to emulate some country which is 'better endowed' with skills, and projects growth in the supply to meet conditions in the reference country. The third is more detailed. It utilises some technical or engineering and other educational, organisational and economic coefficients or relationships and estimates the needs as they would have to be in order to satisfy these relationships. Thus, it can be said that a petrochemical or a textile industry of a certain size and technology requires so many engineers, foremen and skilled workers of certain specifications. This process can be extended to include all economic and educational activities where coefficients can be established by experts. These coefficients are then applied to the activities, the requirements ideally defined are determined, and then aggregated for the whole country. A variant of this method is to establish the coefficients for the population, or for whole groups or sectors, and then to make the necessary calculations.

It is obvious that the third method, like those preceding it, suffers from the discrepancy between the rigidity or insufficient flexibility of the projections or demand estimates made, and the continuous change or fluidity in the actual demand. Furthermore, the training of the manpower to meet the requirement estimates is a slow process. This would call for liberality in the projections or estimates in order for the supply of skills to keep abreast of the demand as the latter unfolds. Indeed, other disturbing factors set in. Supply itself can never be rigidly planned and controlled, even in a centrally planned economy. Therefore discrepancies between supply and demand are bound to surface; the difference between countries and between sectors within the same economy also reflects itself in the size of these discrepancies and imbalances. Likewise, investment plans and programmes, be they in the private or even the public sector, change, and change drastically at times, without notice, while the numbers of those in the education and training pipeline cannot be as easily altered.

In the final analysis, the planners and economic decision-makers have to resign themselves to such discrepancies and imbalances. They will perhaps have to find comfort in the fact that in the medium run, market forces (rewards and incentives, and economic penalties) will bring about some adjustment. But more importantly, and mercifully, a variation of Say's Law is probably relevant and not fallacious in the present context, in the sense that supply is likely in the long run to create its own demand, given enough time.

It will be noticed that we have moved gradually from the aspect of academic education to that of vocational training of manpower. (The two are inseparable in an examination of the aptitudes of the work-force.) Training involves the imparting of vocational (technical) skills, and it can be effected in formal institutions at the intermediate and secondary levels in the second cycle of education, as well as through on-the-job training. The institutions can form part of the general system of education, and can be independent, or yet tied to some economic ministry or authority. Training at the university (third-cycle) level of education is professional training. This can be in universities properly speaking, or in university-level institutions and specialised centres.

Finally, the quality of the labour force is closely related to labour commitment to work and the strength of the work ethic which it espouses — in addition to the education and training acquired in vocational and professional skills. The commitment and the work ethic reflect themselves in the acceptance of factory and workplace discipline, the minimisation of absenteeism and job turnover, pride in work and performance, co-operation with other workers, acceptance of the principle that — corrective wage increases apart — wage increments, promotions and other rewards must be tied to merit and increase in productivity. The possession of these and related traits and attitudes makes for a smoother flow of work and greater production, improves the climate of investment and economic activity, and generally promotes economic development by making manpower more dependable.

Even before the occasion arises for a discussion of the remaining aspects of the 'quality' of manpower — namely mobilisation and commitment to the objectives of development arising from the sense of participation, and manpower motivation in general, which will be treated under another heading — it can be seen that manpower constitutes a strong determinant of development. The examination of the aspects of size, quality and labour commitment and its work ethic suggests that manpower is a direct and active determinant, particularly when its quality is of strong relevance to economic modernisation. But this can only be true if the supply of manpower resources does not fall very short of the demand, in the various skill categories but particularly in the critical, strategic ones.

This supply must be responsive to the requirements, otherwise there will be a serious gap which will not only create imbalances and strangulating bottlenecks, but in due course will be more damaging: it will cause a realistic scaling-down of developmental sights and reverse the process of growth. When that occurs, the gap will look smaller, but this superficial simplification of the problem only arises because the much weightier problem of stagnation would be allowed to loom larger. In the final analysis, therefore, compatibility between supply and demand in a setting of brisk growth is of paramount importance, as it is not sufficient for the available manpower resources to be of satisfactory quality, if they are grossly inadequate for demand requirements, and if they do not show alert and commensurate response to the pressures of demand.

It is time to ask how well-endowed the Arab countries are with respect to manpower. In reply, it can safely be said that in terms of mere size, manpower resources are more than adequate for present needs at the prevailing level of economic activity. Indeed, we estimated earlier that there is a very severe and large-scale under-utilisation of available labour. It will be recalled that in the Arab world the effective labour force is a small proportion of the population — about 25 per cent in fact. This is essentially because of three main reasons: the exclusion of a large number of women from the active labour force, the high rate of dependency among the population, with about 50 per cent being under 20 years of age, and the large size of the rural community in most countries and the underestimation of the work-force in the countryside, especially when it includes a nomadic component. Physical fitness does not seem to bar a notable proportion from labour force estimates, although health conditions in general are still far from satisfactory. If adjustment were made in such a way that all able-bodied men and women, say between 15 and 64 years, were counted in the labour supply, then the proportion would amount to about 53 per cent of the aggregate population;[24] the activity rate among those between 15 and 64 years of age is some 75 per cent (against 85 per cent for industrial countries), which amounts to about 40 per cent of the total population, or some 55.7 million.[25] The difference between 53 and 25 per cent would amount to some 21 million of 'unutilised supply' for the whole Arab world (on the basis of the population in 1974), or for 18 million for the twelve countries included in this study. These figures have serious implications, even if they were considered merely indicative.

But there is not much to gain from such an exercise, as the unqualified size of man-power resources is of little significance for present purposes. The resources have to be differentiated according to quality, as this term was defined earlier. If this is done, it will be seen that the manpower resources are much less abundant than crude size would suggest, and distinctly short even of the present needs of Arab economic life. Invariably, the research and interviewing showed that, with the exception of the category of unskilled workers of whom there was no overall shortage (although structural shortages existed here and there, owing to low mobility, insufficient motivation, the sudden emergence of demand unmatched by local supply, and like reasons), there was a noticeable shortage in every other category of labour: semi-skilled, skilled (technical-vocational), supervisory, clerical and professional.

One important qualification ought to be made to this statement in so far as certain categories are concerned. Thus, there are some types of university graduates that are not in short supply in every country, such as lawyers and the holders of degrees in litera-ture, history and other liberal arts — indeed, some countries such as Egypt and Lebanon have an exportable surplus in these areas of specialisation. Likewise, there are hundreds of thousands of the holders of the *baccalauréat* or its equivalent of pre-university diplomas, who have pursued an academic course of study but have not acquired any vocational train-ing that can make them employable except in clerical jobs, where the manpower supply far outstrips the opportunities. Strictly speaking, this exception or qualification to our generalisation with respect to the shortage of skills is not relevant, to the extent that the categories of skill which are abundant are not of immediate and direct relevance to economic development except marginally. The phenomenon of plenty in the midst of scarcity is one of misallocation of resources, of young men and women obtaining the wrong training, in the sense that their skills are not in sufficient demand.

Egypt is the country with the largest supply of manpower in the various skills — those of immediate use for development as well as others. It constitutes a huge manpower reservoir for the Arab world at large, one which no country has failed to draw upon at one time or another. The Lebanese and the Palestinians come next with respect to the availability of some surplus manpower in several technical, administrative, supervisory and professional skills. But even in the very few cases where the shortages are not serious, or even a surplus exists, the partial compatibility between the supply and demand for manpower resources has to be accepted with caution and with some reservations. Thus, the compatibility only exists at the present low level of performance: expansion in the economy at the prevailing technological level produces serious shortages in many critical categories of skill. The shortages will certainly be more serious at a higher technological level, with speedier development and greater diversification and sophistication in the economy. The quantitative and qualitative economic transformation that has begun to take place or that promises to take place in large measure in several countries of the region threatens to create serious supply-demand imbalances in most areas of skill — technical, professional, supervisory, administrative or executive.

The imbalance is all the more serious in view of the country-by-country approach to the problem which largely characterises the situation. Viewed from a regional standpoint, the imbalance is less handicapping, but not considerably so, as the overall, regional situation is itself one of imbalance, particularly once the eight Arab states not included in this study, and which are much less developed, are taken into full consideration. The corrective measures currently undertaken are far from satisfactory or sufficient though this judgement must be somewhat qualified, first with respect to Algeria, where the education and training of manpower are proceeding satisfactorily, and then with respect to Egypt, Iraq, Lebanon, Syria, Jordan, Tunisia and Libya, more or less in that order.

The other countries are also making some efforts, but are handicapped for one reason or another. Thus, Sudan is handicapped by the shortage of financing resources, and by the very low platform from which it starts. Saudi Arabia has the same problem of a late start and a very inadequate 'stock' of skilled manpower to begin with, but also the added socio-cultural resistance to vocational training, manifest in the substantial excess capacity of training centres and institutions, and hesitant acceptance by Saudi youth to go into technical (vocational) training. (Indeed, some occupations are considered unfit for men, or 'shame' occupations, and expatriates have to be made to take them.) Kuwait suffers from the socio-cultural handicap also. Morocco suffers from shortage of financial resources, though it had a more favourable start than Sudan, Saudi Arabia or Kuwait. Furthermore, its economy is not characterised by drive and dynamic growth, which inhibits its youth from turning in large numbers into vocational training.

The response by the various countries under consideration, commendable as it is in some instances, still falls short of the requirements that threaten to be very pressing in the few years to come, much more so than demand has been pressing in the past two decades. In the oil countries where the pace of economic transformation and development has been fast in the last few years and shows every indication of becoming much faster in the several years to come, and in such non-oil countries as Lebanon, Jordan, Egypt and Tunisia — and probably Sudan — where investment seems to be heading for intensification and diversification, the response to the pressure of demand, both actual and potential, will have to be greatly strengthened, if the several economies involved are not to forcibly slow down their transformation. In fact, the 1975-80 development plan of Saudi Arabia calls for an immense inflow of labour that is neither possible nor desirable, considering that it would constitute (with dependants) about a quarter of the population, with all that implies in social and economic strains and stresses. Elsewhere, the labour shortage will be serious, but not as pressing. The response to short supply will have to be not just quantitative, but qualitative as well. The expanded supply has to be better designed to suit the structure of demand envisaged, and to be better planned and co-ordinated as between the various ministries, sectors and private business groups. And it has to take into account many supportive facilities and services such as housing and public utilities — to say nothing of the institutional changes that will have to be likewise undertaken.

Attention to other pressing problems must likewise become strong and effective. They include the inadequacy of 'organizations and institutions for mobilizing human effort, and lack of incentives for persons to engage in activities which are particularly important for national development'.[26] To these problems must be added the fast population growth which exacerbates the already massive problem of urban unemployment and rural underemployment, as well as the cultural blocks to certain types of employment, and the insufficiency of mobilisation and of motivation. At the regional level, attention must be paid to the need for a better allocation of manpower resources, though this could only be a temporary and marginal palliative to the serious overall shortage of critical skills.

Furthermore, the considerable brain drain of high-level manpower from the Arab world into the industrial countries must be halted, and if possible reversed, if a significant component of the category of high-level manpower is not to be lost to the region.[27] The handling of the problem of the brain drain must also be undertaken both at the country and the regional level. Finally, manpower planning, which has so far been one of the weaker aspects of overall planning, must be taken more seriously and fulfilled more intelligently; and the appropriate policies must be formulated and implemented. Foremost among such policies is the creation of a suitable work atmosphere, especially for persons in the more critical categories of skill from the standpoint of development. This atmosphere includes not only income and benefit incentives, but also proper research, workshop and laboratory facilities, and the community of scholars and scientists which is essential for the promotion of science and technology. This last area has received least attention so far in the Arab world, despite the recent passage of laws in Iraq and Libya purporting to pull back high-level manpower that had 'drained' with the promise of attractive terms of employment.

We are ready now to sum up what has been found with respect to manpower. This factor is a strong determinant of development, once it has the relevant education and training, and is in sufficient supply — or, if it is not, once there is brisk and effective action to expand the supply. The Arab world is woefully short of most critical categories of skill, and the shortage threatens to become more serious if the march towards economic expansion, diversification and sophistication acquires greater momentum, as it is expected to do. This is so because the response to the problem is not in the dimensions required. Furthermore, the handling of the problem is mostly on a country-by-country basis, although a regional approach can be more effective.[28] Manpower resources will prove to be one of the major direct determinants of development. This distinction makes it all the more necessary to enable this factor to have its full play.

8. Entrepreneurship and management is the last to be examined in this category of economic determinants. First, entrepreneurship will be considered with respect to its role, locus, spread, quality and effectiveness in the Arab world.

A great deal has been written about entrepreneurship since economic science emerged as a distinct discipline. It constitutes one of the 'factors' of production in standard textbooks. Furthermore, it has been given prominence since Schumpeter accorded it a central place in his theory of development early in the century.[29] The literature dealing with it has been truly voluminous, although in the last decade or so less has been said about it, probably because of the great expansion in the role of the public sector in the economic life of less-developed nations. In fact, however, this structural shift has not reduced the significance or role of the entrepreneurial function, but changed its locus from the private to the public sector.

It would take us far out to examine the entrepreneurial function, the history of thought surrounding it, its manifestations and related questions. For our purposes, it is sufficient to state that this function is essentially understood to include innovation or adaptation, and the building of the appropriate organisation capable of translating the innovation (or adaptation) into an operative, efficient economic unit. Basically, the entrepreneur perceives new opportunities, and in building establishments embodying these opportunities he expands the economy and introduces new products, techniques or organisations, or discovers new markets. Once the societal setting in which he operates undergoes some important changes in technological, social (including demographic) and political institutions and ideas, and economic growth is registered, development is said to have been set afoot.

The entrepreneur is highly sensitive and responsive to motivation. According to some writers, the 'need-for-achievement' motive exerts the strongest pressure on him. As indicated in the previous chapter, McClelland (and members of his 'school') and Hagen have underlined this need very strongly.[30] The present writer, in an empirical study covering the entrepreneurial resources in Lebanon, found the sense of a desire for achievement to be one of the strongest motives — indeed, the strongest according to the entrepreneurs' own declaration.[31] In seeking the satisfaction of what they set as objectives or in responding to their innermost motives, whatever these are, the entrepreneurs promote economic development and modernisation. Evidently, their self-interest might lead them to the expansion of the economy in directions that may not be developmental in the social sense — in the sense that these directions might mean the setting-up of activities or industries of very little significance for the long-term comprehensive development of the economy.

However, even in this latter case, the technical innovations or improvements of which the entrepreneurs prove to be the carriers, and possibly the promoters, cannot fail to have a strong beneficial impact on the economy. Where the entrepreneurial function is fulfilled by the public sector, that is, by decision-makers in public service, this function will be developmental in effect to a more discernible extent, since the directions it will take will be developmental, and probably the scale of promotion will be much larger. In short, it is readily demonstrable that entrepreneurship is of paramount developmental significance to the economy; indeed, many serious writers contend that it is the central determinant and that its impact is direct, strong and profound.

Yet the matter cannot be dismissed as easily as that. The active developmental role of entrepreneurship is closely and causally tied to the locus, spread and quality of entrepreneurial resources. The locus will have to be explored with respect both to the sector or sectors, and the groups or communities, manifesting the entrepreneurial function in strength. It would seem arguable, both conceptually and empirically, that the sector of industry is the one where the function finds the best soil for its growth and fruition, although the other sectors too — particularly agriculture, banking and finance, transport and communications — also provide great scope for its unfolding. Trade is generally considered a dubious case, inasmuch as the impact of the entrepreneurial function in this context is restricted to the example or demonstration effect, namely, to the developmental value of the importation of new commodities which then inspire the entrepreneurs to produce them locally and thus introduce innovation through import substitution. In doing this, the entrepreneurs also advance technology and organisation, and encourage the financing institutions to expand their operations. Likewise, it can be said that the opening up of new markets for exports will enable businessmen to have access to more funds and foreign exchange, which can then be translated into capital investment in new fields. In brief, it can be seen that trade seems to provide some avenues for entrepreneurship, though indirectly.[32]

A great deal has been said about the groups or communities that from time to time, and between one country and another, have shown or show particular entrepreneurial talent. Minority groups have often been said to be especially endowed with this talent; a qualification of this assertion has been that 'deviant' groups are so endowed. At the root of such assertions is the belief that such minority or deviant groups are usually not sensitive to the inhibiting cultural factors to which the majority is exposed. These factors might be the hesitation to undertake certain activities, or high social valuation placed on land ownership, military careers or the priesthood, but not on business careers. Conversely the deviant group might be positively urged by such factors as strong business orientation; or the desire to excel in business and thus reach positions of prominence while the national majority reaches such positions via land ownership, the army, or mere inherited social status; or yet the psychological pressure to compensate for some earlier national calamity and loss of fortune.

The spread of entrepreneurship is closely related to its locus. What is involved here is the size of entrepreneurial resources, and whether they are adequate for launching enough new enterprises embodying innovational ideas to stir the economy enough to bring about substantial growth and, given the right conditions, to promote development. Furthermore, the question of spread relates to the sectors affected, inasmuch as entrepreneurship should make itself strongly felt in several sectors if it is to bring about notable growth and then development.

Admittedly, potent entrepreneurship in a leading sector might be sufficient for a start. But this would be conditional on the sector being truly a leader, its having strong impact on the rest of the economy, and finally on entrepreneurial talent emerging in response in the other sectors influenced by the leader. It goes without saying that a major sector in the framework of dualism will not play the role of a leading sector, if it is insulated through alienation and minimal interaction and linkage with the rest of the economy. (We have had occasion earlier to refer to this aspect of dualism.)

What is meant by quality of entrepreneurship is the extent of research, rationality and calculativeness it manifests, its power to innovate, its daring and defiance of inhibiting factors in the economy and society, its flexibility and power to adapt to new situations, particularly to change character from being fulfilled by daring individuals conforming to the 'robber-baron' prototype, to being fulfilled by teams of innovators in the modern corporation or the public development agency. Another aspect of quality is the power of entrepreneurial resources to be replenished through the rejuvenation of the entrepreneurial spirit. The resources will be unlikely to enjoy such qualities unless the social, economic and technological setting provides scope for their activity and material incentives with a strong enough pull, and unless the inhibitions of the setting are not totally strangulating and paralysing. (A military dictatorship with unstable government and frequent upheavals would be a case in point; so would a situation where law and order could not guarantee safe and remunerative economic activity, or where the population was largely hostile to innovation in the economy and in technology.)

Before we assess the adequacy of the entrepreneurial factor in the Arab context, it will be useful to recapitulate our observations so far. In one sentence, our position is that entrepreneurship is a very effective determinant, but that it should manifest itself and operate in sectors and industries which provide adequate scope for it, and from which it can have its impact spread into many directions. The entrepreneurial resources should be large enough to bring about such an impact, should be capable of defying the inhibiting socio-cultural factors in the social setting, but should be assured certain minimal political and economic prerequisites such as law and order, financial institutions, and reasonably sound economic policies.

The situation in the Arab world varies considerably from country to country, with respect to the entrepreneurial factor, although the unevenness was greater in the years immediately after World War Two, or after independence, as the case may be. Earlier on, the availability and distribution of entrepreneurial resources was such as to give credence to the thesis that these resources were to be found mainly among minority deviant groups, though this picture had notable exceptions. In the late forties and early fifties, it was in Lebanon that the most dynamic and effective resources existed and operated. Additionally, the country attracted hundreds of ambitious and energetic entrepreneurs who left their countries upon the advent of socialism (or state capitalism) into the region. It was not any one minority group that excelled, as Lebanon can be said to be a country of several minorities. The abundance of the resources and their wide spread among sectors and among groups made entrepreneurship a phenomenon characterising the country as a whole, not any one specific group. (Empirical research has shown that the Christian communities had more entrepreneurs than the Mohammedan communities. But the imbalance was more characteristic of the first part of the post-war period than of the latter part.)[33] Furthermore, Lebanon has projected this talent on to other Arab countries, whether in widening the scope of its activities from bases in Lebanon, or in launching new, independent activities abroad which embody entrepreneurial innovation.

Three other countries could claim entrepreneurial activity of note after the war: Egypt, Syria and Jordan. While many original Egyptians displayed such activity, it is also true that in an important measure minority groups excelled in this field. These included Greeks, Italians, Jews, Lebanese and Syrians.[34] In Syria, the resources were mainly Syrian Arab, though the Armenian community and some Christian minority groups (originally immigrant) were active in the northern city of Aleppo and in the vast virgin plains of northeast Syria. In Jordan, the active resources were predominantly Palestinian, and to a lesser extent Syrian.

Nowhere else was entrepreneurial activity very substantial, or were the resources abundant, with the exception of the Maghreb countries. But then these resources were European — mainly French in Morocco, Algeria and Tunisia, and Italian in Libya. The exception is significant, inasmuch as these large European communities did not fit into the type of resources encountered in the Mashreq, nor were they similarly motivated, as they were not weak minorities seeking some form of compensation for the loss of national existence or for their insecure status. Quite the opposite: in the Maghreb the European entrepreneurs were part of the ruling entity, and an extension of the metropolitan country's advanced economy. They were endowed with the power, material resources, business tradition and self-assurance of the huge entrepreneurial reservoir of the metropolitan country. In addition, the colonial authorities provided them with protective shelter — with brute force, legislation and institutions in their favour. Finally, the metropolitan home markets and financial institutions were open to them and conducive to expansion and prosperity. It is no wonder, therefore, that the national entrepreneurial resources did not emerge under colonial rule.

Furthermore, wherever a national bourgeoisie began to form, it was destroyed in the savage military repression of national independence movements. Thus, upon independence, the indigenous entrepreneurial resources were very inadequate and unable to fill the gap created by the withdrawal of a substantial part of European entrepreneurial capability.

This account has so far left out Iraq, Sudan and Saudi Arabia. The first has been notable for its poverty in entrepreneurial dynamism and activity. Indeed, its resources of managers, accountants and administrators are still today notably short. Erratic economic policy and frequent political upheavals since 1958 quite understandably have not been instrumental in widening the entrepreneurial and managerial bottleneck, although economic expansion has characterised an important part of this period. Indeed, some observers believe that the country has not yet fully compensated for the exodus of the Jewish community in 1952 and the loss of much of the country's accountants, managers, financiers and craftsmen.

Sudan was equally poor, if not poorer. In addition, it has not witnessed the expansion that Iraq has had, and therefore has not generated great incentive for entrepreneurship. The country has relied mostly on foreign entrepreneurs: West Europeans, Greeks, Syrians, Armenians. The loss of these entrepreneurial capabilities has proceeded faster than the emergence of national capabilities. The expansion of the role of public enterprise has disguised the entrepreneurial gap, but this is none the less large and real. Finally, Saudi Arabia has until recently witnessed only mercantile enterprise among Saudi businessmen, with foreign elements active in the initiation and conduct of activity in industry and other sectors. Even where new businesses have had substantial participation by Saudi nationals, these have by and large been the suppliers of capital rather than entrepreneurial ideas and talent or managerial capability. (The Palestinian community has been generally active, and has in particular pioneered the introduction of new agricultural crops, especially around the major cities.) Currently, however, there has been a brisk emergence of Saudi entrepreneurship in most fields of activity, including industry. But this tangible improvement is still considerably short of meeting much of the country's vast and fast-growing needs. Indeed, even today, with Saudi entrepreneurs becoming prominent in every field of economic activity, there is a strong presence of non-Saudi entrepreneurs, both Arab and non-Arab.

Dramatic transformation in the situation with respect to the private sector has not occurred anywhere. Thus, while Lebanon has kept its lead and has witnessed a vast expansion in the quantity and quality of its entrepreneurial resources, more modest improvements are observable in Kuwait, Morocco and Tunisia, as well as among East Jordanians in Jordan (that is, apart from the Palestinians there). On the other hand, private entrepreneurship has not grown considerably in Iraq, Syria, Egypt, Libya or Algeria.

The cause for the different course in this last group of countries is not far to seek. It derives from the ideological orientation which characterises them and the adoption of a social system espousing socialism and relying heavily on the public sector as the engine of economic activity. Thus, both Egypt and Syria witnessed an entrepreneurial drain over the past two decades, while Iraq never had a substantial entrepreneurial resource in any case. In all five countries, the entrepreneurial function has in large measure been assumed by the public sector in all but small-scale economic activities. The ideological, economic and institutional ethos is not welcoming or conducive to large-scale entrepreneurial activity by private business leaders; economic uncertainty in the Knightian sense is high;[35] but more significantly, there are explicit constraints — whether in legislation, regulations, institutional limitations or in political credo — on the unfolding of private economic activity on a large scale. Understandably, it is only where such large-scale activity is permitted and encouraged that the Arab world has witnessed quantitative expansion and qualitative sophisticaion in private entrepreneurial resources.

In conclusion, it can be said that it is in a few countries that private entrepreneurship is exercising a strong developmental influence. Elsewhere, this influence is attributable to public entrepreneurship. This factor is all-powerful in the five countries that have opted for socialism. Yet it will be a serious under-statement to ignore the important role that the public sector is also playing in Kuwait, Saudi Arabia, Morocco, Tunisia or Jordan. This role is far larger and more potent than that of the private sector in the socialist countries. But whether residing in the private or in the public sector, or yet in the mixed sector which is not to be ignored or underestimated, the entrepreneurial function was and is a determinant of great significance for development.

Understandably, the motives that influence each of the sectors and the implications for development of the entrepreneurial function in each of them are quite different. Thus, the emphasis on the profit motive and on personal achievement in the private sector, which can be said to make this sector rather indifferent to development at large, is to some extent compensated for by greater concern for efficiency. On the other hand, the emphasis on social needs and ends in the public sector can be said to be somewhat counteracted by this sector's inability to achieve a high level of efficiency. But this differentiation ought not to be carried to extremes: private-sector efficiency is not general, and it is often accompanied by waste if the whole sector's allocation and use of resources is considered; likewise, the public sector has in many instances shown an ability to achieve a notable level of efficiency. Furthermore, concern for the profit motive by the private sector does not necessarily preclude the harmonisation beween private-sector activity and overall developmental objectives; this can be achieved through the design and implementation of proper indicative planning and of sound economic policies, as well as through the modality of the mixed sector. Equally so, the public sector, in its concern for social need and social objectives, need not preclude concern for profit-making, if only as a criterion of efficient operation. There is more convergence than divergence in reality, between the two sectors. The hybrid mixed sector is the meeting point, and it carries great promise for development.

2. POLITICAL AND ADMINISTRATIVE DETERMINANTS

There has been no economist, from the early times when economics emerged as a science until today, whose angle of vision of the factors of economic growth or development has not been wide enough to include some non-economic, and specifically some political, factors.[36] There is unanimous recognition of the importance of the role of government in determining the direction and intensity of economic life, and of the multiplicity of channels through which this role moves or is transmitted. Where economists disagree is in their recognition of the necessity of externalising the political and other non-economic factors in their discussion of development, as against keeping them implicitly under the convenient *ceteris paribus* cloak. Obviously, in this study, these factors are stated explicitly, their operation is explored, and their impact evaluated.

There is one broad aspect of the activity of government designed to further development, whether this activity falls in the specific field of politics or that of public administration, which raises no controversy and finds ready acceptance by all economic schools of thought. This is the provision of law and order, the setting up of public institutions and services relating to money and finance, regulation of trade, education and health, and like components of the framework within which economic activity takes place. What stirs controversy is the legitimacy and/or the effectiveness and efficiency of *direct* governmental participation in economic activity, through the ownership and use of directly productive assests which produce or serve in the distribution of goods and services—particularly ones whose nature does not bar private businessmen from producing or distributing them. The difference therefore is essentially one between the regulatory functions which are universally accepted, and the directly productive functions which are debated.

However, whereas what is accepted is the subject of consensus by the classical, neo-classical, Marxist and other schools, what is questioned is not clearly defined and, even when and where defined, falls into a narrowing territory. Thus, there are many more today who prefer to see public utilities (water, electricity, urban transport, and the like) in the hands of government than in the hands of private businessmen, even though the goods and services they produce have a cost that can be precisely estimated and are marketable at prices that are easy to determine. The preference goes even further to include some 'strategic industries' such as fertilisers, with their basic function in the production of foodstuff; armaments, with their central place in national security; or medicines, with their crucial significance for the health and well-being of the populace.

The broader area of the mechanism of resource allocation, whether viewed from a sectoral angle or more generally from that of the whole economy, has also been a question for debate and discussion. But here again there are today many more economists and other social thinkers who accept that resource allocation should be undertaken through planning and government action, than through the operation of the market mechanism. Belief in the 'Invisible Hand' is losing ground, especially in the Third World countries, to belief in the 'Visible Hand' of the state reaching out into different directions and areas of action.[37]

Yet the issues to which some reference has so far been made are not the only ones that are raised in the context of development. Certain other issues relate more appropriately to the question of political development and how it shapes as the economy progresses, how such political development influences the progress of the economy, or yet how economic development itself influences the course of political development. The position taken here is that these areas and processes of development interact, and that they all are of great significance. But what interests us is the one-way action of political institutions, forces, ideas (and ideologies) on economic development. As our research showed in the course of the extensive interviewing undertaken, and as library research had already suggested, the political determinants are of great significance for development. How significant in fact they are will become clear as we proceed with our discussion.

Six components of the political framework, or six determinants, occupied us in the enquiry. One of these in particular, the role of the public sector, represented a cluster of determinants, all closely interrelated, as we will have occasion to indicate. Another, planning, could have been placed under 'economic determinants' equally legitimately, but we chose to place it here because essentially we wanted to examine it as one aspect of the determination of the political leadership to pursue its economic development and to inject rationality into it and to express its system of economic values through it. On the other hand, at least one determinant which has been left for discussion among the socio-cultural instead of the political determinants, namely the role of the military, has been thus placed because it fits well into the enquiry undertaken later of the role of various agents of social change in development (including élites, the middle class, etc.). It was thought preferable not to fragment the discussion of these agents of change (or of conservatism, as the case may be), and to treat them all as social factors.

Finally, it is necessary to remind the reader once again that our whole enquiry into the determinants and their operation is narrowed deliberately to include the more active factors. In other words, we are not merely examining the indicators of development, but its determinants. The distinction is clear from the semantics of the terms used. Indeed, as we are finding in the process of analysis, the items selected and examined prove of different degrees of force and effectiveness. Without totally anticipating our conclusions, it is becoming abundantly clear that whereas some determinants are active prime movers, others are supportive or complementary factors, while yet some others provide a foundation or milieu for development. All these types are of close relevance and immense interest to this study, in so far as they either initiate, or support and enrich action of developmental content and implications.

The discussion that follows does not unfold in different parts, each in the context of a different economic system. Yet, differentiation as to type of system in operation is indicated where necessary, and the relevance of the system in existence is never absent from the perspective, and is never ignored. The leading studies that have appeared in the last two decades or so have centred on the interaction between economic and political development, or the politics of development or of modernisation, and have attempted a systemic approach to the understanding of the relationships between the process and/or the stages of economic development on the one hand and the form and level of political development on the other. To this end they have classified the many countries examined in accordance with the system of thought formulated[38] — but unlike those studies, the present one pursues a more pragmatic, particularistic approach.

Accordingly, reference is made to the distinguishing socio-economic and political system or the characteristics of the various Arab countries covered; and the political determinants selected are examined in relation to these countries, with a view to exploring how the determinants operate and influence development in the context under reference. This is done without aprioristic theorising based on an almost global or universalistic system of relationships between political and economic development. This approach was initially chosen when the study was being designed, because of the supposition that it would fit more comfortably into the realities of the Arab region and would help in a better understanding of the operation of political determinants. The field-work that was to follow, and the analysis of the country findings, have confirmed this supposition, as the latter part of this chapter will indicate.

1. The first determinant to explore in this section is the development orientation of the political leadership of the country concerned, or its commitment to development. The orientation or commitment is deducible from a few indicators, such as the emphasis placed on development in the post-war constitutions or their amendments,[39] the place of development in the platforms of leading parties, as well as the major pronouncements of the leaders who have unquestionably enjoyed top decision-making power, cabinet programmes, and generally the philosophies, strategies and policies of the powerful groups that have determined the content and direction of politico-economic action in the various countries under consideration.[40]

We have had occasion in the country chapters to refer at sufficient length to the leaderships thus broadly defined or determined, and to their different expressions of position relative to development. To this extent, there is scant need to repeat the references. Instead, concentration will focus on the impact of these expressions (and the policies and measures that constitute their effective translation into concrete terms) on the process of development. These expressions have been made within different political frameworks, ranging from parliamentary democracy in Western style at one end to military or authoritarian governments at the other end, with or without one-party systems, and with varying degrees of popular political participation. Furthermore, the leaderships vary as to social origin, composition, political experience and motivation. They range from a dynasty that combines the highest religious status with absolute monarchy, as in Morocco, where the King is also commander of the faithful, to Iraq or Syria where the top leadership consists of lower-middle-class army officers and/or party members who, however they reached power, had not done so through inheritance, social class distinction or financial opulence.

In the Arab world, and presumably in most other Third World countries, the developmental 'philosophies and strategies' declared are not necessarily those that the leadership is intent on translating into concrete policies and measures, and on executing. A certain element of unreality must always be allowed. This is true whether the leadership sets out deliberately to mislead the population and to endear itself to it, or it is short on seriousness and makes statements lightly and with insufficient responsibility, or yet it is sincere in its avowed intentions but overestimates its power to make good its promises. Again, this is also true even when the system of government is autocratic, as in this instance as well, the leadership seems to want to please the population. In any case, the leadership's desire to ingratiate itself with the population in advertising its development-mindedness and its determination to promote the welfare of the populace provides evidence of the high social valuation placed by the people on development, though of course their understanding of 'development' will not be abstract or global, but will boil down to a new school in the neighbourhood, piped fresh water, cleaner and cheaper bread, or more secure jobs.

Likewise, the developmental philosophies and strategies of the leadership may not be explicit at all. True, the leadership might not have a coherent philosophy or strategy for development to begin with, but the observer and analyst can always impute such a philosophy and strategy to the leadership — that is, he can reconstruct it from the policies laid and measures taken. What is relevant and central to the discussion here is that the leadership should in fact be committed to development, and that this commitment should be expressed in concrete reality, not just in pronouncements.

The pronouncements by themselves are not to be despised or belittled. It is true that the leadership can make its developmental message reach the masses via the actual improvements it can bring about in the volume and range of goods and services produced, and in the more equitable distribution of these goods and services. Thus the fruits of development are the most effective transmission lines to pass the message. But governments can find to their distress that the population must not be left in the dark, uninformed about the developmental efforts deployed and results achieved. Indeed, the efforts, like the results, can be substantially expanded and enriched if there is large-scale mobilisation of popular support for the efforts. We will have another occasion to talk of the significance of participation for development, but we must at this point underline the simple truth that unless the population is mobilised behind the drive for development, the results will not be maximised for a given effort and outlay.

The leadership's commitment to development can be manifested in many ways, some direct, some indirect. Broadly speaking, the manifestation takes the form of an active programme of investment in the public sector, with all that goes with such a programme in terms of institution-building, encouragement and establishment of facilities for research and feasibility studies, the furtherance of the education and training of manpower, the modernisation of organisation, and other measures purporting to expand production and improve its quality. Likewise, the commitment takes the form of distributive measures aiming at achieving a fairer distribution of income and wealth — one which better reflects the contribution of the various categories of manpower to the economy and the rise in productivity. Finally, in a broader sense the leadership's commitment can take the form of changes in the socio-economic system designed to provide a framework more conducive to development and the achievement of its objectives. This list is by no means exhaustive, but should be sufficiently indicative.

As far as the private sector is concerned, the commitment of the leadership takes more indirect forms. In general, the commitment is translated into two broad sets of policies and measures. The first is designed to be promotive of entrepreneurial drive and investment in the directions thought to be aligned with the overall vision of the leadership of how the economy should progress, that is, in line with the investment and growth and employment patterns (in terms of sectors and industries and activities) desired by the leadership. The other is designed to be inhibitive or prohibitive of activities and investments that the leadership wants to be discouraged because the sectors, activities and industries to which they would otherwise be directed rank low in the leadership's valuation.

However, apart from these translations of commitment in the context of the public and the private sector, there are other, overall avenues of action that are chosen in order to reach certain desiderata. A development-oriented leadership is usually seized with several desiderata, four of which seem to be most recurrent. The first is to achieve, or to maintain, a reasonably high rate of overall economic growth with a reasonable rate of economic stability. The second is to raise the level of employment (and, conversely, to reduce the level of unemployment and of underemployment). The third is to reduce the degree of dualism, especially where it is associated with economic exploitation or socio-political incursion into the community's life, arising from the presence of a large foreign-owned and -operated sector or industry. The last desideratum to be brought out here is the reduction of imbalance in the economy and society. This imbalance could be between regions, sectors or social classes or groups. The four desiderata and their rationale are too well known to call for further discussion here.

As already indicated, the area of action within which the leadership's commitment to development manifests itself is vast. Likewise, the action takes different forms, at different levels. One prominent and far-reaching manifestation of the commitment is development planning and the allocation of the necessary resources. As a determinant of development, planning is important enough to be discussed separately further down. At this point we need only underline it as the expression *par excellence* of the commitment to development. Certain other expressions will be mentioned in the rest of this section. But planning remains the mechanism and avenue, or the modality, through which not only commitment to development is expressed, but also some of the other political and administrative determinants. It has received vastly increased emphasis in the post-war period in the Third World at large, and in the Arab world in particular. How well it has vindicated the promise vested in it remains to be seen in the discussion to come.[41]

It is not only with respect to planning that the effectiveness of the commitment of leadership to development has to be assessed. Indeed, avowed commitment, no matter how sincere and well-meant, remains insufficient, though necessary, for development to materialise. Understandably, many other factors have to be present and to operate, both as active, initiating determinants, and as contributive, supplementary determinants. But given suitable circumstances, and given the presence of these other determinants, it remains crucial for commitment to development to satisfy certain conditions for it to be fruitful. There is need only to mention a few of the salient conditions without elaboration. Thus the commitment must show continuity, and not be erratic. It ought further to be expressed in terms of sound strategies, policies and measures. Likewise, other areas of political action must not be in contradiction with the developmental policies pursued. In other words, the general economic climate created by the political leadership must be inviting to developmental effort; and this climate relates to the politico-social as well as economic spheres. Often, policies and measures in the political field proper block the delicate developmental drive which is launched alongside in the economic field.

How do the Arab countries fare with respect to the commitment of their various leaderships to development? There will be no attempt to take one by one the various points raised so far in what is meant as a conceptual framework, and to examine the degree of conformity of each of the Arab countries to the conditions and specifications laid down. Instead, a global evaluation will be attempted which is believed to be an honest round-up of the variety of specifications and the degree of fit in each case.[42]

The attitude of the Arab countries comprised within this study varies from one of lukewarm commitment in Lebanon to one of profound commitment in Algeria, Iraq, Kuwait or Libya. However, leaving Lebanon and possibly Morocco aside as rather special cases, the remaining ten countries do not span a wide range but all generally reveal degrees of commitment close to each other. The exclusion of Lebanon and Morocco calls for some explanation. The economic philosophy espoused in Lebanon is one which involves a low degree of involvement by the government in development effort. Indeed, even the more obvious areas of activity, such as infrastructural investments, do not all fall in the public sector, nor are they all the recipients of adequate attention and investment, although the country's prosperity and position as commercial, financial and tourist centre (and as the most effective centre for communication and mass media operations) depend on certain aspects of the physical and service infrastructure. Furthermore, the degree of seriousness in Cabinet statements, of continuity in the pursuit of the limited developmental objectives, and of discipline in the planning, execution and follow-up of projects is in all instances very low. Given this situation, it can be said that the economic growth achieved in the postwar period has come about in spite of the low level of real commitment to development by the political leadership, but mainly thanks to the entrepreneurial drive of the private sector, which bursts with energy, and which has to a large extent compensated for the failings and shortcomings of government.

Morocco, the other country excepted, presents a different and more complicated situation. Here, hesitancy and slowness characterise official attitudes. This is best seen with respect to the slow and half-hearted take-over of the rich land that was in the hands of the *colons* upon independence; in the resistance to the nationalisation of extractive industry which is of paramount importance to the country; and in the equally hesitant measures of Moroccanisation of industries and public utilities in European hands.

Hesitation and the avowed concern for efficiency explain the official attitude to *colon* land, the phosphate mines, and much of industry. But only in part. These attitudes must also be understood in the light of certain aspects of economic and social policy. As in pre-1952 Egypt or pre-1958 Iraq, development efforts have been influenced to a not inconsiderable extent by some special interests, as we have had occasion to indicate with reference to dam construction policy in Chapter 13 of Volume I, and to the slowness in liberating the national economy from the grip of the French. In brief, there is a conflict between socio-political *malaise* and economic development — as in most other Arab countries. Hence the restiveness among a certain proportion of the articulate, politicised population (students, labour unions, opposition parties) — a restiveness which creates some cynicism even with respect to sound, bona fide projects of development. The motivation of the paternalism proclaimed and practised by the authorities is at times unjustly questioned; this no doubt dilutes popular initiative and participation, and under the circumstances is unwarranted.

Algeria can claim a reasonably good score, both with regard to commitment to development by the leadership, and to the results in the economic and social spheres. This presents a paradox to a certain extent. Morocco enjoys a degree of freedom of the press, the labour movement and the political parties not enjoyed by Algeria, yet Algeria has given scope to political participation at the grass-roots level, and has achieved creditable economic results, which seem to compensate for the freedoms curtailed. (This does not mean that creditable performance and freedom are mutually exclusive — only that the latter has been sacrificed for the former by the leadership.) Basically, the explanation must lie in the fact that the 'system' in Algeria is not designed to benefit a national bourgeoisie, or an oligarchy, or yet a military élite whose social origins go back to the bourgeoisie or to powerful tribes, and which therefore does not provide a counterpoint to the other power élites but a tributary in the mainstream of power. The virtual classlessness of Algeria and the determined effort by the leadership to achieve economic *and social* development, combined, spell the difference between it and most other Arab countries. (The emergence of a powerful civil service and a ruling party qualifies the description of Algeria as largely classless only partly, owing to the narrow economic range of socio-economic differentiation.)

The developmental orientation and commitment of Tunisian political leadership is a distinctly positive factor. The country has had a conjuncture of influences all pouring into one mainstream. The first is a development-minded, progressive, strong leader who has been occupying the top place in influence and later in power for over forty years: Habib Bourguiba, first a rebel and fighter against colonial rule, then since independence unchallenged President and leader. The constitution, the laws and the ruling party all emphasise development and social justice, no less than the opposition and its platforms (whenever such opposition has appeared).[43] The 'flavour' of the leadership, as of the young in the urban centres — intellectuals, labour, students, civil servants — is modern. The urge to modernise has revealed itself in many areas: not just in the building of economic and social infrastructure, planning and development work, but also in the emancipation of women further than anywhere else in the Arab world, in secularisation, and in legislation in general. Nowhere else in the Arab world has a leadership so oriented been in power for so long. Were Tunisia's resources to permit it, the country would have achieved one of the most brilliant records of economic development.

On the other hand, Libya, with abundant financial resources available for several years now, and with a fresh leadership very eager to develop the country, suffers from the absence of a few critical ingredients in the determinant under examination. Thus, not only is the leadership new, having come to power late in 1969, but it has set out to undo much of what had been attempted or begun earlier. Furthermore, its eagerness for development is not matched with steadfastness of vision and concentration of focus. It allows itself to be drawn into side preoccupations which are wasteful of energy and of resources. This is not to belittle its performance or its purposefulness, but to suggest that its commitment to development has yet to be combined with a few of the prerequisites to which we alluded earlier as necessary conditions to be satisfied, for commitment to bear fruit. Furthermore, time has to be allowed for the leadership's commitment to benefit from the maturing effect of time and experience.

The Egypt of the Revolution has enjoyed most of the advantages associated with the determinant now being considered, but has had three major setbacks since 1952. The first is the basic shortage of material resources and the heaviness and bureaucratisation of the civil service, both of which have counteracted the beneficial effect of the leadership's commitment to development and rendered this leadership's means distinctly short of its ambitions and determination. The second is the series of wars and political setbacks the country has suffered, in 1956 (the Suez war), 1961 (the break-up of the union between Egypt and Syria), 1962 (the involvement in the Yemen war which lasted for a few years), 1967 (the brief but bitter and destructive war of June 1967), and 1973 (the October war).

The third major setback is associated with the two just cited, but is of distinct significance as well. This is the weakening of purpose that befell the development effort after the 1967 war, but more particularly after the death of President Nasser in September 1970. The determination to develop remained strong in official pronouncements, but it has been definitely bedevilled by hesitation and some confusion, particularly in the past few years. This most recent period is singled out because it has witnessed rather contradictory orientations: the application of real control over the economy, along with widely advertised policies of 'opening-up' or liberalisation; adherence to socialism, along with permissiveness towards (if not encouragement of) the mushrooming of private fortunes and of millionaires; and, most significantly, the continued insistence that development continues to occupy top priority and should receive the utmost of resources available (especially foreign exchange resources), along with a new permissive import policy and equal permissiveness towards consumerism in all its forms.

As a result of these and other associated developments, Egypt now has what looks like a confused system of priorities, a tendency to change course frequently and widely, little effective planning, and seriously inadequate resources for its urgent and longer-term needs. To an appreciable extent this is a reflection of the inconsistency between the avowed commitment of the leadership to development, on the one hand, and the real developmental vision, strategies, objectives and policies chosen, on the other hand.

Post-war Sudan shares very little of Egypt's experience. Sudan's wars and political turmoil have been internal, not external. Its economic potential is immense, given its present sectoral structure, whereas Egypt's is limited, unless it undergoes vast change. And Sudan has not enjoyed the long stretch of determined and effective developmental commitment which, for Egypt, lasted till the middle of the sixties. If one were to dramatise Sudan's post-independence experience, one would describe it as a series of flashes of developmental zeal, alternating with another series of political preoccupations that have diverted attention from development into political survival for the leadership. In fairness, the leadership has shown clear signs of an ingrained interest in and desire for development. But these qualities fall short of an effective commitment, in the sense in which we have qualified the term in our introductory observations. As in the case of Egypt, even given apposite development orientation and commitment, Sudan is seriously short of investible resources. Nowhere else in the Arab world is the gap as wide between potential and immediate investment possibilities. Here lies the country's sorrowful present reality; but here also lies the challenge to its leadership which is full of promise. Most recently, there have been clear indications that political stability, coupled with a strong government and a strong commitment to development, are going together to permit the country to have access to considerable resources for the integrated development of its vast agricultural sector and the associated sectors of storage, transport and irrigation.

Lebanon has already been examined with respect to the operation of the determinant under consideration. No more need be said at this point except to draw attention to the irony that the country with the political system nearest to the Western model — elective, parliamentary representation; multiplicity of parties; a free press — is the one country where the leadership's commitment to development is the least in evidence and not surprisingly the least effective.

Syria stands in contrast. From its independence three decades earlier onwards, and under different socio-political systems, it has shown a strong developmental orientation and commitment in its complex of leadership. Even when this leadership shared much of the outlook of its Lebanese counterpart, as far as its option for a system of free enterprise and parliamentary government was concerned, its seriousness of purpose was more distinct, and its commitment to development more purposeful and more effective.

Furthermore, since the union with Egypt started in early 1958, and despite a record of political unrest and deep involvement in two wars with Israel in 1967 and 1973, the commitment has become stronger and more effective. The major discernible difference lies in the direction of this commitment. For, whereas essentially it aimed at the activation of the private sector before 1958, since then it has opted for the public sector as its major engine for development. Except for the October war of 1973, the country has been on a course of stability and greater purpose since the early 1970s, and there is great promise, if the present course continues, that the determinant now being examined will have yet vaster scope to show positive developmental results.

The experience of Jordan, Syria's southern neighbour, is one of part convergence, part divergence, when set against that of Syria. Jordan has had some serious internal political turmoil, and has suffered even more heavily in the June 1967 war with Israel. Its leadership can be said to have consistently had a strong commitment to development, but this leadership has not been as concerned with considerations of social justice as that of Syria since 1958. Another major difference between the two leaderships is their option of socio-economic system. In Jordan, private enterprise still plays the major role in the economy, and it is entrusted with many more tasks related to economic growth than the public sector. However, unlike the Lebanese leadership, the Jordanian has undertaken its developmental responsibilities seriously and steadfastly. It is to the credit of Jordan that it has pursued this course of action with more meagre resources than Lebanon. In brief, it can be said that the developmental commitment of the leadership of Jordan has been a strong factor and has produced positive results in the socio-economic areas of action.

Evaluating the effectiveness of the commitment to development of the leadership of Saudi Arabia calls for a careful look at some of the distinguishing features of development in this country. To begin with, there was little serious work in this direction until the early 1960s, as we indicated in the country chapter on the kingdom in Volume I. It was only then that the overspending and mis-spending of King Saud and the thousands of members of the extended royal family was curbed, under the firm leadership of Crown Prince Faisal who had been asked to become Prime Minister and salvage the situation. Until that time, it can be said that the commitment of the leadership was very weak — indeed, there was a commitment to block development, if the overall picture of the leadership's behaviour is to be considered.

The situation was gradually reversed under Faisal, first as Prime Minister and Crown Prince, and later as King. However, two features of Faisal's rule deserve emphasis before the impact of the determinant under examination can be assessed. The first is that, over the period 1963-75 when development work gained momentum until it attained its present immense thrust, development has meant the building of roads, the installation of factories, and the establishment of more schools and hospitals. These things are creditable in themselves, but they do not go far enough. Thus the social content of development is restrictive, and the process is largely limited to its material, purely economic aspects. What is as serious is the oversight of the necessity to strive for self-reliance and to gradually reduce the dependence on powerful foreign economic interests. The transnational corporations are not only tolerated; they are welcomed and taken as partners in every conceivable enterprise. The policies formulated in the fields of petroleum, industrialisation and transfer of technology often reveal the concern that the Western world and the international economy at large should be inconvenienced as little as possible in the process. This is commendable as a manifestation of a sense of international responsibility.[44] Yet at times it means lower oil prices and a smaller revenue to the country than could be set and obtained; it also often means the acceptance of a slower enhancement of the capability of the country to generate the internal forces that are the true propeller of solid development.

The second feature that qualifies the commitment to development in Saudi Arabia is the parallel adoption of two conflicting philosophies and policies: the opening of the economy to the world as completely as possible, along with the limited exposure of the society to outside social and cultural influences. This is not to deny the social influence of the introduction of a modern technology and its products, of commercial dealings with and travel to the Western industrial world, or yet of the introduction of modern education. However, the strictness of the control over the entry of books and magazines, and the careful limitation of the despatch of bursary students abroad (whereby the number is kept very small compared with such other countries of lesser means as Kuwait, Iraq or Jordan) provide an illustration of the desire to expose the country to the outside world socially with rationed dosage, in contrast with the large-scale economic exposure. To sum up: the commitment to development must be understood within the constraints and qualification indicated. There are yet other ways in which the quality of this commitment influences the course of development. The accumulation of immense financial reserves and the record of very high rates of growth in national product must not lead the observer, any more than the concerned Saudi, into satisfaction that the country is achieving the quality of development which it deserves and is capable of bringing about, were there to exist a more harmonious blending of economic and social philosophies and policies.

Kuwait presents a different picture. Its resource mix is different; it is much more open socially and culturally to the outside world; its leadership leans heavily on an elective representative base; and it has not had the experience of misallocation of resources to any comparable extent that Saudi Arabia had before Faisal took effective power. Examining the commitment to development against the yardsticks and within the framework formulated earlier, it can be seen that Kuwait ranks commendably high. The commitment by its leadership has been strong, continuous and largely enlightened; and it has been supported by some effective institutions, including a National Assembly, by a relatively large measure of participation, and by a development-oriented, well-established and strong merchant class. This overall favourable evaluation can be made despite the controversial, even faulty, policies with respect to population and naturalisation, land purchases by government and industrialisation that have been adopted. (The country chapter in Volume I discusses these policies and their implication in some detail.)

Finally, Iraq. It can be said that this country has had a strong awareness of the need for development and concern with it for several decades, long before oil revenues became an important source of state income in the early 1950s. Thus the commitment to development, defined loosely and unambitiously, has been a characteristic of the leadership for a very long time. However, it gained considerable strength at the beginning of the 1950s, and has continued in evidence ever since, though with severe fluctuations in the degree of effectiveness of this commitment and its satisfaction of the conditions and prerequisites we set earlier for it.

This commitment has been curtailed in effect for much of the quarter-century 1950-75, owing to internal political strife, including the Kurdish rebellion in the north and north-east; to the country's involvement in the Arab-Israeli wars; to the insufficient concern of certain components of the leadership — namely in early parliament and party circles — with developmental issues; and to the protracted struggle with the Iraq Petroleum Company, a struggle which seriously restricted the flow of revenue to the country from the export of crude. However, underlying these destabilising factors which have of necessity caused serious digressions from the leadership's commitment to development, runs a strand of continuous concern for development in the circles of government and top leadership. That this concern has not always manifested itself in the formulation of sound priorities and policies, or that it has at times been coupled with counter-productive policies and measures, qualifies the statement but does not totally negate it.

Although the composition of the leadership has changed considerably and has narrowed since the revolution of July 1958, this can be said to have been compensated for since the mid- or late sixties by an intensification in the commitment, coupled and supplemented more recently with three propitious factors. These are the steep increase in oil revenues in the seventies, the elimination of knotty conflict with the concessionary oil companies through the nationalisation of their assets, and the solution of the Kurdish problem and the ensuing cessation of hostilities. As things stand today, Iraq can claim that the determinant under examination is a strong positive and promotive factor in development — one which is all the more effective as it is coupled both with a clear vision of overall development in its several dimensions, and with sufficient resources to put this development afoot.

2. The second determinant to examine is planning and plans. The main question to be answered is how effective planning has been as a prime mover or factor determining the course of development. In attempting to provide an answer, we will not survey the planning experience of each of the countries covered in the study, nor the plans formulated and implemented. (This was undertaken in the country chapters.) Instead, we will examine the role of planning as a determinant from a number of angles, drawing illustrations or providing concreteness by referring to the various countries as we move along.[45]

(a) Conceptualisation of the Future

The function of the planner or the designer of planning policy is — or rather ought to be — very much like that of the architect; both start from a certain conceptualisation of what it is desired to create or shape. The sound approach to planning ought to be teleological, thus emanating from the future vision of the economy and society for which the plan is to be formulated, no matter how broad and general this vision is. Without it, planning remains mechanistic, without much horizon or depth. Obviously, planning into the future must involve some significant transformations in the economy and society, otherwise it would fail to justify the effort put into it.

Arab planning experience shows that such conceptualisation is missing from most plans; where it exists, it is partial, or else implicit and hesitant. The least unsatisfactory in this respect are the plan documents of Syria, Iraq, Kuwait and Algeria, where the desired future image of the economy is externalised. But beyond the conceptualisation, there is need for an elaboration of a strategy capable of enabling the economy, while implementing the plan to achieve the targets set — however these are defined or expressed. The strategy involves, *inter alia*, a careful definition of priorities; the identification of the strong as of the weak points in the economy; the determination of the sector capable of leading the drive for development; the formulation of policies capable of activating this leading sector and enabling it in turn to activate much of the rest of the economy. Arab experience here again, though dissimilar in detail, largely betrays the absence of a carefully thought-out strategy, and not infrequently shows an insufficient concern with, or explicit presentation of, the policies called for by the plan.

(b) The Political and Institutional Framework

The second angle of vision is the political and institutional framework of planning, which it is necessary to understand if the nature and effectiveness of planning are to be assessed. Four major elements are most relevant to the framework: political stability in the context of a political system amenable and welcoming to planning; development-orientation of the political leadership; an efficient civil service which is not overburdened with bureaucracy and fragmented loyalty; and appropriate planning institutions and instruments. The first three are discussed separately as political determinants in the present section of the chapter, while the fourth has received attention during the discussion of planning in the various country chapters in Volume I. We need only make some general remarks here on these four points.

The political stability required is one which is seasoned with political participation; otherwise, the stability would be the product of autocratic rule which would defuse potential popular enthusiasm for the plan and co-operation for its success.[46] Most of the Arab countries have missed this kind of qualified stability in the post-war period, and planning has suffered as a result. Furthermore, political stability cannot be assessed in isolation from the socio-economic system and its objectives, to the extent that the stability that flows from free political expression and the ability to achieve orderly change in government cannot be had unless the socio-economic and political system attaches a high value to this type of stability and the forces behind it.

We need not add anything to what was said earlier in connection with the development commitment of the leadership, which was the first determinant to be discussed in this section, except for one point. This is that one major aspect of this general commitment is the specific commitment to the plan, which takes many forms. In this respect, it can be said that the Arab countries can be classified with respect to the degree of seriousness with which they take planning. Accordingly, Egypt (until 1965), Syria, Iraq, Tunisia, Algeria and Morocco rank ahead of the remaining six countries with regard to planning seriousness; Lebanon and Kuwait tail the list, although in the latter the government treats development with the earnestness it requires.

The civil service, which is the third factor to consider in the present context, has on the whole been characterised by lethargy, inefficiency and unpreparedness for the economic tasks assigned to it by the greater recourse to planning.[47] The improvement of the service at the top of the hierarchy, through the introduction of professionalisation and the recruitment of well-qualified elements, has not gone down the pyramid far enough to make a tangible difference. Furthermore, questions of political appointment, divided loyalty, frequent change of government and insecurity — among others — have made this factor's contribution to the success of planning and development much more modest than it could have been.

Finally, planning agencies and instruments. These, as already stated, have been discussed in the various country chapters of Volume I. All that is to be added here is that by and large these institutions have been short of qualified staff and of reliable statistics, insecure owing to the general political instability and frequent change of government, at the mercy of frequent and sharp changes in policy handed down from the political leadership at the top, and generally frustrated because of their inability to see through the outcome of any plan.

(c) Planning and Some Major Economic and Social Issues

Planning and the planners have had to face several major issues, five of which will be mentioned here. These are: the conflicting claims for priority or ascendancy between the objective of increasing production, and that of a more egalitarian distribution of national product; the philosophy and priorities of education, involving the pressure for universal education and the provision of opportunities for all those who want to go to secondary and then higher education, as against the concentration on the education and training of manpower categories that are critical for the process of development — given the shortages in all countries of teachers and/or financial resources and facilities; the pattern of allocation of investment resources, among the various sectors and regions, in such a way as to correct imbalances without spreading the resources too thin and losing the advantages inherent in lumpy or concentrated investment in satisfaction of the 'big push' principle;[48] the competition between development and defence for short physical and/or skilled human resources; and the harmonisation, or at least the removal of contradiction, between country plans on the one hand, and the developmental and planning needs and requirements of the Arab region as a whole. Merely to list these issues is to suggest how serious and difficult to resolve they are, and how taxing for policy-makers and planners alike.

(d) The Horizons of Arab Planning

This aspect relates to the quality of planning, its sectoral and regional comprehensiveness, the allocation of the economic burden it creates, and its realism. An examination of the Arab plans from this angle permits a number of observations.

The first relates to the social burden arising from planned development, and the degree of consistency or parallelism between the investment programme planned, and the mobilisation of the domestic resources called for by such a programme. Stated differently, the question is one of the weighing of economic and social benefits against economic and social burdens. One concrete embodiment of this issue is the tax policy adopted.[49]

The Arab experience in this regard indicates three different trends. The first is seen in those oil-rich countries which do not impose taxes on their citizens, namely Kuwait and Saudi Arabia. (Where they do, as in Libya or Iraq, the tax burden is not equivalent to the benefits advanced by the government plus the development effort expended.) The second tendency can be seen in the countries that have opted for socialism, namely Egypt, Syria, Iraq, Algeria, and to a much lesser extent Tunisia, where the tax burden is higher, and where the higher-income groups find it difficult to escape their tax obligations. The last tendency is encountered in the remaining countries, where no heavy tax burden is imposed because of development planning, and where evasion is relatively easy anyway.

The second observation is that planning has often been characterised by over-ambitiousness, both in the investments projected, which have almost invariably been well beyond the spending and executing capacity of the country, and in the expectations of returns or achievements. Frequently the frustration and disappointment that have followed have been caused as much by the underfulfilment of the plans as by the initial over-ambitiousness. The underfulfilment in the period surveyed as a whole has been experienced in Egypt, Syria and Iraq, but more so in Morocco, Tunisia and Sudan.

Thirdly, one aspect of comprehensiveness which has not received the attention it deserves in virtually all the Arab countries over the stretch of their planning experience is manpower planning, with regard to education, training, health and labour supply in general.[50] This oversight, or weakness in the plans, is all the more surprising considering that the population is at the same time the beneficiary of development, as it is its brain and muscle. Partial explanation can be found in the scantiness of demographic and manpower statistics. But the scantiness itself reflects the insufficiency of effort exerted in respect of statistical improvement.

Finally, the quality of planning and its reach must be assessed not only in the degree of sophistication of the plans, but also in their coverage. Thus, do they take into account all economic sectors, as well as both institutional sectors — the public and the private? Do they take into account all resources available, and all resource uses? The most important question in this broad context is the place of the private sector and how businessmen are made to conform to plan expectations, and whether or not the policies and measures taken are consistent with the desire to bring about a large measure of such conformity.

The experience of the Arab countries in this regard consists of two strands. One of these, which characterises most countries, is that the policies adopted have been far from instrumental in making the private sector behave as expected and planned. Indeed, most frequently these policies have been outright counter-productive. The second strand, which characterises the experience of a few countries for a part of the period covered, is that the private sector has been assigned a larger role than the socialist option suggests. Iraq and Syria, and more recently Egypt, are cases in point. Whether or not this is a healthy development does not concern us here; what does is the necessity for internal consistency in order for the public and private economic decision-makers to take the appropriate stand with respect to investment, expansion and technological change.

(e) The Methodology of Planning

There are two sides to this question: the method of actual plan formulation, understood from the point of view of institutions and participants in the process of plan design and formulation; and the technique of planning, including the degree of professionalism and sophistication. Both relate to the role of planning as a determinant, but the first is much more relevant, as we shall see.

With respect to the first aspect, there is still preponderant emphasis in the Arab world on what one might call 'Central Inspiration' in plan conceptualisation and the setting of overall targets, plus actual design and formulation. This is to say that the plan is prepared in the central government by the ministry or specialised agency, with little or no consultation with the 'periphery', that is, with local administrations on the one hand, and with the consumers and the private sector on the other. Planning can thus be said to be largely a 'one-way' process, instead of being a 'two-way' process involving a give and take, consultation and subsequent adjustment, back and forth, until consensus is reached.

The significance of this matter is not just one of form; it relates to the degree of participation by various public and private bodies in plan design and formulation (including the setting of financial and physical targets), and thus to the degree of realism of the plan and its reflection of the actual needs of those who are its beneficiaries and instruments alike. Furthermore, to the extent that participation is weak, mobilisation for the plan and commitment to its targets are also bound to remain weak. The dictum can be suggested here that there can be no strong commitment without strong participation and mobilisation.

The second aspect to be examined under 'methodology' need not detain us long here. We can briefly say that considerable progress has been made in the techniques and sophistication of plans and planning in all the countries of the region. Egypt, Syria, Iraq, Morocco, Tunisia and Algeria have marked most progress in this respect. Likewise, the statistical services which are indispensable to sound planning have advanced considerably from the early post-war years.

(f) The Continuity of Plans and Planning

It would not have been realistic to expect the early plans to have had their full span, considering the novelty of planning then, the scanty experience possessed, and the changing world around the plans. Consequently, a very high turnover of plans can be seen in most of the period covered, say from its beginning to the early or mid-sixties. This turnover was not merely the outcome of a desire for improvement, or in satisfaction of changing economic conditions, but also because of political upheavals and changes of system, or yet of personal predilections associated with the change of minister or heads of planning outfits. Notwithstanding the causes of frequent change of plans, the record shows that Egypt has shown the highest continuity, and Iraq the lowest, the latter having had eight plans between 1951 and 1975. The remaining countries fall in between, with the exception of Kuwait, which has not had a single plan approved by the National Assembly in spite of the fact that there have been three formulations of a plan, and of Lebanon, which has had a few plans but has not adhered to them.

While it is true that rigidity ought to be avoided and alterations within the plans, or even plan changes, ought to be undertaken where necessary, it is also true that frequent alteration and change, no matter how worthy the declared cause, lead to hesitation in decision-making, especially with respect to investment, in the private and the public sector alike. Indeed, where perfectionism is used as an excuse for change of plan during its course, it is still arguable that a plan which is 60 or 70 per cent satisfactory, is better, and ought more strongly to be pursued, than a plan that promises to be 80 per cent satisfactory, if the change threatens to be frequent and to disrupt the decision-making process and to cause unnecessarily frequent institutional changes. In this latter respect, the Arab world has witnessed excessive experimentation with institutions, in planning but also elsewhere in government. Even with the best of intentions, excessive change is harmful to the institutions themselves and to the work for which they are designed.

(g) The Structure of Investment Programmes

The experience of the Arab countries espousing planning reveals a large measure of realism in the structure of the investment programmes of development plans. Even when the shortage of statistical information and of planning experts was very pressing, these programmes by and large reflected a great deal of common sense in the allocation of resources among the economic sectors. Hence, agriculture and irrigation have generally received a respectable share of investments, while industry has received a rising share but one not as large as the pronouncements in praise of industrialisation would have suggested. (Indeed, the share of industry has suffered fluctuation in relative terms, particularly in Iraq.) In all the countries with operative plans, investment in infrastructure has received major emphasis, both in its economic, physical category such as transport, communication and energy, and in the social category such as education and health. Again, the general shortcoming that can be discerned with very few exceptions (notably Algeria) is the direction of adequate resources to the development of manpower and population, in the fields of training and job provision.

(h) Plan Execution and Follow-up

With the exception of the brief experiences of Iraq in the early fifties and of Libya in 1952 and again in 1960, the function of planning has been kept separate from that of execution in the Arab world. This writer endorses the principle of separation for various reasons to which reference has been made in Volume I. Foremost among these is the danger that the function of proper control of execution cannot be performed if the planning agency is itself plan executor. For, even with the separation of functions, the control is slack, and the timing and allocation of investments, as well as the quality of work undertaken, seem in most instances to have been out of line with plan specifications.

There is no uniform picture for all the countries examined with respect to the effectiveness of follow-up; however, the one generalisation that can be made is that follow-up has been weak, but that it has improved somewhat over the years. The improvement has been the outcome of three factors: greater recognition of the significance of follow-up for the avoidance of waste of resources and time, and of frustration; growing experience within execution agencies charged with follow-up; and increased setting-up of specialised bodies for follow-up coupled with improvement in follow-up techniques and records. Indeed, a number of countries — in particular Syria, Iraq, Morocco, Tunisia, Egypt and Algeria — have started the sound precedent of preparing careful reports in which the plan results are evaluated and published. Publication is essential, in order for the public at large to be capable of assessing the performance and the failings, and of discussing them and generally exercising some healthy control over the plans. The accountability of planning and executing authorities to the public is necessary, and it complements the participation to which we referred earlier.

(i) Achievements Compared with Plan Expectations

The final, integrative look at planning and its role as a determinant lies in the comparison between what had been originally expected or aimed at in the plans, and what was actually achieved. Understandably, a shortfall, like an 'overfulfilment' of plans need not, indeed must not be totally attributed to plan implementation. So many other factors intervene and interfere — political, economic, climatic. However, the comparison remains necessary and useful. The experience of the Arab world viewed from this angle permits four inferences.

The first is that the achievements have been clearly below the expectations or objectives set, except for most of the major oil producers and exporters. The gap between growth rates projected and recorded has been small in Jordan, Syria and Egypt, but large in Iraq, Sudan, Morocco, Tunisia and Algeria (in the seventies). No plan in Lebanon included such growth rate projections until the six-year plan published in 1972; the Kuwaiti plan never became operative as a plan; and the Saudi five-year plan 1970-5 was actually started in 1971 and no results are available as of the time of writing. In Libya, the growth rates have been much higher than all plan expectations owing to the steep rise in oil exports and revenues.

The second inference is that the measurement of growth rates achieved versus those projected is inadequate as a criterion of performance, because, invariably in the Arab countries concerned, it conceals behind it wide variations among sectors and among years.

That is to say, the variations between projections and achievements which may be small globally for the whole economy, are substantial per sector and per year.

In the third place, there are many factors behind the performance gap, whether global, sectoral or temporal. Probably the strongest of these is that of frequent and sharp change in political authority and system, and therefore in the degree of stability, in a number of the countries studied. But to this, and to unpredictable climatic changes, must be added: the inadequacy of statistical information and related studies which constitute essential inputs into plan formulation and provide protection against guesswork and rule-of-thumb planning; permissiveness towards over-ambition and over-optimism in the definition of plan expectations and projections, and unwarranted neglect of base year data and the realities of the background period to the plan; and generally the failure to lay down realistic assumptions with regard to the plan framework and its political, social, institutional, manpower and economic components.

Finally, examination of the Arab planning experience betrays not only a discrepancy between growth rates projected and achieved, but also between investments planned, allocations cited in the budget, and investments actually and finally made. In all the countries comprised here except Egypt and to a lesser extent Syria, where the performance is reasonably good, the ratio of investments actually realised ranges on the average between half and three-fifths of programmed investments. This suggests that the shortage of investment resources is not the main bottleneck, although in some instances it was the direct cause of slow actual investment. Instead, the main bottleneck is probably the ability to absorb investments for virtually the whole Arab region. A limited absorptive capacity is attributable to the weakness of the planning authorities and mechanisms, inadequacy of statistics, insufficiency of pre-investment studies, shortage of technical and managerial/ administrative/advisory manpower resources, weakness of organisation, and unsuitability of the climate of investment and the political/institutional framework, given the size of the plan and its investment programme.

What can be said in conclusion with regard to the effectiveness of planning as a determinant of development? The answer to this question requires the prior emphasis on three matters related to planning: that planning mentality and methodology require a more advanced state of economic rationality and political purposefulness than the Arab countries have been able to claim; that planning calls for a greater recognition of the importance of time discipline and commitment to time-tables; and that planning implies the definition of clear targets within a clear system of priorities and a clear strategy, instead of aimlessness and arbitrariness.

Bearing these points in mind, we can say that planning has led to some acceleration in the pace of development and made it somewhat more rational and purposeful than it would have been without planning. This can be said without losing sight of the drawbacks and serious shortcomings and failings of Arab planning experience. In general, the planning process, in spite of some positive aspects, is still in need of a great deal of improvement and tightening — from the stage of conceptualisation down to executions and follow-up — if the returns of planning are to justify the effort and expenses involved. Furthermore, two other matters of great concern have also to be attended to if planning is to be an effective determinant. The first is the provision of the appropriate politico-institutional framework. In the absence of such a framework, planning cannot be effective, no matter how sophisticated it is, and how elaborate its growth models are. In this respect we generally witness more tangible improvements in the methodology of planning than in its framework.

The second matter is the mobilisation of the populace. Its awareness of the significance and usefulness of planning must be heightened, and its energies must be mobilised in the service of plan execution. But this can only be achieved if there is widespread information and 'enlightenment' and wide political and economic participation. The latter must relate both to plan design and execution, and to the sharing of the rewards that development planning is supposed to bring about.

3. The determinant to examine now is the civil service, or the public administration. The examination will essentially aim at assessing the effectiveness of the service as a factor in economic development, and it will be conducted from several angles which include recruitment, promotion and termination; training; attitudes to the job and to the public; loyalty and its object; professionalism; bureaucratisation; allocation of authority; motivation and incentives; operation of group politics on the morale and functioning of the service; and generally relevance of the service to the needs and demands of a modernising economy.[51] We will touch on some other points in the process of the discussion; on the other hand not all these points will be explicitly taken into account, one by one. Instead, an overall evaluation of the civil service will be undertaken which will constitute that one-tenth of the proverbial iceberg which is visible, whereas the detailed scrutiny of the many criteria and measuring rods that have been listed will constitute the invisible nine-tenths of the iceberg. The 'invisible part' has been examined carefully in the research and field-work, but the amount of detail involved in it forbids its reproduction here in full. None the less, there will be many occasions where reference will be made to specific points and criteria that form inputs in the final evaluation for each of the countries.

Before this discussion proceeds any further, it ought to be stated that, like planning, the civil service is strongly shaped by the political leadership and its attitude and commitment to development, in so far as the service is called upon to exercise an effective influence in the process of development. When it is seen further that the factor of commitment also influences the course and operation of other political (and indeed, economic and socio-cultural) factors, it will be realised that this factor is one of the greatest significance — probably the most potent among the ones surveyed in this chapter.

The angles from which the subject matter can be examined, and the number of countries involved, produce an unwieldy number of combinations, given the method of analysis used in this study. (The angles or criteria number at least a dozen, as do the countries.) Therefore, to be able to handle the material on hand and derive intelligible country evaluations, and final generalisations for the region, some clustering will be resorted to: clusters of criteria as they apply to one country, and clusters of countries as they qualify with respect to a criterion. This is a free-hand method which, it is hoped, will give the reader the 'flavour' of the public administrations in the region's countries.

Egypt, to begin with, betrays some striking contrasts. Thus it has a very large service relatively speaking, but one which enjoys a high level of education and a very long tradition in continuous government — indeed, the longest for the region, and one of the longest for the whole world. The high level of education has not made for remarkable efficiency, for neither the quality of this education in general nor its degree of relevance to the tasks on hand have been instrumental in bringing about greater efficiency. Furthermore, the long tradition, and the size in itself, have promoted bureaucratisation of a very heavy type, a fear of taking responsibility and therefore an excessive fragmentation of responsibility, procrastination and slowness. The very low wage level in the context of general poverty has made for a high incidence of corruption and a low motivation. Again, although the 1952

Revolution brought in its wake substantial changes in the higher rungs of the service, the very large size of the pyramid left the bulk of the service unchanged, unmoved and almost immovable. That the political leadership has enjoyed continuity for many years since 1952 has further added to the rigidity of Egypt's public administration. The very capable elements at the top have only had a limited seepage effect. On the other hand, the emergence of new, non-traditional economic ministries and public-sector corporations or authorities has not had a far-reaching radiation effect on the old, established ministries and administrations.

Egypt's experience shows other paradoxes. Thus the civil service is highly disciplined. But the discipline has in a way inhibited personal initiative, the level of which was not high to begin with. On the other hand, at the higher level of government and politics, the country has had an energetic life and has witnessed drastic change in many areas. Yet the civil service does not seem to be likewise activated. Loyalty has not been fragmented as in most other Arab countries, but the object of the loyalty, whether the state or the person of Nasser, did not seem to inject dynamism into the bureaucracy. Contrasted with professionalism and efficiency in many areas at the top, there is generalism, non-specialisation, lethargy and inefficiency in most areas further down. The public administration has all the paraphernalia of modernity: efficiency tests, supervisors' reports, in-service training, public administration institutes, a well-defined web of rules relating to appointment, upgrading, promotion and termination. Nevertheless, it has experienced gross irregularities, under one guise or another, with respect to appointment, promotion or termination. The new efficiency-oriented, better-paid and better-motivated administrations, instead of radiating a healthy demonstration effect, have become sore spots in the overall body of the public administration. They rouse jealousy, frustration and a disgruntled attitude in the old, established ministries, without themselves remaining immune to corruption. Their corruption may be of a different type, but it is indeed on a larger scale, considering the nature of the work of the new administrations, namely the handling of public-sector enterprises.

If a certain measure of detail, and a tone of strong criticism have been allowed into this illustration, this is not to single out the Egyptian civil service for harsh judgement. The choice of Egypt was deliberate because it is the largest country in the group, it has the largest and oldest civil service, and it also has been ahead of the other Arab countries in launching a far-reaching economic, social and political transformation. Yet, examined in its entirety, within the context of the many criteria and angles of vision, the Egyptian public administration in its present state does not seem to be a very promotive developmental factor. The limitation of its effectiveness must be understood mainly from within, as an internal problem of this administration — but not wholly. The political leadership has reduced the usability and usefulness of the public administration, both in the conventional civil service and in the new public sector, through the imposition of frequent institutional change, the weakening of morale through the welfare-oriented policy of appointment, and finally through the failure to devote the energy, attention and resources required for a proper modernisation and activation of the administration.

The public administrations of Morocco, Algeria and Tunisia make a strong contrast with their Egyptian counterpart in many respects. Though the service in each of the three Maghreb countries differs from that in the other two in certain features, there are broad similarities. One of these is the relative youthfulness of the holders of government jobs. Another is the general orderliness, seriousness and pervading atmosphere of discipline. Though on the whole comprising relatively fewer university-educated elements, the services in the Maghreb are distinctly achievement-oriented and give every indication of performing their tasks diligently and conscientiously. Corruption, never absent, is believed to be within controllable and modest limits. In all three countries, but particularly in Morocco and Algeria, the civil service includes a sizeable contingent of European and Arab foreigners, mainly schoolteachers and professionals. But with the progress made in Arabisation, and in the education of nationals, the rate of substitution of foreigners is fast, though higher where Europeans are concerned.

In none of the countries is the size of the public administration very large (including public sector enterprises, which constitute a large component in Algeria). Nor has the bureaucratisation reached serious dimensions. This is probably because the administrations are new, mainly formed since independence. Furthermore, a serious effort is exerted to streamline such matters as appointment and promotion in each of the countries, and to make merit the basis of both. Inevitably, personal factors and party considerations enter into appointment and promotion decisions, and into the determination of the authority exercised. But there is evidence to suggest that these deviations from universalism are less serious than in many of the Mashreq countries.

The public administrations of the Maghreb, though suffering from the relative weakness of financial incentives, display strong motivation. And they attract capable young men in competition with the private sector. (However, this sector is particularly weak in Algeria and provides a very ineffectual pull.) The turnover is not as high as it is in, say, Iraq or Syria, but at least in Algeria and in Tunisia political changes have caused a rise in the turnover, in the former mainly in 1965, but less so at subsequent dates associated with some internal political strains, and in the latter during the days of Ahmed Ben Saleh, but especially during the years 1969-71, when the government was actively undoing what Ben Saleh had done in his era of power.

These disruptions notwithstanding, and taking the situation as a whole in each of the three countries, it can be said that the civil service is a promotive factor of development, one which operates relatively well and effectively. In the case of Algeria and Tunisia, this determinant supplements that of the leadership commitment to development. Furthermore, with growing decentralisation, the civil service performs an expanding developmental role at the local level. On the other hand in Morocco, where the leadership commitment is relatively less strong and effective, the operation of the civil service as a development determinant is handicapped. However, the qualities of this civil service enable it to minimise the damage to the process of development and to make the tasks which it is within the power of the civil service to handle, more likely to be achieved.

Though part of the larger Maghreb, Libya does not partake of many of the qualities of the public administrations in its neighbours to the west. The country inherited a very nebulous civil service upon independence, and its demographic and educational handicaps made its progress very slow. The improvement that began to be felt in the mid- and late-sixties gave place to an uncertain pace when the revolution of September 1969 took place. The new government is avowedly highly committed to development and to the modernisation of the country, but the turnover undertaken in the ranks of the civil service, particularly at the higher levels, plus the 'cultural revolution' launched over the past few years, have speeded up the turnover of staff, reined in initiative, and subjected the civil service to the vagaries of political life.

The modernisation of the Libyan civil service has been slow. For much of the period under consideration, promotion was not conditional on training requirements, and the incentive involved was therefore forgone. Presently, promotion is on the basis of seniority plus a supervisor's report. Recruitment, which used to be effected at the discretion of the head of department, has since the Revolution been based on academic qualifications and experience. The National Center (Institute) for Public Administration was founded as long ago as 1953, but was modernised in 1968. During the period 1968-72 it operated with the assistance of the United Nations Development Programme. However, since 1973 it has been totally Libyanised, and as a result has terminated the services of the expatriate experts and staff. Despite the expansion in the fields of training and number of trainees, its capabilities are very limited, and its educative function is very limited. To sum up, it can be safely said that the civil service of Libya has a low developmental capability. The situation is all the more serious because the 'stock' or reservoir of civil servants, in spite of the presence of many devoted members, is hesitant and handicapped by the overall framework within which it works, while the 'flow', consisting of new recruits or trainees, finds itself absorbed by the much larger body of the service. New recruits are not distinctly superior and, in addition, on joining the service find themselves drawn into the mainstream of its work habits, mores and inhibitions.

This rather critical picture must not be left without some qualifying remarks. One of these is the presence of islands of creditable performance and initiative. Another is the high level of morality imposed by the leadership, mostly through the demonstration effect, and the severity with which deviations are punished. A final remark is that the sobering down of revolutionary zeal will hopefully permit greater initiative and drive within the public administration, and will make it a more effective determinant of development than it is or can be under present circumstances.

The administration of Sudan is generally believed to be 'clean', efficient and devoted, compared with that of a few Mashreq administrations. Although the approach has been mainly to choose the 'generalist' in the old English tradition, recently there has been more emphasis on professionalism in new recruits. The situation presents some contrasts worth noting. Thus, because the country is in a transitional stage between traditionalism and the beginnings of modernisation, features of both are encountered. The civil service by and large owed its loyalty to the state upon independence, but with greater politicisation and party incursion, loyalty is rather divided now. The morale of the service has been eroded with political upheavals, of which there have been a few since the first military *coup*. Again, the erosion has been accelerated by the application of non-professional rules into recruitment and promotion, especially at the higher echelons, as a result of changes in the locus of power.

The modernisation of the service is slow. Recruitment is effected on the basis of interviews, not competitive tests. Political and welfare factors operate, though career or specialisation are taken into account. Promotion also is by seniority coupled with performance as assessed by the supervisor. There are no formalised prerequisites, such as training or retraining, or examinations. The supervisor's report is not necessarily based on impersonal, objective grounds. Kin solidarity and party allegiance play an unduly large part. The Public Service Commission (later replaced by the Public Service Board) and the Institute of Public Administration have been instrumental in some improvement in the situation, but this seems to be marginal. There is still excessive centralisation or concentration of authority, both in the geographical sense and within each ministry or administration. Decentralisation was instituted in late 1971, but the results are slow to appear, and in any case the province capitals themselves have not delegated much administrative power to the local bodies.

Initially upon independence, the public sector narrowly defined (that is, only comprising public enterprises) was very small. It has grown substantially since. The rather sudden shift in functions has imposed tasks for which the civil service had not been prepared. Like almost all other Arab countries faced with a comparable problem, the service has performed its managerial role poorly on the whole. The main and common defects include the weakness of a business sense, of concern for profitability and efficiency, and of sensitivity to the market; inadequacy of the sense of 'responsibility towards a constituency'; padding of staff, employment of army officers who fitted uncomfortably into their new functions, and a preponderance of engineers over economists and other persons trained in business skills; and the tendency to keep authority concentrated in a few hands.

By and large, the Sudanese public administration is thought to be a positive factor for development, given political stability and clear commitment to development by the leadership. Although some observers on the scene claim that the efficiency and integrity of the service are really a myth, and that when the crucial test came the service failed to handle its new developmental tasks properly, it seems to this writer that the judgement is too harsh, at least with respect to the test indicated. The fault did not truly lie with the civil service, which had not been trained for development. Its integrity and efficiency were not unusually high, but not low in comparative terms. This was the situation until about 1960, after which the political strains became heavy, demoralising and disrupting, not only for the politicians, but for the civil servants as well.

The six Asian Arab countries included in this study present each a separate type with salient distinguishing characteristics, except perhaps for Syria and Iraq, which share more features and experiences than any other two countries of the group. In both these countries, the public administration has had to live through a frequently changing political framework; to witness a radical change of socio-economic system and the uprooting of the ruling class that was in power at independence; to experience a high and frequent turnover of staff on the higher rungs of the service, as different political régimes succeeded one another; to be called upon to handle vastly expanded economic tasks as a result of the immense growth of the public sector and public enterprise; and to be forced to become not only highly politicised (which they had not been at independence) but partisan, and to redirect their loyalty towards the group or party in power. This last phase can best be described by the statement that for many years now, in both countries allegiance to the ruling party and dependability in this narrow sense comes ahead of merit both in recruitment and promotion.

Side by side with these developments, there has been considerable professionalisation, especially in Iraq, which is the better equipped with technical and professional skills of the two countries. Interestingly enough, in both, but more so in Iraq, there has been some serious questioning since the late sixties or early seventies of the adequacy of the public administration for its new and expanded tasks. But in neither has there been far-reaching reform. Iraq has been the more dynamic of the two in attempting to institute decentralisation, to raise the level and widen the spread of professionalisation, and to attract back the manpower that it had lost in a protracted and heavy 'brain drain'. As these measures relate to the past three or four years only, they are still too close to show tangible results. In general terms, it can be said of both public administrations that they are development-oriented, motivated, disciplined and experienced in their developmental tasks, enough to be considered an effective determinant of development. They have been 'in apprenticeship' since the late 1950s, and they are not out of line with the strong commitment to development of the leadership in their respective countries. Their integrity has been under strain, but it has not suffered considerable erosion.

The Lebanese public administration stands in sharp contrast. Nowhere else is there such a glaring contradiction between individual skill, qualifications, intelligence, motivation and a desire for achievement, on the one hand, and collective inefficiency, apathy to public interest, large-scale corruption and indifference to development on the other. The high motivation and need for achievement are restricted to the private domain, thus producing that baffling mixture of apathy where the individual's performance in the civil service is concerned, and great energy and dynamism where that individual's personal interests are concerned. That a substantial proportion of the service has a sad reputation for corruption on a large scale can cynically be explained as an attempt to reconcile the two conflicting qualities of apathy and dynamism: apathy as far as the performance of public functions is concerned and dynamism where attention to private interest is concerned.

The confessional system permeates all through political life and the public administration. The division of spoils on confessional grounds and the influence of politicians in the administration together make the loyalty of the civil servant turn to his religious group and the politician whose *protégé* he is; usually the latter belongs to the same sect, and these two sub-loyalties do not present any conflict. This sectarian system makes it extremely difficult for a conscientious minister or head of an administration or a department to punish the slovenly, inefficient or corrupt, even if the latter happens to be a mere clerk or office boy. There is hardly a civil servant who does not have a 'back', as the expression goes — that is, a protector.

Other illnesses beset the Lebanese public administration. These include centralisation in the geographical as well as the administrative sense, that is within the pyramid of authority, on the one hand, and fragmentation of authority, on the other hand, in the sense that the smallest transaction has to be handled by several persons, each affixing his signature to it. To collect a parcel from the post office, 14 such signatures have to be affixed, with an additional one if the parcel contains printed matter. To renew the licence of a car is a nightmare, to avoid which the car-owner hires an agent *and* bribes his way around.

Professionalism has started to make its way. This dates roughly from the era of the third President, General Fouad Chehab, who encouraged the entry of technocrats into the public administration. But a degree in law is still the master key to almost any job, regardless of whether or not it involves the use of legal training. The establishment of a Civil Service Commission in the days of President Chehab whose function was to train, test and rank candidates for office has not been a major improvement. This institution has had to take into account the sectarian balance in recruitment and promotion which Article 95 of the constitution stipulated in the late 1920s. Not infrequently, ministers have not heeded the Commission's ruling. Turnover in the administration is not high, as the socio-economic system has not changed in the country's 32 years of independence, 1943-75. There have been a couple of purges, but these have affected a small number of senior officials, and have constituted mere ripples of reform which left the mainstream of corruption and inefficiency unaffected.

To sum up, it can be said that in Lebanon there is neither a strong commitment to development at the level of leadership nor a public administration which could undertake vast developmental tasks, were such a commitment to be present. Indeed, both factors must be considered strongly negative individually. Their conjuncture accentuates their individual negative effect.

Kuwait, which shows a marked difference with respect to the development commitment of its leadership, also has a civil service which, despite its many shortcomings, is capable of handling the developmental tasks which are currently being assigned to it. The service, as we have had occasion to see in the country chapter of Volume I, is superfluous in size — the largest, relatively speaking, for the whole region. Furthermore, its Kuwaiti component to a not inconsiderable extent offers a performance much less than its proportionate size and its emoluments and other benefits would suggest. Nowhere else has the appointment of nationals on purely welfare or employment-creating grounds taken such dimensions as in Kuwait. The differentials in terms of employment between the Kuwaiti and non-Kuwaiti components of employees have led to some disgruntlement and demoralisation among the latter group who are discriminated against in terms. But this expatriate group none the less shoulders the bulk of the work of government, developmental and current.

Despite the relatively large size of the public administration, it is less bureaucratic and slow in motion than its size would suggest. The degree of its integrity is rather high in regional terms; the level of pay has tended to ward temptation off, except in the last few years with inflation biting deep into the disposable income of civil servants. Furthermore, the better terms offered by the institutions of the mixed and private sectors have tended to loosen the hold of integrity on the service in government proper. Until recently, the public administration had more appeal for young men seeking jobs, both in terms of money incentives and the status trimmings that go with government service. This was unusual for most Third World countries, where the private sector offers on the whole better terms. However, Kuwait has now fallen into the common pattern, with the private sector (and the mixed and public enterprises) providing much stronger financial incentives, especially to the energetic.

By and large, the country can be said to have suffered no serious manpower pressure in its public administration, with its rather liberal policy relating to the entry of expatriates, and its wage policy which is unmatched in any other country, whether or not oil-producing. Though the population and naturalisation policy was and continues to be unduly narrow, restrictive, and unsuited to the country's true interests, Kuwait has managed to staff its public and semi-public sectors quite adequately, and the conclusion can firmly be stated that the public administration is a positive factor for development, particularly as it is guided by a political leadership distinctly committed to economic development. Furthermore, the recourse to advisers in the various ministries and services has enriched the flow of ideas related to the process of institution-building, modernisation and development.

Saudi Arabia's experience over the past three decades manifests a more limited suitability to development tasks by the public administration. The shortcomings of this administration cannot be dissociated from the qualifications already indicated of the commitment of the leadership to development, or from the values and behaviour of the socio-cultural and institutional milieu within which the civil service operates. This milieu has not yet permitted the emergence of a strongly development-oriented and -capable administration.

In fairness, an evaluation of the Saudi civil service in the present context must not be made in isolation from the country's limited experience with statehood, as it was only in the twenties that the Kingdom was united, and until today tribal life, organisation and modes of thought make their incursions into the modernising society. It is understandable, under the circumstances, for the economic aspects of development and modernisation to move faster than the social. Hence the need for greater concern with the social and cultural aspects, in order for the gap between them and the economic aspects not to widen seriously.

In this general setting, the public administration cannot be expected to be capable of coping with the vast demands of fast modernisation, especially with the continued attempt to limit the modernisation mainly to its material aspects, at the expense of its deeper socio-cultural aspects. Furthermore, the modernisation process is very recent, and is superimposed on a foundation of strong traditionalism and insularity. Under the circumstances, it is little wonder that the government is just beginning to introduce into the administration those rules and procedures, institutions and approaches that would make of this administration the machine that can perform the tasks and functions that are asked of it. As of now this machine is manifestly unable to do so. This is evident by its low level of performance, by the need for expatriate staff, but above all by the expectations in the new plan for the years 1975-80 that hundreds of thousands of non-Saudi manpower will have to be admitted into the country during the plan years in order to bring about a semblance of balance between supply and demand. A certain proportion of these will have to go to the civil service proper, but a much larger one into enterprises and administrations in the public and the mixed sectors.

Yet such a voluminous influx will not provide a satisfactory and sufficient solution to the problem of the inadequacy of the public administration. The influx will have to be preceded by a clear vision of the role of expatriates, the web of rules and socio-economic conditions that will have to govern, and form a setting for their life and work, and, above all, how the national manpower resources can replace the expatriates at least at the same level of performance. And all this will have to be achieved within an inevitable exposure to the socio-cultural forces and influences of the world outside which is constrained by the deliberate policy of insularity. It is warranted to conclude that for many years to come the public administration will continue to fall short of the country's developmental expectations, even though these are mainly restricted to the material aspects of modernisation.

4. The next determinant in our list is that of political stability and national homogeneity.[52] Several explanatory remarks are called for here. The first is that stability and homogeneity are closely related, though they do not constitute one inseparable whole. Generally speaking, homogeneity can be expected to lead to stability, if other stabilising factors are operative, or, stated differently, the absence of homogeneity is a destabilising factor. The homogeneity can be ethnic, and additionally it can be linguistic-cultural, or religious. Any of these attributes can be of strong influence in cementing or fragmenting society, particularly as they not infrequently are interrelated, in the sense that linguistic or religious differences are usually associated with ethnic differences.

What is more important with respect to homogeneity is the oneness of outlook, the sense of solidarity and of true community in society. The ethnic, linguistic or religious differences could possibly exist without causing a fragmentation in outlook and in the sense of integration or solidarity. On the other hand, ethnic, linguistic or religious homogeneity might well be accompanied by social fragmentation and the weakness of the sense of integration and solidarity, owing to deep political fissures between parties or economic classes. Consequently, in our subsequent discussion, we will refer to homogeneity or integration in general, and assess the degree to which it is experienced in the Arab countries concerned. This is because it is our purpose to see to what extent there is a sense of national unity and of national purpose, and to what extent this sense is mobilised in the service of developmental aims.

Another remark due here relates to the notion of stability. Different things can be understood by it. One way of understanding stability is to see it as the product of an elective, parliamentary system of politics which permits orderly government and an orderly change of government when the latter loses the confidence of parliament. Likewise, it permits the change of parliament when it demonstrably ceases to assure honest representation. Such a system provides outlets for popular political expression and obviates the need for unrest and instability. A variant of the system is one which does not have elective, parliamentary representation, with two or more parties and scope for free opposition, but which none the less has evolved an acceptable degree of participation in local and central political bodies, through wide syndicalism or elections, but without a multi-party system. Opposition in this instance is allowed but within a one-party system, and is generally rationed. Most of the Arab countries examined in this study do not have an elected parliament with free opposition, but have the variant first mentioned. However, the true extent of participation, and the ration of opposition allowed, vary from one country to another. In general, both the extent and the ration are quite limited.

The second way in which stability can be achieved is through autocracy and heavy-handed force, by a ruler whose base of power and authority is very narrow and who allows virtually no popular participation and no opposition. Such stability is widely different from the first type, even from its variant based on a one-party system. The heavy-handed stability is nearer to a freezing or a paralysis of popular will and the power to act, than to orderliness in political life. The phenomenon is closely related to its basis or cause; therefore great caution is called for in determining whether or not there is political stability, as the form of stability witnessed in a country may well be the product of an optical illusion, turning out to be no more than the paralysis under a heavy-handed despotism.

These differentiations are necessary because they are directly relevant to economic development. Stability can be a determinant only if it is a voluntary stability, begotten of the ability to enjoy political expression, to bring about orderly change in government, and to oppose government without sanction. The other type of stability, the heavy-handed stability or pseudo-stability as it might be called, cannot be a positive and promotive factor of development because it stuns the popular will, immobilises it, and, in forbidding expression and participation, makes impossible the mobilisation of the popular will and energy behind the drive for development. A population conscripted for development, if the expression may be used, by a despot who is development-oriented, will not give its utmost effort for long under this form of forced stability. Alternatively, even if the first form of voluntary stability, born of participation and orderliness in political life, were to lead in the short run to some deviations from the course of dedicated development and to waste some time and energy in opposition and other expressions of protest, in the longer run it would lead to surer and more profound development, since the effort required would then be invited or solicited through persuasion, and voluntarily offered.

The sense of national unity and purpose arising from national integration or homogeneity in the broad sense is at least of equal significance for development as stability. It is of the utmost importance for the drive for development to succeed to have national consensus behind it. Such consensus cannot be forthcoming unless there is a sense of sharing and participation, in the conceptualisation and definition of developmental ends, in the efforts to be exerted for achieving development, as in the rewards that will be reaped. This part of the determinant presently under examination is closely related to the next to be discussed, namely 'degree of political participation by the population', and both are heavily dependent on the mobilisation of popular will behind the developmental effort. Such a mobilisation cannot be achieved without the demonstration that those whose effort is invoked will be the main beneficiaries of the fruits of this effort, and, furthermore, without a certain degree of freedom of political expression. Such freedom makes the response to mobilisation largely voluntary and not forced.

The Arab countries vary with respect to the satisfaction of the conditions of political stability (of the type which is development-positive) and of national unity and purposefulness. Syria, Iraq, Sudan, and to a lesser extent Jordan and Morocco, have suffered most from instability in the post-war or post-independence period, as the case may be. But this does not mean that the remaining countries have enjoyed a large measure of stability of the desirable type which we have specified above. Indeed, there are only two countries where the conditions for this type are satisfied: Lebanon [53] and Kuwait. Taking all the twelve into account, only in Lebanon and Kuwait has there been an orderly political life where governments could be changed without strife *and* in response to the wish of a parliament or of the electorate. (However, political unrest has loomed large on the Lebanese horizon since the early seventies, fed by political, social and economic discontent.) This does not mean that the political system guaranteed true representation of the people's will through elections, as in one of these two countries, Lebanon, the electoral system's ability to reflect the popular will honestly is widely challenged in the country. The same, though possibly to a lesser extent, is true of Kuwait.

These qualifications notwithstanding, it remains true that in the remaining ten countries, even a modicum of free and orderly political expression (witnessed until 1975 in Lebanon and Kuwait) is missing. Whether there are national assemblies of some sort, as in Algeria, Morocco, Tunisia, Sudan, Egypt, Syria or Jordan, or not, as in Libya, Saudi Arabia and Iraq, there is very little free political expression and less free opposition. This is truer of the last three countries, since they do not even have the outward appearances of representative bodies. In the group of seven countries just cited, dissent is possible to a certain extent, if moderate and 'responsible'. Elsewhere in the remaining three countries there is no formal representation. Yet some mechanisms of consultation with political groups exist — in Saudi Arabia, there are crown councils and advisers, as well as tribal bodies with which consultation takes place and forms a continuation of an old tradition; in Libya, the Revolutionary Command Council sits as a legislative and consultative body; in Iraq, the parties meeting in the National Front constitute a consultative body, while the Revolutionary Command Council and the Party local leadership are the real source of authority and legislative power.

Taking the post-war or post-independence period as a whole, not just the still picture of the present, we find that everywhere except in Saudi Arabia at one time or another there has been an elective body with legislative powers, where dissent was possible. In Sudan, Morocco, Syria, Iraq and Jordan the ration of dissent was larger than in, say, Libya, Tunisia or Algeria. Pre-revolutionary Egypt also enjoyed a larger ration. But, whereas the political base of expression existed in all these instances, the socio-economic base did not, in the sense that true representation was not achieved because of the underlying gross disparities in the distribution of political, social and economic power. This points to a sad paradox. Thus, while true political democracy cannot be achieved without economic and social democracy, in practice, when the latter advanced considerably in many of the region's countries, thus providing a more solid base for political democracy, political democracy was drastically curtailed by the very authorities which had promoted socio-economic democracy.

This examination of the situation with respect to free stability and national homogeneity and the sense of national unity and purpose is generally critical. There has been occasion before to point to the disparate march of socio-economic development, on the one hand, and of political development on the other, with the latter being either much slower, or even regressive. How can this paradox exist? Does it mean that political stability and national unity and purposefulness are not relevant to development? And, conversely, if they are relevant, why is it that in some of the countries where these factors have been weak some marked development has none the less been registered, while in Lebanon where stability has been marked, the record of development has not been spectacular?

Some explanatory observations may clear the paradox and make the situation easier to understand. One of these is that stability and the sense of national purpose do not necessarily move and act in the same direction, or to the same extent. It would seem that development could proceed unless the political power centre were outright despotic, and unless it stifled all opposition and free expression through whatever outlet possible, and unless the political leadership were hostile or at least indifferent to development. But what would be achieved in this instance is growth rather than development, in our understanding. Yet even growth, if coupled with some distributive measures in the sphere of social justice, would act as a sedative and a compensation – in the short run at least – for the loss of political freedom. However, the situation with respect to positive stability being what it is, it is the sense of national unity and purpose which has been pronounced. This factor has been promotive for development. Consensus around development might not involve a sophisticated conceptualisation of development in the abstract, but some basic and homely demands for food, shelter, schools and jobs. Viewed thus, development commands general appeal and unified purpose. There are many indicators in evidence of this.

Another qualifying observation is that in several of the countries concerned some favourable, promotive factors have fortuitously operated and helped economic growth, such as oil revenues, politically motivated industrialisation, and energetic education and training. Finally, commitment to development by some political leaderships has also compensated for the curtailment of political freedom and the positive form of stability. In turn, the commitment has enjoyed widespread popular support.

To sum up, in general the countries of the region have not enjoyed a wide measure of that form of political stability which is conducive to development; but on the other hand, the political leaderships have not been as repressive as to stifle the demand for development. Such demand has formed one major object of national consensus and of the sense of purpose. Whether the emphasis on development has been spontaneous and has expressed itself through the outlets available – the press, clubs and other associations, the literature dealing with current affairs, or the limited-purpose national assemblies – or whether it has been placed by the leadership and widely communicated through the means and media at the disposal of the leadership, it has been there in all the countries, though in varying degrees of strength and effectiveness. The results have also varied considerably.

But there is a final proposition to be made – one which enjoys a great deal of circumstantial evidence. This is that although the two components of the determinant under examination (stability and sense of unity) are somewhat effective, and although many of the region's countries have registered some notable development in the post-war period, this development will remain limited and restricted. For development to have the much fuller content to which we referred at length in the last chapter, not only should there be a strong commitment to development by the leadership, but there should also be a wide measure of popular political participation and mobilisation.

5. The degree of political participation by the population, which is the fifth determinant to examine, has received several references already. Its relation to the first determinant in this section, the development orientation and commitment of the leadership, as well as to planning, and finally to political stability and the sense of national unity has been shown to be very strong. Together and in interaction, they have a cumulative effect which is greater than their individual effects. The extent to which participation is exercised in the Arab world has been indicated. Therefore only a few further comments will be made here on the

subject, in order to clarify the situation.

To begin with, in the early post-war years or independence years, as the case may be, most of the countries experimented with the Western type of parliamentary democracy, which involved large-scale participation via elections. This was done without the ground-work for such democracy having been laid, in the way of education, economic security, social liberation and release from the grip of established traditional leaderships, whether the base of their power was political or economic. (Often the two converged to constitute one base.) This democracy failed to bring dignity and well-being to the masses, as could have been expected. The political leaders proved too preoccupied with their personal gains from the system and their relative power and influence to attend properly to the public interest. Fierce rivalries, inability to achieve accommodation to make the political and economic machines operate smoothly, popular disenchantment with the farce of the system of representation in force, and probably a deeply ingrained suspicion of the West and its model all combined to put the system into doubt and to pave the way for a series of military *coups d'état*. The story of these is too well known to recount here.

However, these eruptions interest us to the extent that the new political systems they ushered in became the setting in which popular political expression was now to be effected. It is therefore necessary to understand the new mood and the forces that have led to the present situation which is characterised by very little participation.

One factor which explains the apathy and indifference to the present limitation to participation is no doubt the disenchantment with the abortive and unsatisfactory experience with democracy earlier. The new class in power — the military and their support-ing technocrats — were not slow or ineffective in denouncing that experience and condemning it as a fraudulent imitation of democracy. A second factor was the filling of the vacuum created by the denunciation of the democratic experience, with a whole battery of slogans centring around the priority and absolute necessity of the new socio-economic democracy that was to be introduced by the new systems, for application subsequently but on truly firm foundations of political democracy. The socio-economic democracy was in turn to be based on the dual foundation of development and distributive justice. Except for a part of the intelligentsia and most of the deposed (and often dispossessed) political leader-ship, the change was welcome as a start, and only gave place to indifference slowly and passively. The opposition was easily discounted: the intelligentsia was accused of being naïve, theoretical, or out of touch with reality, as well as a part of the old establishment; the politicians were accused of heeding only their personal vested interests. That both lines of attack had something to substantiate them only served to strengthen the new rulers in their positions and to conceal the weakness of their own political philosophy and of the legitimacy of their succession to power.

The indifference that has followed the welcome to the change has not led to active opposition except in a few cases, and then most ineffectually. Where opposition has been effective, it has come from within the ruling institution, whether an army or a party that first came into power in the wake of army action. There has been widespread disenchant-ment and alienation, particularly among the more politicised and the normally more articu-late. To this factor must be added the readiness of most régimes in this region to use repressive methods; their credibility in this area has never been discounted.

Finally, the 'socialist transformation', in addition to the removal by force of the genera-tion of politicians who had initially applied the models of Western democracy, have together been accompanied by a campaign with a dual thrust: to free the Arab countries from Western democracy as one manifestation of freeing the Arab world from Western hegemony

— whether military, political or cultural — but to accept Westernisation in the guise of modernisation in the economic and technological areas of life.

This digression into the region's experience with political democracy and with participation has been necessary to explain why more participation was not allowed, even encouraged, as a substitute to the formal parliamentary system. Such participation could have found expression through several types of groupings at the local, syndical and professional levels, provided these groupings were enabled to actively debate the policies of the central government in the political, social and economic fields, and to contribute to the formulation and evaluation of policies. Arab society has a rich history in participatory democracy,[54] and it could have been not only desirable but possible to revive the tradition of participation. Had this been done on a large scale, it would have compensated for the absence of parliamentary representation, or else its artificiality where it exists. It remains to be added that with wider political participation, the Arab countries would have achieved a larger measure of, and a truer and richer, development. As things stand today, it can only be said that this potentially very strong determinant has only been allowed to operate to a limited extent. This judgement is based on the realities of current Arab political life. The few exceptions in existence, as in Kuwait, Lebanon and Algeria do not drastically qualify the judgement, since these countries are a minority in the region, and their own participatory freedom has itself to be qualified.

6. The last determinant to examine is a composite one. It was designated in the last chapter as 'the role of the public sector (indicators including economic institutions, area of decision-making, nationalisations, social welfare, budgeting, extent and seriousness of planning)'. Soon after the field-work was started, it became obvious that this determinant had to be understood and examined somewhat differently. The central point was to be in fact the socio-economic system in force, and the public sector was to be a component of the system and to be explored in that broader context.

Two points of explanation are in order here. The first relates to the concept of public sector itself. As we have had occasion to indicate earlier on in this section, the term is understood to include public enterprises and autonomous public economic bodies (like development banks), in addition to the government's conventional economic administrations. The public enterprises include nationalised as well as other establishments set up by a governmental or public sector agency for the purpose of producing a marketable good or service. The second point is that initially, when the study was being designed, the importance of the public sector was taken in large part to lie in its capacity to plan development work, to initiate programmes and projects and to provide financial, entrepreneurial and managerial services to these, and generally to set up development-serving institutions. This emphasis is still strong, but to it has been added the force of the ideology behind the extension of the frontiers of the public sector — that is, behind the change in the socio-economic system.

It is true that a good part of the expansion in the public sector involving the establishment or else nationalisation of existing enterprises came about through force of circumstances — mainly the exit of foreigners owning such establishments, or the hesitation of the private sector to initiate them, either because of their novelty and non-familiarity, or their large size. It is also true that many nationalisations did not come about in response to the exit of foreign owners; in this latter case, the nationalisation involved establishments owned by nationals, or else by foreigners who had not planned to leave the country. In such instances, the nationalisation was motivated by nationalistic feelings, often described as socialistic exigencies. To this latter extent, the move must be interpreted in ideological terms, ones relating to the change of economic and social philosophy and thus influencing or totally shaping the system.

Before we explore the extent to which such a change of system with the ideology underlying it and with its manifestations, including the change in the nature and size of the public sector, has gone in the twelve Arab countries covered by the study, we ought to determine how the system and its components can influence the course of development and serve as a determinant of it. Here one enters the realm of ideas and is called upon to determine the force of ideas in economic life. Although such intellectual explorations have been frequently undertaken, they remain dangerous as they carry the researcher into difficult terrain. In the few comments to follow we will avoid abstractions and theorising, attempting to remain within the realm of the operational to the extent possible, and to approach the enquiry from a practical angle.

One way in which the socio-economic system adopted influences the course of development is through its content. and the desiderata such a system emphasises. Often, the choice of system is motivated to start with, and subsequently justified, because it can promise fast and profound development, the satisfaction of mass needs, the freeing of the economy from exploitative foreign dependency, and the liberation of the groups previously exploited by other groups in society. In other words, often the objectives include development and a drastic change in the mode and relations of production in harmony with the philosophy or ideology underlying the system. Almost everywhere in the Arab world where such a drastic change has occurred — or has been meant or designed, or yet announced, as the degree of credibility of the change varies — it has largely been justified in the terms just indicated. This is true of Egypt, Syria, Iraq, Tunisia, Algeria, Sudan and Libya, though in widely different degrees. The difference arises both from the extent to which the system has changed (being minimal in Sudan and Tunisia, moderate in Libya, and vast in the other countries cited), and from the seriousness with which the new system has been injected with a developmental, egalitarian and liberational content.

There is nothing new in the rationale provided for the change in system, which is often described as socialist but which the critics describe as 'socialistic' or socialist-leaning, and the cynics describe as one of state capitalism. Furthermore, there is nothing new in the claim that the new system is capable of achieving its objectives, and how it is enabled to do so. In brief, the rationale centres around the removal of exploitation and inequality of power and opportunity; the triumph over underdevelopment and backwardness; the provision of entrepreneurial leadership, finance and management where the private sector is unable to do so; the freeing of society from foreign domination in the political, cultural and economic fields; and the curbing of the power of the national exploitative bourgeoisie and therefore the profound alteration of the relations of production. This rationale as presented varied in its explicit use of Marxist logic and theory, but in more instances than not it relies heavily on Marxist terminology. This was particularly so where the intellectuals providing *ex post* rationalisation, justification or explanation supplied the intellectual underpinning — or the frills or sugar-coating, depending on the observer's predilections with regard to metaphor. This is not to say that the new centres of power did not believe in this rationale. Quite the contrary. In this writer's view they were largely and basically sincere, at least at the outset. The subsequent dilution of the sincerity through the introduction of personal or group interests, power politics, renegation on the initial principles, the discovery of errors or excesses, and frustration in general when the objectives proved much further away than earlier imagined, should not becloud the initial sincerity — even though it had an overdose of innocence and ignorance.

The claim that the new system would bring the beautiful social and economic dreams true was essentially based on the belief that the motivation of economic life and behaviour had to be altered. Thus, the profit motive of the hitherto predominant private sector was to be replaced by the motive of satisfaction of social need, that of private empire-building was to be substituted by the building of productive establishments and service institutions for society; the accumulation of private fortunes had to cede its place to the satisfaction of the well-being of the masses; exploitation and privilege were to be removed and in their place just economic and social relations and equality of opportunity were to be instituted.

The pass-key to all this change was to be the ownership by the state, via the public sector, of the major assets and instruments of production, and therefore the undertaking of production and distribution in such a manner as to serve the new social objectives. In the field of social services, particularly in education, the pass-key was the horizontal spread of services along with vertical improvement, and the opening of access doors to poor and rich alike. To achieve this transformation in philosophy, objectives, economic relations and instruments, the locus of political power had to move from the traditionally rich and powerful — the landlords, merchants, the established occupants of the top seats in the power pyramid — to the representatives of the people. These representatives were the army officers of the several countries which we listed above, with a few exceptions.

These exceptions were the ruling party in Tunisia, and the Front that successfully led the liberation war to triumph in Algeria, although the latter depended heavily on the Liberation Army of Algeria and the guerrillas. Another qualification relates to Syria and Iraq, where the army spearheaded the take-over and subsequent transformation of the system, but later handed over to a ruling party. Yet here again, the party could maintain power only because it managed to align the army with itself. It remains to be added that in all the countries cited (except Tunisia, where the army never played an important socio-economic or ideological role) the army officers who engineered the transformation and carried it out and maintained it, belonged to the lower middle class.[55] They identified with their class and with the underprivileged in general, and claimed to be the honest spokesmen of the masses.

Elsewhere in those other countries which also witnessed a notable expansion in the role and power of the public sector and which instituted significant welfare measures, namely in Kuwait and Saudi Arabia, the rationale and motivation for the new developments were different. Here the role of the public sector was justified more on pragmatic than on ideological grounds. Basically, the grounds were: insufficiency of the entrepreneurial resources in the private sector, the size of the undertakings entered into by government which was beyond the capability or the desire of the private sector to initiate, and the nature of some of the undertakings which made them more appropriate for public-sector ownership and management. These reasons were not always given in combination; the choice was determined on the merit of the case. Yet the public interest was also invoked as another justification, particularly in Kuwait. This whole complex of justification can constitute an ideological approach, though the ideology involved differed from that motivating the countries that opted for socialism. In other words, it can be said that the pragmatic option whose advocates assert that they do not espouse an ideology, considering 'ideology' an almost pejorative term, in so asserting and implying opt for a different ideology. Their non-ideological position is an ideological position, if the seeming contradiction is considered. This non-ideological ideology is essentially based on the philosophy, values, tenets and objectives of capitalism and free enterprise; and it adopts their mechanisms and tools, both the intellectual and operational.

In Kuwait and Saudi Arabia alike, the public sector is strong, but with two notable differences in its structure. In Kuwait, this sector mostly operates in partnership with the private sector, within the framework of the mixed sector. The hybrid sector is believed to enjoy the strength of both, and to avoid the weaknesses of both. Or, it is at least believed capable of doing so, given the right circumstances. Thus it can combine concern with the profit motive and with efficiency, which the private sector is reputed to be more capable of assuring, with concern for 'the public good' and the considerations of state and society, which the public sector is reputed of being capable of assuring. Furthermore, the convergence and pooling of entrepreneurial and managerial capabilities will enrich these considerably and make good their shortcomings in either the private or the public sector. Finally, the confidence which the private sector often seemed to lack, and the hesitation it frequently displayed, can be intensified and reversed, respectively.

The present writer endorses most of these arguments in favour of the mixed sector, and lays a great deal of hope in mixed undertakings in Third World countries, not only for the reasons just stated, but also because of the conviction that mixed enterprise, while limiting the scope of state capitalism, widens the base of asset ownership, and dilutes the dangers and loosens the rigidities associated with state ownership.[56] However, a few of the observers interviewed in Kuwait had misgivings with regard to the mixed sector, as we have had occasion to mention. The main ones are two. First, that there is no such thing as a mixed sector: whoever has the majority share in capital, or has the controlling say under the articles of association, is the real decision-maker. This decision-maker is either in the public or the private sector, will be guided by its business principles and ethos, and will suffer its shortcomings and idiosyncracies.

In the second place, in practice, the government has often been called upon to disguise the weakness of the private partner, and to pay for the managerial blunders committed by him. At the same time, as the government in Kuwait is not a very parsimonious partner, the private partner has frequently failed to ask the public partner to account for his actions, knowing that in the end a red balance would be turned blue by this latter partner. There is a great deal of evidence in support of this second accusation. However, it seems that the first is carried to an extreme. The presence of a partner who is the holder of the majority of shares does not at all seem in the case of Kuwait to mean that he dictates to the minority partner. Quite the opposite, there seems to be considerable discussion and accommodation, and consensus is often sought.

It was stated earlier that the public sector of Kuwait differs from its counterpart in Saudi Arabia in two major respects. The first of these has been examined. The second is that in Kuwait, the private-sector partner is invariably Kuwaiti — by law he cannot be a foreigner, as no foreigner is allowed to own a business or shares in a corporation. On the other hand, in Saudi Arabia there is a considerable shareholding by foreigners in joint undertakings. These are mixed in two senses of the term: in having government and private business participation; and in having Saudi and foreign participation. The latter is mainly North American and Western European. Arab non-Saudi participation is very small in comparison. The implications of this structure of the Saudi mixed sector are very serious. For, although the pattern is supposed to lead to the richer inflow of technological innovation and know-how, which it obviously does, it is highly doubtful that it actually leads to the implanting in Saudi soil of the new technology and its acclimatisation. Furthermore, the leakage to the foreign partner in profits, salaries and payments for patents is considerable. Finally, the optical illusion of speeded development effectively disguises the true slowing-down of real, home-based, home-manned and internally propelled development.

This discussion has not so far dealt with three of the countries under examination, namely Morocco, Lebanon and Jordan, where, although there is an active public sector, this sector is none the less secondary to the private sector. This judgement is not based solely on the relative size of the two sectors in each of the countries, but additionally on their status in society, and on the self-image of the economy which in each of the three cases considers itself one of private enterprise predominantly. The regulatory measures to control, direct or otherwise condition the activities of the private sector, and to assure certain basic guarantees in the public interest, are weakest in Lebanon, followed by Morocco and then Jordan. Furthermore, the positive developmental measures taken are strongest and most effective in Jordan, where likewise the commitment to development by the leadership is most evident. The results, in terms of economic growth at least, are also most satisfactory in Jordan.

Before we pass on to a final evaluation of the developmental impact of the public sector, the system in the framework of which it arises and operates, and the ideology underlying the system, we ought to indicate that serious planning is one of the indicators of the size and effectiveness of the role of the public sector. Other indicators were also listed at the start of this discussion. However, as planning has been examined separately, we need not examine it here again. It is sufficient for present purposes to bear in mind the assessment made of planning and its impact as a determinant. Finally, such other indicators as budgeting and the outlay made on development by government, important as they are, do not form a distinguishing characteristic of any one socio-economic system. We have therefore not pursued their examination in our research, and we will not discuss them in this section.

A few concluding remarks can be made in summing up, by way of evaluation of the role of the public sector and the socialist system as applied in the Arab world, as a determinant of development. In drawing our conclusions we rely not merely on the analysis here, but also on our field-work, and our analysis in the country chapters in Volume I of this study. Four conclusions will be stated.

The first is that the account is complex, and not conclusive. This arises from the disparity in performance and achievement between countries with a large public sector within a system with socialist leanings, as it is between the two countries which have a large public sector in a framework of private enterprise philosophy, and between those countries where the private sector predominates. Furthermore, there is disparity between the three groups of countries. The complexity and inconclusiveness grows when we consider not merely the rates of growth achieved, but the more subtle and less measurable indicators of deeper development.

In the second place, the public sector and the system and ideology forming its milieu are not the only factor in operation. So many other factors operate, and in strength, that to impute development (or an identifiable part of development) to any of them is next to impossible — at least as this writer understands the complicated system of causation, and within the methodology he has adopted for the study. However, the examination at length of the twelve countries comprised in the first volume of this study and the analysis in the present volume enable us together to draw some tentative conclusions further down.

Third, oil has added to the confusion of the account. Some oil countries are socialist, like Iraq, Libya and Algeria; some others espouse capitalism, like Kuwait and Saudi Arabia, but with a large public sector. Kuwait has had a high rate of growth almost consistently, and a large measure of development, while Saudi Arabia's growth has also been consistently high but its deeper development more modest. Iraq, Algeria and Libya have had notable oscillation in their course of growth, while the first two have recently had a notable developmental performance. It adds to the complexity of the picture to record that the non-oil countries share in these disparities.

Finally, with respect to the socialist countries proper, which are the focus of this part of the discussion, some tentative conclusions can be drawn, in spite of all the qualifications and complexity to which reference has been made. Thus, although it is extremely difficult (perhaps impossible) to impute specific results to the one factor under discussion, the conclusion is ventured that this factor has been positive in promoting development. The line through which its impact has been transmitted has on the whole not been so much its distinguishing structural and institutional characteristics — ownership of important means of production, central decision-making, far-reaching planning — as its ideology, philosophy, values, objectives and emphasis. The one common feature in this large complex field has been that all the countries espousing socialism (in their own way, admittedly) and assigning a substantial responsibility to the public sector have declared themselves strongly concerned with development and with social justice in combination, have maintained this concern, and have attempted to define strategies, formulate policies and institute measures purporting to serve their overriding concern.

This they have often done in their best light. That their best light has at times been dim, that errors of judgement have occurred, that digressions and deviations — some serious — have been allowed, that contradictions between principle and practice have beset their course of action, that all this has happened does not conceal the basic commitment to development, and the high priority it has continued to enjoy. It might be asked: how, then, can this claim be reconciled with the indifferent results in some countries, the poor results in some others? The answer lies partly in the admissions just made relating to faulty conceptualisation, design and implementation of developmental policies and measures, but more seriously to the deviations from the course that should logically have been pursued, had consistency been sought between the philosophy espoused and actual behaviour. The fault basically lay in the men, not in the ideas and the system. The separation between the two will no doubt be refused and denounced by many. Yet even if it is not attempted, it can still be said that given more experience, given more popular political participation and therefore more accounting, the men will have to live more by the ideas. The greater the identification between the two, the more operative and positively promotive this determinant, the more influential the other positive factors, and the less powerful the restraints on development. This conclusion is less an act of faith than a reading of the experience of the Arab world in the post-war years.[57]

3. SOCIO-CULTURAL DETERMINANTS

The socio-cultural framework, broadly defined, comprises a large number of components that are all demonstrably relevant to the process of development, although their influence varies in intensity and its incidence varies in timing and phases of development. These components fit into large categories such as social organisation, social forces, institutions, values and value orientations. Wilbert E. Moore's set of four groups, the ideological, institutional, organisational and motivational framework is probably one of the most suggestive and useful categorisations.[58] But however identified or selected, and however grouped, they go far in determining and shaping the genesis of development as well as its ongoing course and its maturing.

It was with great difficulty and after much hesitation that the determinants to be examined in the context of this study were finally selected. There was, to start with, the inhibition the writer felt in trespassing outside his familiar territory of economics, even if into friendly territory. This feeling persists, although it is true that several economists concerned with development have examined certain socio-cultural factors involved and have therefore mapped parts of the terrain for others. Yet the economist remains on the whole in awe of a discipline not strictly his own, and most economists have in consequence preferred not to tread beyond their bounds. It is probably in large part a gesture of gallantry for a noted sociologist to say that the 'standard complaint by many sociologists and anthropologists that economists do not adequately take into account "cultural" or "social" or "institutional" factors is scarcely justified as applied to those economists studying economic growth'.[59] This kind judgement did not apply to many of the then well-known development economists as early as 1961, when it was made.

In the second place, the array of relevant socio-cultural factors was very wide, with widely differing degrees of impact on development. As in the case of economic and of political-administrative determinants, the distinction had to be made between indicators, factors and determinants, the last being active and strong factors, more of the type of prime movers than other factors that are distantly influential. Furthermore, socio-cultural factors in general are subtle in their operation, and their impact is extremely difficult to identify or impute.[60]

Another problem beset the design of this part of the study. This was the selection of those determinants that are of close relevance and strong impact on the course of development, which can be said to have a *prima facie* case to be included. A further condition was that the operation of these determinants could, on the one hand, be observed and followed with relative ease, without, on the other hand, indulgence in professional, deep analysis of the determinants selected as areas of study by themselves, which would turn the exploration into one in sociology and culture and not one in development. To illustrate: it is one thing to examine the family system in existence in a certain country, or the power of motivation, in their relevance to development; but it is another thing to examine theory relating to the family system, or to motivation, in its own right, and to get involved in its subtleties and controversies. The first, limited task can be undertaken with some reading, some thinking, some observation and a concentrated focus on development. The second further-reaching task calls for much more reading in and much deeper knowledge of socio-cultural areas, and much more analysis of the various aspects of theory. But the latter task could conceivably lead — one might say would probably lead — to a more limited understanding of the impact of the phenomenon studied on development, as the nuances, subtleties and sophistication of the latter approach would necessitate endless qualifications, caveats and hesitations and end with even more tentative conclusions.

The writer encountered other problems and anxieties in this part of the study — ones that are of a more general nature. One of these was the passing of the era of comfort with sociological theory in its relevance to development. Reference is made here particularly to the 1950s, when characterisations of traditional society and analyses of social structure and social change by leading sociologists were more clear-cut and assertive than they have since become. That era can be called the Parsons era, but with contributions more or less along the same lines as those of Talcott Parsons by Bert F. Hoselitz, Neil J. Smelser, Wilbert E. Moore and others.[61] This era was to a far extent dominated by clear-cut formulations of types in pairs: tradition-bound and development-retarding, versus development-oriented and -promotive types. (This polarisation is reminiscent of that of Indians versus cowboys, or bad versus good guys.) We refer here to a number of formulations, typologies and schemes. One of the best-known of these puts in juxtaposition achievement versus ascription as types of value orientation; universalism versus particularism as modalities of the social object; specificity versus diffuseness as to scope of interest; and affectivity versus affective neutrality with reference to the gratification-discipline dilemma.

It is not implied here that this schema was presented as universally applicable, without reservations or caveats, by Parsons and those others who accepted it. (Indeed, Hoselitz does not consider the last confrontation as relevant to an understanding of economic growth.)[62] Nor is it now claimed that it has lost all usefulness 20 or 25 years after its formulation. What it is our purpose to indicate is that there has since been much wider questioning of the schema and less comfort with it as a key to the understanding of members of a traditional versus a modern or modernising society.

Indeed, the whole concept of traditionalism versus modernity has undergone considerable change in one basic respect. Thus, there is an acceptance today of the claim that wider differentiation exists than was initially admitted. Furthermore, societies are not believed to be in a continuum leading from primitiveness to traditionality to modernity, but to have islands of modernity alongside and concurrently with ones of traditionality, while others stand in a distinctly transitional stage. This spottiness and differentiation denies implicit one-directional motion or relationship.

The last point can be illustrated in the greater questioning today with respect to the notion accepted earlier that individualistic, achievement-oriented values are more development-promotive than communally oriented values. This is far from acceptable to many writers today who insist that development must be mass- and need-oriented, and that a society seeking profound development in this sense should develop communal goals, *and* pursue these communally. The evolution of thinking probably derives from the liberation that social thinkers concerned with development today have achieved from Western models and values (usually subsumed in modernisation as Westernisation).[63] In other words, an individualistic, achievement-oriented typology is more suited to the values of Western capitalism and free enterprise, whereas a communally oriented typology is more suited to the values of Third World socialism or state capitalism.

Another illustration can be taken from the area of social institutions and organisation. This is the size of family, and the argument that the nuclear family is more suited than the extended family for the requirements of a developing country. The argument is heavily qualified today, as the functions of the extended family still make it an institution of service to most Third World societies. Finally, social mobility, with all the power it has in helping promote development through strengthening motivation, is none the less vulnerable in its Western context to serious criticism from the viewpoint of Third World societies.[64] Social mobility, as understood in the context of the Western world, emphasises and relates to individual mobility along the vertical ladder of economic wealth and social influence. Essentially, it is individual-oriented. One can at least question the relevance of this force in the Third World context, where what is needed is group orientation to halt, or at least retard, the pursuit of individual power and wealth materialising at the expense of the bulk of the community — with ambitious individuals callously climbing on the backs of the many in their eagerness for vertical mobility.

A different problem, but one which strongly beclouds the observer's vision, is the slowness of change in socio-cultural forces, institutions and values, which also makes for their slow operation in society as determinants of development. They are more slow-moving than political determinants, if only because the latter can be shaped almost suddenly, particularly when political institutions and forces make a sharp departure from one course, or from one modality, to another. While political change is change in society and therefore occurs slowly, it can also be willed by a determined group taking over power and bringing the change about by decree, drawing legitimacy from force or violence.[65] Obviously, change thus effected is change in institutions (in the sense of organisations), and in the restructuring and relocating of power. Yet this type of change should not be underestimated; it can be so designed and steered as to bring about the slower type of change in society at large: in its political attitudes, values and objectives.

This comparison apart, there is no doubt that the social framework is slow-changing, and to that extent its transformation which necessarily spans over a long period of time can well witness many economic, technological and political changes. But within a narrow time span, socio-cultural factors seem to be unchanging; in contrast, economic and political factors are distinctly less 'stable' or sticky. This disparity in pace of movement complicates the assessment of socio-cultural change and the attribution of socio-cultural factors to developmental change. That socio-cultural transformation looks minimal or even absent over the short run is at the same time deceptive and grossly underestimates the power of socio-cultural factors to influence the course, intensity and content of development. The necessity of recognising that development is a slow process itself thus looms larger, since the transformation which constitutes development includes as part of its fabric socio-cultural transformation.

It was stressed further back that the condemnation of traditionalism in the literature on development and on social questions in the early post-war period implied — or stated explicitly — that traditionalism was 'bad' for development, and that societies moved more or less in a continuum from the traditional to the modern state.[66] It was also stressed that this view is much less accepted today, having been replaced by the wider recognition of the coexistence and interaction of islands or pockets of traditionalism and modernity at the same time in the same society. This, plus the recognition that socio-cultural forces, institutions and values are changing content and shape, poses two questions. Is this change spontaneous, or is it engineered and/or influenced by groups and individuals acting deliberately through the media, the educational system or the literature? And if deliberate (as against spontaneous, subconscious) change is possible, does development require across-the-board modernisation, or is it compatible with selective modernisation?

These questions seem to us of great significance. Yet they will not be explored directly here. Instead, there has been occasion, and there will again be in the course of our analysis, to indicate that the active forces and institutions in society potentially can and actually design socio-cultural change and modernisation, and that this can and ought to be selective. No better field can be suggested in which selectivity can be exercised than education. Yet the choice between sweeping and selective modernisation reaches into every aspect of society's life. Fortunately for the Arab world, an earlier polarisation which caused the advocates of the two opposing views to be locked in a pointless and wasteful verbal duel has ceded place to greater acceptance of differentiation and a multi-sided approach to the question. But to say this is not to say that there is near-consensus on what of the past to discard, and what to preserve. The present period is one of debate around this issue, and the issue embraces a wide area of enquiry. Apart from the obvious socio-cultural institutions and values, the debate includes such questions as the very purpose and objective of development, motivation, socio-economic system and even technology and the production mix. Nevertheless, it must be admitted that that party in the debate which challenges the concepts and notions of modernisation as handed down by scholars preaching 'modernisation-as-Westernisation' is by far smaller and less heard than the other party.

The last point to stress before we proceed to an examination of the socio-cultural determinants selected is that of interaction between economic and socio-cultural change. The discussion has so far concentrated on the impact of socio-cultural factors on the course of development. This suggests a one-directional movement. But in fact there is a two-way movement, with economic change also influencing the socio-cultural factors. Economic development has its own logic and force, and in turn it influences the shape, direction, content and power of the socio-cultural forces. However, important and basic though this point is, it will not receive consideration here, as our emphasis is on the impact of socio-cultural determinants on development. But there is throughout an underlying realisation of the interaction and interrelationship. The two sets of forces act on each other and determine each other very much as the two sides of a simultaneous equation do. Yet in the present context we are interested in the action of the side comprising the socio-cultural factors.

Five socio-cultural determinants have been selected for examination in this study. The first four, namely education, acceptance of technological change, the agents of change and motivation are individual determinants or homogeneous clusters. The fifth is in fact a composite item or a basket with several items thrown in together. These are social mobility, family and system of authority, traditionalism versus modernity in attitudes, and status symbols. We recognise now at the time of the final writing-up of the study that the lumping together of these factors was an error in design. Yet the error, when first committed, was justified on the grounds that a basket was indeed needed to take care of a number of items, none of which could or would receive extensive examination in the relevant area literature and in the field investigation. This expectation has largely proved realistic in the subsequent library and field research. But that does not totally absolve the design of the study from the adverse consequences of the lumping together of four different items.

The five determinants or clusters will now be examined in the order in which they were listed in the last chapter. As in the case of economic and later political-administrative determinants, the operation of the ones that now occupy us is investigated via area studies and field interviews undertaken. The former source proved to be extremely frugal and general in nature. Hence the greater dependence on the latter source.

1. The first determinant is education: its level and spread; content and philosophy; methodology (including extent of experimentation, research and intellectual exploration); and relevance to development. This is the most obvious socio-cultural factor in development, particularly if it is understood to include vocational and professional training, as it is in this study. In this instance, what is acceptable on grounds of common sense is also provable in more rigorous and scientific terms. At the first, common-sense and perceptive level, education is not merely a means, but also an end for development. The acquisition of knowledge and skills, of analytical power, and of the capability to master the environment are obviously tools in the achievement of development. Likewise, they are symbols and manifestations of development.[67]

What is acceptable at the level of perception remains acceptable at the level of conception and analysis. However, some qualifications are in order. These relate both to the function of education as a means, and as an end for development. We will restrict ourselves to two such qualifications. The first centres around the content and quality of education, and the methodology used in education. The second centres around the real beneficiaries of education, and how their formal education serves in their broader socialisation.

There have been several occasions in the country chapters of Volume I, and again in the present volume, for underlining the significance of the content and quality of education, and of the methodology used in it. This underlining has been motivated by the belief that the relevance of education to development derives essentially from its content, quality and methodology. (This relevance is also predicated on the spread of education to reach as many beneficiaries as possible, but this second point will receive attention further down.)

The relationship that is at the root of the relevance can best and most readily be seen if education is considered as a means for development. It is here that the type of knowledge and skills imparted, the mental exploration encouraged, the capability to master the environment, the habits of team work — and other aspects of the 'right' quality, content and methodology — become particularly relevant. The requirements of relevance vary from one stage of development to another, as well as between one cycle of education and another, and between education and vocational or professional training.

Some thought was given to these requirements in the first section of this chapter when manpower was examined as one of the economic determinants. Yet, high as the relevance of the quality of education is, as a means for development it must not conceal the significance of the quality of education as an end in itself. It is of the utmost importance to society what kind of educated men and women it has, what their knowledge, skills, world-view and values are, and how they have acquired them. These men and women (and, in the final sense, all their compatriots) are the ultimate object of development, and the quality of life they are capable of living constitutes a forceful judgement of the education, and more generally the socialisation, they have had.

This last consideration is the bridge that connects the first qualification to the second. The latter underlines the spread of education and attaches great significance to its beneficiaries. It is highly pertinent to ask exactly who in society does get educated. The question is not rhetorical, in spite of the apparent vast spread of Arab educational facilities geographically and across population groups. Indeed, the availability of free education at all levels makes the question seem much less urgent than it was in the early independence years of each of the Arab countries considered here.

Yet the theoretical spread of education in both senses indicated, its costlessness, and the apparent equality of opportunity must not disguise the fact that the spread is still very limited, the cost inhibiting to many, and the equality constricted. In reality, in most Third World countries universal education is still far off in the future. We have seen that in the Arab world as a whole only a little over half of school-age youth are actually in school, with girls representing a much smaller proportion. Furthermore, the drop-out rate is very high, leading to the fact that only a tiny proportion of pupils in the elementary cycle ever finish the secondary. Likewise, the vocational training provided draws what can only be said to be a negligible proportion of youth in schools.

The costlessness of education is a reality (or nearly so) in the national system in the Arab countries, but only for those who actually go to school. Furthermore, the economic pressure on numberless parents forces millions of children either to forgo school altogether in order to work and support their families, or else to drop out at a very low level of schooling, and regress into illiteracy after a few years of schoolessness. In other words, the cost of education must be viewed not merely as the school fees charged, but also the income forgone that a parent will have to incur if he sends his son to school. If he cannot afford to forgo such income, then the cost to him is in effect prohibitive.

Finally, opportunity is not equal. While it is true that there is no explicit restriction or discrimination, this exists in reality. Thus the question of cost to which reference has just been made constitutes an effective limitation of opportunity. Political, social and economic power and influence still play a large role in admission, particularly where openings are restricted in institutions of higher learning. And, given the handicaps under which university education labours and the adverse effects these have on the quality of education, equality becomes further circumscribed to the extent that the rich can send their sons and daughters to better-quality private universities abroad or at home. The graduates of these expensive universities are later favoured in the job market, they earn higher incomes on the average than the graduates of national universities, and are enabled in their turn to send their own sons and daughters to better-quality universities. The narrow cycle is thus completed.

The implications of these constraints on the true spread of education do not receive adequate attention in the Arab world. Even in those countries where a socialist transformation has been initiated, education has not yet acquired its full role as a social function, but is still treated as an individual affair. The emergence of an educated élite capable of accumulating power, influence and wealth in the service of their personal interest stirs no social opprobrium, and hardly draws mild reproach. Obviously, from the standpoint of the social values implicit in our approach in this study, education cannot be strongly contributive to development (whether as a means or as an end) unless it has a much more pronounced social content.

The evaluation which follows of the role of education and training as a determinant of development largely focuses on education as a flow, that is, on current education involving its values, content and methodology as they exist today, as well as on current enrolment in the three cycles. The 'stock' of the educated, that is, those already out of the system, ranging from the sub-elementary to the post-graduate category, remain largely outside our account. The stock is at least as relevant for our enquiry as the flow, considering its size and the fact that it constitutes the educated component of total manpower gainfully engaged in the economy and generally active in every aspect of society's life. However, it is not possible to discuss and evaluate the role of this stock, since the relevant data are not available. There are guesses, or estimates if the observer wants to be charitable, relating to different years for the different Arab countries, for the number of the literate. However, even when these estimates are restricted to a certain age-interval, such as 15-24 years, they remain mostly out of date and of low reliability. Furthermore, the background of the 'literate' varies widely, not only in so far as their individual levels of education are concerned, but also as the systems under which they had acquired their education, the courses taken and their content, and finally the methods of instruction experienced are concerned. The investigator is therefore compelled to consider the flow only, that is, the students 'in the pipeline' and the educational systems currently in force.

In one important sense, this flow is of greater significance for development than the stock or reservoir of educated and trained men and women, since it is the former which will influence the course of development for the many years to come. However, to a not inconsiderable extent, the stock and the flow do not differ much in their aptitudes, since over the short or even the medium term, the content and methodology of education varies but little. This is all the more true if the last few years are left out of the account, since the post-war period down to the late 1960s did not witness as significant a change in the quality as in the quantity of Arab education.

Viewed globally, the national educational systems in the twelve countries embraced here reveal a few salient similarities. Within each country, the system shows very little differentiation, if any, between one school curriculum and another, and even one university programme and another. Almost invariably, education is still viewed as a one-directional process: the teachers impart knowledge, and the students absorb it, often via their memory. Again almost invariably, there is a shortage of laboratory material, of library books and journals, and of audio-visual aids. With few exceptions, knowledge imparted has a sanctity:

it is poured out by the teacher who possesses it to the pupils or students who absorb it with hardly any challenge. This derives from the atmosphere inherited and preserved within which the belief predominates that there is one channel to truth, and this runs through the books used as texts or the lectures delivered. Furthermore, the pupil or student is placed by the firm and sure hand of the teacher or professor in that channel.

To approach imparted 'truths' as propositions that can be confirmed or refuted, is generally shunned; only in the natural sciences, and here only recently, has the idea of challenge begun to take root. Yet even here, in one country after another the interviews confirmed that the students feel much more at ease when 'final truth' is handed down to them and all they have to do is to entrust it to memory. This is almost universally true of the social sciences and the humanities. Finally, in a list of generalisations that can be extended, the lecture or presentation form still enjoys the largest frequency and occupies the place of honour among the methods and techniques of education. Discussion, the give and take between students or between them and their instructor, only enjoys restricted usage, particularly at the sub-university level. Yet even at the university level, when seminars or workshops are conducted, professors still tend to lecture — not to say to pontificate.[68]

Where vocational and professional training are concerned, the ailments of the national systems were not until recently totally unrelated to or different from those of academic education in general. Thus, the aids available for training were virtually in every country less than adequate. Furthermore, the instructors in most instances showed a preference for lecturing over demonstration and the guidance of the trainees in experiments. The training books, manuals and aids were on the whole foreign-produced and insufficiently adapted to local needs, and the translations left a great deal to be desired. Indeed, to this day some of the training manuals are still in foreign languages, thus creating a double hardship for trainees: becoming familiar with the content, and grappling with an unfamiliar medium. Finally, trainees heading for a profession like engineering hesitated until recent years to get their hands dirty with machines; at a lower level, foremen wanted to reach their status without having to rise from the lower rungs of labour.

As in many other aspects, Lebanon stands out as untypical among the twelve countries in this study, with respect to academic education. While it is true that its national system of education is quite similar to its counterparts in the other countries, the scope and capabilities of its private educational system are unique in comparison. The private sector until recently monopolised *all* education in the second and third cycles, the public system restricting itself to the first cycle, but even here performing at a much lower level than the private system. The latter still predominates with respect to elementary, secondary and higher education, both in quality of education and in number of students. Though less important than in the early post-war years, the foreign private system is still of great overall significance, and an inordinately large proportion of the *dirigeants* of the country have had their schooling and university work at foreign private institutions of learning.

The current structure continues by design. Although there is a rising pressure to have the public system rise in relative importance, few voices ask for the reduction in absolute terms of the role of private schools and universities. The private system in the primary and secondary cycles conforms broadly to the public system, although there is flexibility with respect to the textbooks and the techniques and methods of instruction. Further flexibility is provided by the permission that those schools which prefer to prepare candidates for the international *baccalauréat,* the French *baccalauréat,* or the English GCE (General Certificate of Education) may do so. The degrees of freedom at university level are much wider. Nowhere else in the Arab world is there nearly so much flexibility.

These special features of the Lebanese overall system of education have important implications for development. The climate of liberality and flexibility supplements the general atmosphere of liberality and the scope for initiative. Inventiveness and enterprise are encouraged, and there is less tendency to monolithism in the search for solutions to problems or in the design of frameworks for the understanding of academic and other intellectual or social issues. Furthermore, Lebanese intellectuals are the least inclined to fear intellectual exploration, heresy, challenge of the traditional wisdom, or iconoclasm — whether this is religious, social, intellectual or economic.

Yet education in Lebanon suffers from a few very serious shortcomings and ailments. It is exaggeratedly individual-oriented. In encouraging social mobility, it also encourages excessive competitiveness, downgrades co-operativeness, and is permissive towards selfishness. The variety and flexibility which are commendable at one level lead to a disjointed social mosaic, reduce national cohesiveness, and weaken the sense of national purpose. The sectarian identity of many of the private institutions deepens sectarianism which is already serious and very menacing to the social and political fabric. That many of the private schools are foreign-owned and -run accentuates the fragmentation. Finally, much in the content of educational material eulogises the structure and values of Lebanese society and the economic system, and therefore breeds a services-oriented mentality which emphasises verbal prowess at the expense of commodity production.[69] In brief, the strong, like the weak, points of the system cannot fail, each in its way, to influence the developmental performance and potential of the country.

If Lebanon has been allowed unduly large space, it is because of its 'differentness'. The other Arab countries share many of the characteristics to which reference has been made in the country chapters, in the regional (final) chapter of Volume I, and in section 1 of the present chapter during the discussion of 'manpower' as a determinant. At this point it is necessary only to draw some broad features in large strokes of the educational public systems of the region.

(a) In all twelve countries except Lebanon the private system occupies a very narrow space. This restricts flexibility greatly; nevertheless, it enhances national unity and narrows differences of outlook among different social groups.

(b) In almost all cases, the public system draws heavily on the European continental system, but mainly on its French counterpart. This is largely because Egypt, the leading country, adopted and still maintains a French-like system, particularly in university education, and the other Arab countries have patterned their universities and much of their first- and second-cycle schooling after the Egyptian example. The Maghreb countries, which had been under French rule, inherited the French system and to that extent did not follow in Egypt's footsteps. But since independence and the spread of Arabisation, the three countries, but particularly Algeria, have had recourse to a large number of Egyptian teachers who have tended to preserve the system to which they were used. There are some notable exceptions to this generalisation in Saudi Arabia, Iraq, Jordan, Sudan, and lately Kuwait, but they relate on the whole to parts of their university system. The main areas of difference include greater emphasis on smaller classes and greater scope for discussion, the use of the term or semester and the credit system rather than the utter dependence on a final examination, as a result of which the student passes or fails.

(c) There is growing dissatisfaction with the systems of education in almost all countries, and some effort is made to re-examine the curricula and the techniques and methods of instruction.[70] These efforts vary in seriousness and effectiveness, but are most notable in Algeria, Tunisia and Iraq, although Morocco and Egypt are also engaged in re-examination.

(The last-named country undertook some important changes in the sixties in the faculty of political science and economics.) The focus of the re-examination is basically to make education more modern, to emphasise experimentalism, to have greater resort to smaller classes and seminars, and to encourage more students to go into science — both theoretical and applied. (However, it must be admitted that so far much of the reform in the first two cycles has affected the appearance of textbooks — their design, covers and general attractiveness — rather than their content.)

(d) Everywhere there is a marked determination to expand education horizontally as far as resources and teachers allow, and to provide more facilities for secondary and higher education. The large budgets channelled in the direction of quantitative expansion and qualitative improvement testify to the determination. Yet much more is still called for, in terms of resources, time and the reorientation of the teaching staff.

(e) Foreign languages are given less attention than they deserve, or even than they used to get before independence. Enhancing national education is not inconsistent with better mastery of a foreign language, but it seems to be taken that the two are incompatible. This has the deleterious effect of narrowing the student's horizon and restricting his capability to appreciate and learn from other cultures, limiting the range of outside readings, and disadvantaging students travelling abroad for graduate training.

(f) The research facilities are very limited in practically all institutions of higher learning, and the climate of research is not very encouraging, with political insecurity, suspicion of field-work and job insecurity. Furthermore, the professors have very little time to supervise and/or conduct research, pressed as they are by their generally low pay to seek additional lectures in other colleges, or even non-academic work in their spare time. The students suffer as a result, both because they receive minimal training in research methods, and because they are deprived of the potential benefit of the research that could be undertaken by their professors. Associated with this shortcoming, there is the added one of very limited recourse to essay-writing by the students, again because the professors are too busy to supervise such writing, and the large size of the classes is inhibiting.

(g) The vast expansion in the number of university students and of universities and colleges and the incompatible growth in the number of professors has led to very large classes and to overcrowding in general. Likewise, this phenomenon is encountered at the sub-university level of education. And, in addition to the shortage in teachers, there is the low level and insufficient training of many teachers. The teacher training institutions are simply unable to cope with the need, and the pay for teachers has not been enough incentive to establish balance between supply and demand. To these problems must be added the associated problem of crowded premises in most countries, inadequate library and laboratory facilities, and the limited benefit the student or pupil gets from these facilities.

(h) There is insufficient co-ordination between secondary and higher education, which is one manifestation of the insufficient planning of education as a part of general planning. Were the planning and co-ordination to be better designed, more rational, and more closely suited to the endowments and needs of the various countries, there would probably be more incentives for technical training resulting in less overcrowding in universities. It would seem that Algeria heads the list in concern for better co-ordination and educational planning, followed by Tunisia and Iraq.

(i) Much of the 'learning' at the primary and secondary, and even at the university level, is still by rote. The writer has seen students on the grounds of almost every university walking back and forth memorising notes from professors' lectures or passages from books, and reciting them aloud. When questioned regarding the usefulness of this method, many of them indicated that they knew of no other way of learning. A few indicated dissatisfaction with the method, but felt that that was what the teachers expected.

(j) There are too many political appointments, promotions, or else dismissals of professors, deans and presidents in Arab universities. The damaging interference of political rewards or punishments in academic life cannot be condemned enough, and the harm it brings to education and its quality cannot be overstated.

(k) Finally, training. With few exceptions, technical and vocational training still fall far short of the needs of the expanding economies of the twelve countries. The most notable exceptions are Egypt, Algeria and Iraq, but serious efforts are also being exerted to the same end by Tunisia and Syria. The oil-producing countries are the best situated as far as the provision of incentives and resources is concerned. But, Algeria and Iraq apart, they are handicapped by the very limiting shortage of trainers and by the weak response by trainees and would-be trainees.

The rather large space devoted to education is well justified by the great relevance of this determinant to development, and its parallel significance as an object of development. However, the discussion must have suggested the existence of a sad paradox: that education is potentially a very powerful determinant, but that in effect its operation has been seriously handicapped in the Arab world by the many shortcomings and defects in the educational systems in force.

The role of education and training as a major determinant spreads over all the cycles of education, from the three Rs to post-doctoral programmes, and from plumbing to the most sophisticated field of engineering. Each of the levels has its relevance and its special function, and its capability to contribute to development. Arab education on the whole has yet to have its role and function re-examined, and its content, directions and methodology re-adjusted to fit the role and function. But above all, its social function has to be discovered and asserted. As of now, we can only venture to say that Algeria has started the difficult, demanding, but rewarding, search for the proper values, content and approach that its education is to have if it is to serve society at large and the economy in particular. Some shy steps are being taken in a small number of other countries, such as Tunisia, Iraq, Jordan and Egypt. But for the Arab world at large, the journey is still very long. This means that far-reaching and profound transformation will have to occur before education can act as a powerful determinant — that is, for its potency to match its potential.

2. The determinant to be examined at this point is acceptance of technological change. This comprises the areas and indicators of such acceptance and how it is translated into concrete behaviour, including the sophistication of production and distribution methods and of business organisation, the extent to which research is resorted to, and like manifestations. No doubt technological change is almost always occurring, and the acceptance of such change as a phenomenon of everyday life cannot be considered a particularly meaningful determinant of development.[71] Furthermore, the outward appearances of such acceptance are encountered almost always and everywhere, in the form of improved tools and equipment, new machines, new ways of doing things, new factor mixes, and improved or more modern forms of organisation. Evidently, what is meant by the determinant in question is something more than what is commonplace and familiar.

Three conditions are emphasised in the choice of the acceptance of technological change as a determinant of development. The first and easiest to satisfy is the acceptance of more modern and more efficient tools, machines, equipment, forms of organisation, factor mixes, and ways of doing things, whether in a farm or a factory or research institute. To this extent there is scant resistance to the 'newness' or modernity. But the scale of the newness or modernity, or yet advancedness of the technique or technology (as the case may be) which is involved in our understanding of the determinant must be large. Indeed, it must be so large that the quantitative change will be such as to amount to a qualitative change. Only in such an instance will the acceptance or rejection be a test of development-proneness by a society. Otherwise, without such a test the act of importing the more advanced technique would involve very little adjustment and will not necessarily indicate a decision or a stance of developmental significance.

The second condition to satisfy is that society should show an active eagerness not just to import a more advanced technology (or components of it), but to adapt such a technology to local conditions, endowments and aptitudes. No doubt there is a certain element of adaptation in every country, to the extent that the orders for large machines or factories have to include specifications which often call for special adjustments in the design and manufacture of the capital goods ordered. But this is only a first approximation to adaptation. What is needed beyond it is for the engineers of the importing country themselves to suggest certain adjustments, and secondly to introduce changes to the capital goods and the methods of production and organisation in their own milieu, and subsequently to be able to design and make the adaptations on the spot. It is through passage along this process that a country ultimately moves from pure importation, to adaptation, and finally to creative contribution to technology and to innovation.

With these steps in the process of adaptation during the transfer of technology, which increasingly emphasise self-reliance, the third condition will be gradually satisfied. This is the occurrence of change in outlook and attitude towards technology as a means to development. This internal, profound transformation involves a new attitude towards the physical environment and its taming for the service of the economy and society, and it likewise shapes a new attitude to science and its usability, and the capability first to know how to use it, then to be able to contribute to its evolution in the service of development.

It is obvious that 'acceptance of technological change' is a continuum beginning with some very simple decisions like willingness to experiment with a fertiliser in agriculture or with a new wheat breed, and reaching into research in nuclear physics or the development of new forms of energy. The situation is never one of comparative statics, but of dynamic, continuous transformation. Even in the same country, pockets of modernity and high acceptance coexist with stubborn resistance. The Third World countries which permit technological change to occur speedily and which therefore permit this factor of change to influence the course of development are ones which expedite the transition from traditionalism to modernity in the sense in which the latter is used in this section, and which make the area of transition as large as possible and the process of transition as smooth as possible.

The twelve Arab countries examined are all now witnessing this transition. But in the early postwar years, only a few of them were. For instance, Saudi Arabia, Kuwait, Sudan and Libya were, if at all, at the very threshold of the transition. The three Maghreb countries under French rule then were witnessing technological change, but it was being introduced by a colonial power and therefore it was resented, particularly as it was predominantly in the European *colon* sector that the change was being introduced, for its own benefit. Elsewhere, Egypt and Lebanon were ahead, followed closely by Syria and Iraq. Today, the picture is quite different in several respects. Our research has brought out the main features for the various countries. But it must be admitted that invariably the distinction ought to be borne in mind between the appearance of change or the acceptance of the superficial marks of change, and the deeper, more profound transformation in attitude to advanced technology and organisation and what that implies.

Probably Lebanon leads the list with a high degree of acceptance among a very large segment of the population, along with noticeable deeper transformation. This is true of manufacturing industry, as of banking, air transport, the hotel industry and agriculture. However, along with the marked advances made by the private sector in the directions indicated, there has been a marked stickiness in the public sector with respect both to the introduction of technological change, and to the resort to research and the application of its fruits. (Indeed, the downgrading of research is common both in government circles and in the business community, although the latter increasingly resorts to feasibility studies made by foreign or local consulting firms.) The explanation of the large measure of acceptance of technological change is not far to seek. It can mainly be found in the country's openness to the outside world for centuries now, the spread and high level of education, the intensive travelling undertaken, the dynamic enterprise of the Lebanese, and their trading tradition which familiarises them with more advanced technologies and whittles away their fear of innovation.

Sudan stands at the other extreme. Here even the first, most superficial aspect of the acceptance of technological change is still slow and partial. The introduction of modern gadgetry and durable household goods has been effected, but only within a very narrow social and economic circle in the cities and towns. However, there is evidence that where financial rewards and incentives have existed, and where the groups concerned have become aware of these incentives — and awareness is a most important condition — technological change has been accepted and new modes of work and life have been adopted with little maladjustment. Instances of transference from dry to irrigated farming, involving new crops and the use of new tools, have been witnessed around the irrigation dams, and the transference has taken only a few years. The vastness of the country and its relatively small and sparse population will remain a handicap to the radiation effect from the islands of technological change to the rest of the country. Hence the great importance of the modern means of transport and communication, as we shall see when we come to discuss the agents of change next.

The other countries fall in between, but the experience of each has its own flavour, and this justifies some specific observations. Thus, Saudi Arabia, also a country large in area but with a small population and a low educational level, witnesses today a much faster technological change than Sudan, and will most certainly witness a faster acceptance of this change. This difference arises from its oil revenues which permit an almost forced modernisation in technology, in the sense that the government is importing an advanced technology wholesale and large-scale. The population is hardly at all prepared for this sudden transformation, and very serious manpower problems already exist, and threaten in our view to lead to resource waste on a colossal scale, and to strangulation because of the manpower bottleneck. Yet the population cannot but feel the impact of this vast exposure to the new technology, with its machines and tools, its organisation, its power, and its gripping magnificence to a community not yet very far from tribalism or primitive urban activities. The scale of the technological importation and the almost total unpreparedness will necessitate the passage of some time for the first phase of acceptance to be gone through. The second and third phases, namely those of adaptation and indigenous creativity, and of profound transformation in attitudes to science and technology, are in this writer's view matters for the distant future.

Be this as it may, it ought to be stated that the Eastern Province of Saudi Arabia has by now traversed a long distance in accepting modern technology. This is thanks to the presence for decades now of the Arabian American Oil Company (ARAMCO) there, and its radiating leavening effect. As in Sudan, awareness of rewarding economic returns has led to speedier acceptance of change. And whereas the early manifestations of this acceptance did not go beyond the transformation of camel drivers into truck drivers, today the Saudi work-force in the Eastern Province possesses a much wider range of skills, and its concept of technological change goes much deeper than driving cars or using the telephone. But in most other parts of the country there are strong pockets of resistance. (The first human landing on the moon in July 1969 was disbelieved and the report was condemned as out-right blasphemy. This attitude changed gradually, from perplexity finally to resignation and acceptance.)

Here as elsewhere the transistor radio and the television set are great carriers of convic-tion. The man in the distant village whose acquaintance with modern technology was restricted to a water pump a few years ago, and to whom the economic benefits of modern technology were an abstraction, if he ever heard of them, could not be blamed for a low degree of acceptance. Indeed, the word 'acceptance' is not relevant in his case. The test comes when the truck can reach his village, as well as electricity and piped drinking water, the radio and the television set, and money for the effecting of commercial exchange. All that can be said at this point is that it is probable that he will be quick to adopt some of the consumer and the durable household goods, but slower to adopt new techniques and machines and inputs in production — such as a new crop rotation or breed of vegetables, a tractor, or fertilisers. The slowness will be more marked the further away he is from the centres of radiation, and the less the attention devoted to his education and socialisation.

Algeria, Tunisia and Morocco, in that order, show a marked degree of acceptance, and for very much the same reasons. All three had been exposed for a long stretch of time to European influence through colonisation and direct rule, all three had large European communities that were not only active but predominant in economic life, and all three witnessed the building of an economic infrastructure which was not matched in any of the other countries under examination. Algeria leads in these respects because it had the longest association with Europe and is very close to it geographically, the French were determined to turn it into an extension of France, and the European community was the largest in absolute and in relative terms. Furthermore, today all three have a large body of workers in Europe who keep in contact with the mother country.

Yet the long direct contact with Europeans cannot and must not be taken automatically as a factor for a high degree of acceptance of technological change. As already indicated, the colonialist-colonised relationship is not conducive to learning by the latter from the former, nor does it imply eagerness by the former to teach the latter. In all cases, the most painful manner in which the colonised become familiar with the colonialist's more advanced tech-nology is the latter's well-organised and -trained army and its modern weapons — hardly a welcome medium for the transmission of technology. Nevertheless, the demonstration effect has been powerful. The three Maghreb countries, though seriously handicapped upon independence because their social infrastructure had been as thoroughly and deliberately neglected as their physical infrastructure had been built and their resources exploited, have not failed to become ready to absorb modern methods of production and to show a readi-ness to apply them that would otherwise have been distinctly less pronounced. Yet in all three countries this readiness centres mostly around the outward, physical manifestations of modern technology. Even Algeria, while the furthest ahead in technological change and the most serious in widening the scope and reach of this change (with respect to territory and to sectors), is still much more concerned with the economic, material and technological aspects of modernisation, than those of deeper attitude and of basic scientific transformation. It seems likely that its strong eagerness to achieve fast economic growth and to industrialise is usurping the attention of the leadership, at the partial expense of the intangible aspects of development.

We need not go on with this sketch country by country. Some broad generalisations apply to the countries not specified, as to those to which reference has been made. The first is that basic research and research aimed at the application of science in technology are both deficient and receive much less attention, resources and manpower than necessary. It follows that there is still a very limited application of scientific methods to problem-solving. Though significant in itself, this deficiency is of further grave significance for the passage from the first to the subsequent phases of acceptance of technological change and techno-logical transformation. Secondly, modern organisation still creeps slowly, in business as in government, in factory as in university. Thirdly, almost invariably the Arab countries are still within the first phase of technological transformation, mainly in the process of importing modern technology with very little adaptation and hardly any creative contribu-tion or innovation. The imported technology is also mainly embodied in tools, equipment, machines and spare parts, as well as certain inputs. To a much smaller extent it comprises intangibles like organisation and research. The saddest aspect of this failing is that the Arab world has thousands of very capable and well-trained men and women who can bring about adaptations to machines as to tools and forms of organisation, and who can put basic and applied research to the service of development, but who are not assigned the right place or given the right incentives or allowed the right climate for their skills to be put to optimum use.

In brief, it can be said that the acceptance of technological change, and the more profound technological transformation, which have a manifestly important role in the process of development, are still at an early phase of materialisation. Their potential is great, but the present state is modest. The much greater availability of financial resources today can help considerably in the training of a new generation capable not only to know what technology to choose and import, but what specifications to make, what design to suggest or make, what adaptations to introduce, and what innovations to contribute. Such training, and the education and research to support it or guide it — as the case may be — is essentially in need of the proper vision at the decision-making and leadership level, and of the proper understanding of the conditions creative men and women need for their talents to be put into technological transformation. But the leadership, whether in govern-ment or in business, must also realise that such transformation must spread to reach the whole society. It may start in isolated islands, but these will have to expand and to touch and interact, if it is to be meaningful for development.

Finally, all decision-makers who have a say in this technological transformation have to free themselves of the current overwhelming tendency to emphasise the importation of technology indiscriminately and wholesale, and to attach primary importance to self-reliance and creativity. While financial incentives are significant for the acceptance of technological change, and while travel and contact with more advanced economies are powerful instruments for the transfer of technology, and while the demonstration effect and the spread of the mass media of communication at home will facilitate the diffusion of modern technology, it remains true that fundamentally, Arab society must develop its internal capability to advance science and technology, if development is truly to benefit from technology as a determinant. As this internal capability expands, the problem of acceptance recedes; as technological transformation is internalised, the resistance to technological change is overcome and expelled.

3. Closely related to the acceptance of technological change as a determinant is another which also focuses on change: the agents of change — change here specifically identified as developmental. As the study was being designed, the agents that were to receive special attention were military and party élites, political leadership, the middle class and minority (deviant) groups.[72] These agents represent a more directly-acting determinant than the acceptance of technological change and technological transformation, to the extent that the agents are actors or potential actors, human decision-makers, and do not simply involve a change in attitude or in organisation. As elsewhere, the position taken here is that wherever human actors are concerned, we are face to face with direct prime movers. This emerged most strongly from our earlier discussion of entrepreneurs and the developmental orientation or commitment of political leadership.

In the field investigation undertaken, questions with respect to the agents of change were open-ended; it was left to the respondent to identify what in his view were the major agents. Consequently the replies came up with other agents. Some of these were groups of inhabitants, some were non-human forces, as the reporting on the responses will show. It is obvious from the original wording of the present determinant in the last chapter that emphasis had been mainly laid on human agents, groups with particular concern for develop-ment or power to influence the course of development, although non-human agents had not been outside the preview of the writer. The field-work somewhat qualified the initial emphasis.

It is necessary to indicate that the present enquiry was not launched from the assumption that the agents listed were active determinants of development in the Arab world. Instead, the enquiry was to show to what extent each of the agents listed could be so considered, in one country after another. In other words, the listing was no more in effect than a proposi-tion which the investigation was to confirm or refute. And, indeed, it did. Without anticipa-ting the country findings, one illustration can be given to show how the findings drastically corrected one preconceived idea. This relates to the role of the military in development, which the present writer had assessed as very significant, projecting from the case of Egypt into several other countries.[73]

The investigation proved the error of such projection for, although the governing groups in Syria, Iraq, Sudan or Algeria had had their access to power initially cleared by military take-overs in the fifties and sixties, and although these groups still retain very powerful military figures, the commitment to development at leadership level is to be found essen-tially in the prevalence of developmental concern shared by members of the leadership, both military and civilian. In other, more direct, terms, this concern is not a function of the presence of former military officers in power, but in the developmental orientation and commitment of the group that is in power as a matter of personal conviction, not as part of the values of the officer corps.

One comment each is called for with respect to the middle class and minority groups as agents.[74] In our view when designing the study the former comprised professionals (lawyers, physicians, professors) as well as industrialists, bankers and large merchants. The list did not exclude senior civil servants. But it excluded the traditional élite, the large land-lords, upper-class dignitaries or rich *rentiers*. Although we did not explicitly list trade union leaders we were intent on looking for their role, which, it was hoped, would be identified where applicable in the responses to our open-end question. The enquiry set out with some reservations with regard to merchants and their role, but it was left for the interviews to justify or dispel these reservations.[75] As far as minority groups were concerned, we had started under the influence of Hagen[76] and others in so far as their developmental role was thought to be activated by their sense of deviance, and with the expectation of finding them still contributing considerably to development. The enquiry again corrected this expectation substantially, as we have had occasion to state earlier on in this chapter in the context of the discussion of entrepreneurship. With these observations stated, we can now turn to an examination of the findings of the study.

Quite a large number of agents were listed by the respondents in the countries surveyed. It was found difficult to see the distinct features of the picture emerging from the surveys without some schematic aid. Consequently, we tabulated the findings with respect to the agents listed, under country headings. The picture now emerged clearly; its main features will first be described, and then some of its peculiarities.

The one point on which there was total agreement for all twelve countries was the importance of the political leadership as an agent of change. In the cases of Jordan, Morocco and Saudi Arabia, the King in person was mentioned in each instance as a strong promotive factor which sets the general tone of development, whereas in Kuwait the ruling family as a whole was strongly emphasised as a force for development. But this is where agreement ends. In the view of the respondents, the army made a most distinct contribution to development in Egypt, and specifically under Nasser. Libya and Sudan were listed as two other cases, but with reservations about the latter because of its instability, the spottiness of the performance of the officer class in power, and the absence of a clear programme with developmental content subscribed to by this class. Also with respect to the instruments of power, it was found that leading or ruling political parties that had acted as a determinant were to be found in Syria and Iraq (where it was the party rather than the military that was given credit), and to a lesser extent in Tunisia. In this last case, it was emphasised that only recently did the Socialist Destour party begin to show serious concern for development, its earlier interest having been mainly political.

Finally, in the present context, religious and land-owning élites were not credited as a determinant except in a few cases. These were the landowners in Syria in the early post-war years, and to a lesser extent in Egypt, certain elements of the religious leadership in the Sudan, and the King of Morocco, in his capacity as 'Commander of the Faithful'. Tunisia deserves special mention here, to the extent that Zeitouna Mosque (and school of thought) shaped a religious élite of importance in the history of leadership; likewise, the Sadiquiyya College graduates were to emerge as a developmental force with a traditional (religious) background but with modern education and outlook.

The middle class was not cited as a significant determinant in Morocco, Algeria, Saudi Arabia or Libya, and was cited with some reserve as a force in Tunisia, Syria and Egypt. But it was considered an important factor in the remaining countries, particularly Lebanon. Yet in these two categories where the middle class was not listed, or where its role was considered modest, the technocrats were cited as a very important factor. It would seem that we are faced here with a definitional question for, if the technocrats (as a component of the senior civil service) are excluded from the composition of the middle class, the findings become plausible, but less so if they are not so excluded in the case of Syria, Egypt and Tunisia. Yet even elsewhere, a clear definition of the components that constitute the middle class would probably have produced a different response for Libya, Morocco and Saudi Arabia, particularly given the attachment of the last two countries to the system of private enterprise in which the middle class is allowed to play an important role, and given the emergence of a middle class in both of them, though with different composition.

Because of this questioning of the responses and of the underlying definitional ambiguity that is being assumed, all that can be said is that a broad definition that takes into account senior civil servants, technocrats, industrialists and the leaders in such other private sector activities like transport and banking, can justify the attribution of substantial credit to the middle class as a strong factor in development. But this is only possible if the industrialists and other private-sector elements in the middle class succeed in tempering their private profit-making with concern for the general development of society, and put their entrepreneurial drive in the service of, or in line with, national development plans and policies. No doubt it is the duty of the state to provide some indicative planning for the private-sector middle class so that it may conform, and to permit a fair financial reward to the business community for its activities so that it may have an incentive to pursue such conformity.

A final word must be said in the context of the middle class about Sudan. An influential group which played an important role in the intellectual ferment of pre-independence and early post-independence days is a grouping of middle-class educated men known as the Graduates' Congress. Although this group was concerned more with political issues, it had a moderate modernising effect among the civil service, the educated community and the parties. But its current influence is almost totally absent.

The senior civil servants can be included in the middle class, but can also be considered an agent of change in their own right. The civil service was investigated as a determinant under the political-administrative cluster in section 2 above. Thus we do not have to examine it here at length, but only in so far as some respondents identified it separately as an agent of change, or subsumed it under the middle-class group. The influence of the senior civil service was not denied in any country, but there were qualifications and reservations in a few cases. Thus, in Saudi Arabia it was under-played, while commoner ministers received greater recognition as an agent of developmental change. In Libya and Lebanon its influence was considered weak, with emphasis on its deterring effect in the latter case. Finally, in Kuwait it was emphasised, but the point was made that when credit is given, it should mostly go to expatriate senior civil servants and advisers of government, to the extent that this group has been influential in creating a climate of change and in supplying many ideas of developmental impact and significance.

The last group among those we started with in the investigation was the minorities. In support of our earlier finding in section 1, the responses were negative in ten out of the twelve countries examined. One exception was Jordan, where some respondents said that if the Palestinians in East Jordan were to be considered a minority in the sense that they had taken refuge there subsequent to their escape from Palestine upon the establishment of the state of Israel in 1948, then it must be underlined that they are a very powerful agent of change. The second exception was Kuwait, again where the expatriates were admittedly a powerful agent of developmental change. But in Jordan as in Kuwait, the paradoxical point is that the minority is a numerical majority of the total population. The 'minority' can be considered a minority only in the sense that it has gone into the country in the post-war period in search of a refuge or of remunerative employment. In Jordan, the Palestinian refugees have come to enjoy equal political and economic rights with the original inhabitants, although the highest circle of power where final and effective decision-making is made remains East Jordanian. In Kuwait, the expatriates (whether Arab or non-Arab) are allowed no political rights and are denied the ability to own land, houses, businesses, or even shares in corporations. We need not do more than remind the reader that the erstwhile very powerful European agents of change in the Maghreb countries have virtually disappeared from the scene. Likewise, the Europeans in Egypt, the Jews in a few of the countries, the Armenians in Syria and Lebanon — all have lost any claim they might have had to being an agent of developmental change.

A few other recurrent agents which we included in the tabulation to which reference was made earlier on are education, the mass media of communication, and travel abroad. While education was cited in every single instance, with special mention of education abroad, its impact was declared weak or limited in Libya, Sudan, Saudi Arabia and Morocco. In several countries, the emphasis on education was supplemented by references to the schoolteacher. In one instance, education was thought to rouse ambition and to sharpen motivation. In the case of Kuwait, this reference was further qualified by the insistence that the expatriate schoolteachers and university professors have played a specially meritorious role. The mass media were cited in nine countries, that is, excluding Morocco, Egypt and Iraq. In the case of Iraq and Sudan, the influence of this agent was stated to be present but weak. The silence about it in Egypt is rather puzzling, inasmuch as our general knowledge of the country suggests that the spread of these media and the attention given to them by the authorities cannot but be an indication of their potency as an agent of change.[77]

Foreign travel was not cited in Libya, Sudan, Syria or Iraq, where it was considered not to be of a scale justifying its inclusion in the list of agents. In the case of Lebanon and Saudi Arabia, emphasis was placed on the large flow of incoming travellers for tourism and holidays to the first, and pilgrimage to the second. Furthermore, strong influence was attributed to the foreign companies doing business in Saudi Arabia, in generating entrepreneurial ideas and in bringing about transformation in skills and technology.

In this latter respect, it is important to add that the five large oil-producing countries considered oil and the revenue it brings in as a major agent of developmental change. Its influence ramifies in many directions, including that to which reference was made in Saudi Arabia. But in another more significant respect oil revenue creates a pressure for the search for opportunities for developmental investment. And, in the nature of the case with oil and gas as a basic input in a large variety of new industries, this resource is a factor of innovation and diversification. Finally, in their desire to find alternative sources of income to replace oil when its reserves are depleted, the oil countries seize the opportunity of the still abundant flow of oil revenue to diversify the economy and develop many new industries and activities, and to promote education, science and technological transformation.

We are now ready for some individual observations that escaped inclusion in our tabulated generalisations. In the case of Sudan, the railways and the lorry were emphasised as modernising agents. The role of the army was expanded to include the introduction of modern equipment, training and transformation of thousands of youth, and the carrying into the remotest parts of the country of the only marks of modernisation like vehicles and machines. For Kuwait, a small 'think tank', mostly expatriate, around the strong man of the ruling family in the tender and critical years of early independence, was credited with significant developmental ideas relating to institutions, legislation and projects. The presence of the expatriates, acting as instrument and initiator of change, acted on a willing and open society which had been made receptive to change, thanks to a long tradition of trading with other countries and active navigation. Furthermore, the large merchant families were cited as a strong agent of change in the first years of independence.

In Iraq, the post-war pressures for development on a world-wide scale were considered an important agent. The influence of neighbouring and other Arab countries was added. In both instances, the underlying factor was access to information thanks to travel and the mass media. Some of the Saudis interviewed emphasised the sedentarisation of the tribes as a factor for change. Associated with this was the employment of tribesmen in the army and their introduction to the world of machines, discipline and literacy. The same observation was made of Iraq, Jordan and Kuwait. Again, in Saudi Arabia government projects themselves were considered a factor for change, since they familiarised thousands of Saudis with new structures, machines, work plans, and new methods of doing things, and made them readier for further transformation and modernisation. The same factor, but with particular emphasis on industrialisation, was cited in Tunisia. But in this latter country, emphasis was placed on political participation as another factor, coupled as this participation has been with the impact of other factors like communication, travel, widespread education, and contact with the advanced countries.

For Morocco, the army was not considered as a promotive factor in the present context. Its security orientation was thought to involve a misallocation of resources. As far as the role of the parties was concerned, credit was given less to those in power, while the ones in opposition were described as a 'social lash' which was instrumental in heightening the concern for development among the parties in power. However, a probably more balanced view was that the almost continuous tug-of-war between the two groups has been wasteful of time, resources and energy. Also in juxtaposition are the traditional élites (the large landlords, the tribal chiefs, the senior army officers who were originally tribal chiefs or large landlords) and the lawyers and professors (many of whom are in opposition). Because of the wastefulness involved in political dissent, the latter group have had little power to act directly as agents of social and economic change; their impact has mainly been to keep developmental issues alive and pressing.

The officers who took over power in Egypt in 1952, and like them those in Syria, Iraq and Algeria (but less so those in Libya) have all benefited from interaction with many technocrats and a smaller number of intellectuals. But in Egypt the relationship was longer and more fruitful. Yet the role of the army as a modernising agent has been qualified, even for Egypt, by the judgement that the officers had very little experience, a very narrow world-view, and good intentions without a clear programme of action. Their low capability to conceptualise and to see socio-economic problems from a wide angle, and their rigidity and excessive security-mindedness reduced their impact on development. The last element, namely security-mindedness, made them — in Egypt as elsewhere where army officers took over — prefer the loyal to the competent.

For Algeria, the great urgency after independence to improve conditions, coupled with the discipline and devotion to the national cause learnt the hard way during the bitter war of independence, proved a very forceful factor for change. The presence of a middle class was denied, mainly because the national bourgeoisie had been wiped out by the French, but also because the new middle class was not composed as the old had been. In its current state, it consists mainly of intellectuals and technocrats. This phenomenon of the constancy of the factor, but the drastic change in its composition, reminiscent of Pareto's notion of the 'circulation of élites', does not negate the existence of the factor.[78]

A final observation to make relates not to the identity of the agents of developmental change, but to the intensity of the desire for change, the ability to translate it directly or indirectly into action, and the scale of the desire. The desire must be strong, it must be felt by agents capable of such translation, and the desire must be on a large scale. Each of the Arab countries examined has more than one agent, and in each instance the agents include some with the strong desire and the capability of translation or transmission of the desire. But in only a few is this desire widely diffused. Yet, taken together for each of the countries, the agents of change are clearly in operation as a determinant of development.

However, it seems to us warranted to say that it will be some time before this determinant will gather strong momentum and reach a large area of the society, taking into account a number of counteracting forces and tendencies.

4. Reference has been made to motivation and the importance assigned to it by many writers. This applies to entrepreneurs and managers, as well as to lower rungs of the manpower pyramid of authority. Indeed, a few social scientists have assigned to the 'need-for-achievement', which is a motive that is supposed to influence *all* human behaviour, the highest place among the determinants of development.[79] Consequently, we set out to examine the relevance and operation of motivation and incentives as a determinant. At the same time, some exploration was to be made of the significance attached by the respondents to development-oriented social tension, which has engaged the attention of a few economists and sociologists concerned with development.

Motivation, the fourth determinant to consider in the socio-cultural cluster, is essential to all human action. Sensitivity to incentives is indispensable to behaviour, even when such behaviour is attributed to lofty, idealistic urges, religious injunctions, or philosophical explorativeness. Whatever the area of action, there must be an incentive for action — whether it is to please God or to counteract Satan. In a study undertaken by the writer on the entrepreneurs of Lebanon in 1958-60, one respondent reacted to the list of motives suggested as explanations why they went into business.[80] The list allowed for additions, but included such items as profit-making, satisfaction of the urge for achievement, the desire to build a business empire, and so on. The respondent stated that none of the motives listed suited his own purposes. In reply to our enquiry, he stated solemnly and without the flicker of a smile that his objective was to 'serve the Lord Jesus Christ'. Much later in the interview, asked about the minimum annual rate of net profit on turnover he would consider adequate for him to stay in business (the Marshallian notion of 'normal' profit), he stated that it was 25 per cent. A member of the interviewing team later declared this respondent as probably the only surviving Calvinist.

The point of this incident, other than its anecdotal interest, is that there invariably is a motive, and this motive, even in the realm of economic action, need not be only financial. Indeed, beyond a certain high level of riches, the businessman may be motivated far more by non-economic rewards such as power or prestige, than by further profits; this is the more true the lower the marginal utility of money becomes. Yet, if motivation is universal, the question can legitimately be asked: why suggest motivation as a determination and explore its operation?

In answer, it might be said that the investigation aimed first at assessing the *intensity* of motivation in general, and second, at assessing the intensity of financial motivation. It might be added that the motivation of political decision-makers, top civil servants, or party leaders — all of whom were considered as possible agents of developmental change — is not financial, as they are supposed not to seek personal gain in their commitment to and action for development. To this extent, they are motivated by concern for the social good in general, or for development more specifically. Consequently, it can be affirmed that non-material personal motivation has not been ignored in the study, and the narrowed focus of the present part merely serves to help us appreciate the sensitivity of the economic actors in the various Arab countries to economic motives. These actors are taken to mean the private owners of productive assets as well as labour. However, this narrowing does not mean that the motivation of groups not in business, such as civil servants, has not received consideration — indeed, there will be some references to it — but that such groups will remain marginal to the general territory explored.

One further point needs to be made, before some general observations flowing from the field-work are presented. This is that the connection between sensitivity to economic incentives and the exertion of effort to obtain them ought to be borne in mind. Thus, to say that motivation is high, but that the inhabitants of a certain country are reluctant to put the effort required to obtain the incentives, involves a contradiction, or at least a misunderstanding. If the incentives are fair, in the sense that they conform to the general level of return for the action involved, then the refusal to exert the effort required is a sign that motivation is low at the normal, prevailing level of return. (In the case of Kuwait, for many Kuwaitis the returns are excessively high and far out of line with the effort involved; indeed, the welfare payments involve no work at all. Consequently, where effort is withheld, this must be taken as a specially low level of motivation, considering the high level of returns.)

The field research undertaken enables us to make a number of generalisations and observations on motivation in the Arab countries. The first is that most respondents showed some hesitation in answering the questions on the subject, declaring that it is extremely difficult to measure motivation, and risky to make broad, impressionistic generalisations. One aspect of the difficulty of generalising is that different economic and social groups react differently to motivation in the same country. However, almost all respondents stated their conviction that, given an attractive economic reward, motivation becomes operative. But two conditions must be satisfied: that the group being considered be aware of the existence of the rewards, and that this group itself consider the rewards satisfactory. Both points seem to us to be very significant, for what matters is not an economic reward which the subject is not aware of or familiar with, or one which seems to him unsatisfactory or below his critical level of response. The latter question may be declared irrational by the observer who applies his own criteria of rationality and consistency. But what is relevant is the subject's own system of rationality and what he himself considers satisfactory. Only if he behaves in violation of his definition of 'satisfactoriness' can he be considered irrational and his action inconsistent with his standards.

The difficulty of measurement apart, and bearing in mind the qualification just stated, some specific observations are in hand with regard to individual countries. Thus, Lebanon seems to be the country that shows the highest intensity of motivation, both at the level of entrepreneurs and capital-owners, and of labour in the skilled, semi-skilled and unskilled categories. One particular aspect of this country is that often when the Lebanese does not respond to the financial incentives available, even though they are adequate at the going rate, this is because he is very ambitious and eager to earn more. His reaction in such an instance is not merely to refuse to undertake the effort involved, but to emigrate in search of a higher reward. On the other hand the intensity of motivation is thought to be low in Sudan. As proof, it was stated that there is substantial underemployment in the country along with the immigration of about one million non-Sudanese African workers.

However, this illustration, striking as it is, ought to be qualified. Other factors that have to be introduced are the shallowness of agricultural tradition among many Sudanese who are far from the areas of irrigated or dry farming, compared with the incoming Africans; likewise, many Sudanese prefer pastoral and fishing activities and 'status jobs'. Yet, in defence of the responsiveness of the Sudanese, some respondents cited the example of the real nomads, who, in five years, became farmers in irrigated land in the Manaqil extension. All this goes to show how complicated the assessment of the intensity of motivation is.

Indeed, the picture is quite confused, and well worth deep and careful investigation if a large-scale development programme is to be launched in the rural sector involving the land

and its occupants. For, along with the illustration just given, other equally eloquent illustrations are offered that point both to the opposite direction and to the same direction. Thus, subsistence farming is widespread, yet there are huge under-utilised but accessible resources. On the other hand, there is great geographical mobility, from one province to another, in search of improved conditions. We can only venture the hypothesis that motivation operates up to a certain level — satisfying hunger for instance — but is weaker beyond that level.

Kuwait too offers other paradoxes. One of these is the parallelism between high motivation among the businessmen, particularly those with a long tradition of foreign trade and shipping, and low motivation among lower-income groups. The latter phenomenon is probably explainable by the largesse of welfare aid, in cash and in kind; the ease with which the Kuwaiti can satisfy his basic needs, even though these are defined to include many semi-luxury items like a second-hand car, a TV set, modern furniture; and the vast scope for employment in government, in a country with one civil servant for every ten inhabitants — Kuwaitis and expatriates combined. Given the enormous fortunes made in the past two decades, and the example effect that that must have, it can only indicate a low level of motivation to observe the very hesitant and modest spirit of enterprise of most Kuwaitis. The non-awareness of opportunities can be suggested but only in part explanation; another part must be understood through excessive dependence on the government.

The implications of the situation for development are both obvious and serious. The Kuwaiti of today shuns activities with which he or his father used to be familiar, such as fishing, shipbuilding and seafaring. The modern counterparts of these activities are available and well-paying: fishing in motor boats, merchant shipping work, freighters and tankers. No doubt the 'work culture' has been debilitated in two decades of increasing oil revenues and extensive government welfare spending and public service expansion. The Kuwaitisation of a large number of tribesmen from the neighbouring desert has had its effect in shaping the work ethic. Though driving a large, modern American car, the bedouin still has much of his original culture, with respect to status, abhorrence of work that is not clean or manly (as he uses the terms), and non-respect of time and work discipline.

The impact of the desert can be seen in Iraq and Saudi Arabia. An Iraqi sociologist drew attention in an interview to the still-prevalent fishing by spear in the rivers, not by net. The spear permits the tribesman/fisherman to fish for his own needs; if he were to have a larger catch, he would have to sell his surplus, but he would resent that as undignified for a man. Instead his wife will have to do the marketing. The tribesman/farmer will grow wheat, but only for his own needs; he is reluctant to grow vegetables, because these are essentially cash crops. (Among other things, to sell vegetables diminishes the marriageability of daughters to fellow tribesmen.) Though the fishing illustration does not apply to Saudi Arabia, the one about farming does. The growing of vegetables on a large scale has had to await the influx of expatriates in considerable numbers, and it still depends on them essentially. Both in Iraq and in Saudi Arabia, as in those other countries with tribes or semi-settled tribes in desert areas (such as Sudan, Libya, and the Maghreb countries) the degree of monetisation is of great relevance. The tribesmen do not take money to be very important; it has little value in a drought or famine.

As far as the Iraqi business community is concerned, motivation has had a relapse, as a result of the repression of the private sector since the launching of the socialist transformation. Even the farmer is now intensely concerned with exploiting the government's almost uncritical support for him, whether with respect to the provision of land, agricultural machinery, fertilisers, credit or other inputs.

Reference has been made to tribesmen in Saudi Arabia, or to recently settled tribesmen. Other groups show a higher motivation and a more intense work ethic, the more exposed they have been to foreigners, the nearer to seaports, and the more travelled they are. This generalisation applies to all the countries examined. The exposure need not be direct, in the sense that it involves work associations and the learning of work habits and of responsiveness to material incentives. It can be indirect, in the sense that familiarity with new consumption patterns and new gadgets and household tools and durables can be a strong incentive for emulation, and therefore for harder work in order to earn the income with which to buy the new goods. The mass media play a very significant role of demonstration in this respect — even the advertisements which on almost every other count are a disutility to the viewer. Rostow had a strong point when once he recommended the circulation in the Third World countries of vans with transparent glass sides, carrying new kitchen utensils and gadgets, as a strong factor for the search for income, for work, and for development.[81]

Among the Maghreb countries, Tunisia leads in the intensity of motivation. But this intensity is frustrating, inasmuch as work opportunities and investment resources are limited. (Only since late in 1973 have the investment constraints been eased, as a result of the steep rise in the price of phosphates and of petroleum, the country's major resources.) In Algeria, the desire to make up for the destruction and the time lost during the struggle for independence seems to be highly motivating. On the other hand, the air of waiting and hesitation in Morocco dampens the motivation that exists, and the strong element of tribalism introduces the factors to which reference has been made in the context of tribes elsewhere in the region.

In Libya, the repressive Italian rule had both dampened the spirit of enterprise and motivation, and narrowed opportunities to strangulation point. Since the oil boom, opportunities have expanded considerably, but there have been counteracting factors. One of these is the strictness and sternness with which the private sector is treated. The expectation of employment in the oil sector and in government has reduced interest in agriculture and even caused a serious drain of skilled farmers. These factors have come to further weaken an already damaged motivation. Fortunately for the country, the authorities are eager to re-activate the agricultural sector, and to create favourable pull factors in non-oil sectors, in order to have a more balanced and healthy sectoral structure and distribution of employment. To this end, several institutional and financial incentives have been provided. Unlike Saudi Arabia and Kuwait, Libya frowns on subsidies and largesse in welfare benefits, and emphasises gainful employment instead. Furthermore, the government is attempting to increase the attractiveness of technical and vocational training and jobs in order to reduce the dependence on clerical jobs. It is clear from the evidence on hand that there is official awareness of the weakness of motivation and a desire to intensify this motivation.

There is a final observation to make with respect to motivation in the Arab world. This relates to the influence of the prevalent sense of submission to God's will which Islam, the religion of over 92 per cent of the Arab region's population, imparts. It is presumed by some orientalists and social scientists that the contentment with one's destiny, which is an injunction of Islam, is inimical to material motivation, and therefore to enterprise and development. The present writer is not qualified to examine this question in depth; only a few general comments will therefore be made here in this connection.[82]

The first is that both Judaism and Christianity ask the believer to put his trust in God, but this has not at all dampened the spirit of enterprise of the adherents of either religion. Indeed, seeking the Kingdom which is in Heaven has hardly weakened the Protestant or the Calvinistic ethic. Furthermore, in the case of Islam, the submission to God's will, the contentment with one's destiny, and the endeavour to earn entry into heaven are not tied, as in Christianity, to very demanding spiritual commands. In all three religions there are injunctions against usury, but theologians have not failed to find ways around them.

However, the more important point is that Islam has concerned itself with the organisation of economic life to a much greater extent than either of the two other monotheistic religions. It also contains many injunctions enjoining the faithful to work hard, to seek education wherever it can be found, to pay the *zakat* (a form of income and capital tax), and to share with the needy. The absence of a formal, institutionalised 'church' in Islam further allows it great flexibility. The wide doors of *ijtihad* (independent judgement in theological questions and interpretations) have permitted, and to a certain extent still permit, further flexibility. In conclusion, it can be said that Islam, like Christianity or Judaism, in effect is neither strongly promotive of nor strongly inhibiting to economic activity and entrepreneurial drive in particular. As a cultural factor influencing development and enjoining concern for the poor, it is far from neutral. But the point at issue is that economic behaviour, except for a very small fringe of believers who are literal in their textual interpretations, is very minimally shaped, directed or influenced by religion.

The same applies to the literary component of Arab culture, poetry and prose, as well as to popular proverbs. Here one can find ammunition for two opposing arguments: one claiming that this part of culture enjoins hard work, achievement, enterprise, and energy and decisiveness; the other claiming that it enjoins abstinence and contentment, patience and caution, and ascriptive honours. Here again in the latter part of the twentieth century, we see no reason why a significant influence can be imputed to the cultural factor under reference in determining the course of development. For, the same Arab societies, with the same religious and literary culture between the early post-war years and the early 1970s, have shown widely different degrees of change in their attitude to economic activity and enterprise, in their economic motivation, and in their economic behaviour in general. If motivation has been seen to be on the whole weak, this is mainly because of certain restrictive social and economic factors which tend to weaken the responsiveness to incentives; of insufficient opportunities and awareness of those in existence; of counteracting factors like the desire for social aggregation working against mobility in search of more remunerative employment; or finally constraints in the regulatory and institutional framework laid by government, as in the case of nationalisations dampening the motivation of businessmen in the private sector.

In conclusion, a qualification must be made to the finding that motivation is a very powerful determinant of development in principle, that is, in abstraction from its presently low intensity in most Arab countries. This is that for motivation to operate in strength, it ought to comprise a certain measure of public spiritedness and concern for social needs. Otherwise, it would only lead to individual acquisitiveness and fortunes, which may or may not be in line with the common good.

5. The final determinant to examine in this section is, as already indicated, a composite item. As stated in the last chapter, it includes social mobility, the family and (broader) system of authority, traditionalism versus modernisation in attitudes, and the place of status symbols.[83] These items relate to different values. Thus, social mobility relates to motivation and the satisfaction of the desire for achievement; the degree of modernity of attitude relates to the value attached to tradition as against modern ideas, institutions and technology; the family and other systems or structures of authority relate to the grounds for authority and how these promote or retard developmental action; and status

symbols reflect the system of social and individual valuation and the motives for seeking some symbols at the expense of others. In all four instances what is at issue is the operation of the items as promoters of development through the influence they have on economic behaviour.

The field investigation of these four items was far from even. This was partly because it was found impractical to attach equal importance to them, partly because they were found to be unevenly capable of observation and assessment, and mainly because the respondents themselves reacted to the first much more actively than to the other items. However, in reporting our findings, we will leave social mobility to the end and deal with the other three items first, dwelling in all instances on generalisations and broad inferences but supplementing these with specific country peculiarities as the need arises.

The juxtaposition of modernity to traditionalism was pointed to in the introductory remarks made to this section. Emphasis was laid on the error of regarding these two states of mind as being mutually exclusive or as existing in pure form, and on the necessity of recognising the spottiness of the picture, with shades of traditionalism and modernity coexisting in the same society. Furthermore, it was argued that the rather dogmatic assertions of the fifties that all things traditional were inimical to development, and all things modern were promotive or indicative of it, were untenable under careful scrutiny. The field investigation provided support to both points. Indeed, it became more strongly evident during the research that Arab societies were correct in trying to reach a certain mix of the traditional and the modern, especially where cultural heritage and values were concerned. If these attempts at accommodation and coexistence exacted their price in the slowing of economic growth, they also paid a dividend in greater social harmony and psychological integration, and therefore in true development.

A country-by-country examination revealed that Lebanon was the least traditional, followed by Egypt, Algeria and Tunisia. At the other extreme stood Sudan and Morocco. But in all cases, as expected the countryside showed greater traditionalism, and the tribes or tribal societies the greatest. In Saudi Arabia, the manifestations were many, including resistance to the education of girls, the initial resistance to TV and the telephone as instruments of evil, the persistent contention among many persons who have had some schooling that the earth is flat, and not spherical.[84] Yet, even in this country, exposure to education and to the mass media of communication are eroding the resistance noticeably. The father-son clash is itself an indication that the questions at issue are creating tension and that society is in transition. The government is attempting to speed the process of transition and to make it smoother. For instance, a few years ago young boys and girls were never shown together on the TV screen as playing or taking part in folk dances. But gradually this was achieved and today it is accepted without protest except by the most rigid *ulama.* (Oddly enough, the word *ulama* is the plural of *a'alim* which literally means a man of science. In the Saudi context, these are religious judges.) The accommodation to which we have just referred takes the form of some mental adjustments and manoeuvres, but also some external manifestations. Thus an educated and travelled Saudi, Sudanese or Iraqi, who eats with fork and knife like any European in a restaurant, eats with his fingers when at home; the same applies to the clothing that the Kuwaiti, Sudanese or Saudi wears abroad and at home, where he shifts from one to another easily and without embarrassment.

In trying to identify the most appealing status symbols, in order to determine which among them relate to developmental values, we found three matters of interest. First, that there were symbols that satisfied prestige urges, others power urges, and that differentiation characterised different persons and groups. Second, that there is strong class and group differentiation, not only in the identification of the symbols, but more so in ranking them. Third, that there is a large measure of agreement among the different countries, though here again there was a difference in the ranking.

With this last point in mind, it becomes easier to arrange the list of status symbols cited. The items included education, particularly where a profession is involved (a handle to one's name, a title, like Doctor, Maître or lawyer, Engineer); competence or acknowledged excellence in some technical skill; the holding of high office in government; serving as an officer in the army; substantial land ownership in those countries where land reform has not created near-equalisation; being a large businessman, particularly a banker or an industrialist or company president or director, and in Lebanon being a large merchant or importer/ exporter; and, above all, being a Minister in the Cabinet, and better still, the Prime Minister or the President.

Among labourers, it was frequently stated that making a (relatively) high income through vocational skill was a cherished status symbol. In the poor countryside of Sudan a bicycle was such a symbol, but generally TV sets with their proud aerials, radios, Western furniture, and certainly a car are highly esteemed symbols. Likewise, throwing big parties and lavish hospitality, going on pilgrimage, and being able to maintain a second, third, or even fourth wife were cause for esteem. (However, having more than one wife now draws as much sympathy as it stirs envy or generates esteem.) Finally, in spite of the social upheavals in most of the countries examined, and the circulation of the élites, there is still some glamour attaching to the descendants or scions of formerly well-established and prestigious families. For our purposes here, however, what matters is that many of the esteemed status symbols relate to education and the acquisition of technical and professional skills, and to the ownership or control of major economic establishments. This is no doubt of relevance to economic growth. But, unless other symbols relating to or revealing respect for public service and concern for social issues gain wide currency, the status symbols will continue to reflect a much greater emphasis on personal achievement than on societal service and public-spiritedness, and therefore on development.

In asking questions regarding the system of authority and the locus and causes for authority in the family structure, we were interested in identifying those components of the rationale for authority which are of value to the drive for development. In general, the findings show a loosening of the older system which underlined seniority. Furthermore, they show that the young now increasingly choose careers independently, without prior approval of their seniors. However, the shaking of the system of authority, in the family as in larger social structures, is not creating excessive dislocation and tension; the Arab talent for mutual accommodation has permitted a smooth transition. The loss of harmony or identity between role and status has not resulted in the creation of an inordinately large number of misfits, destructive rebels, or psychopathic cases. Four factors have helped the loosening of the system rather smoothly and speedily: education, the emancipation of women (even if partial), military service, and the active drive for development. The last factor has created skills and responsibilities which the seniors could hardly have a say or offer advice about.

Perhaps one quotation sums up the process neatly. One respondent, referring to the leading member of the leading merchant family in his country — a man with intelligence, charm and capability — said: 'Mr X's views used to be respectfully accepted without question; now, they are respectfully challenged when necessary.'

The investigation of the degree of social mobility started from the assumption that high mobility provides scope and opportunity for upgrading and satisfaction of personal ambition; it therefore enhances motivation and development. The field-work and research undertaken showed the need to differentiate between social and economic mobility, and the greater scope for the latter, generally speaking. However, the two are not non-communicating, since climbing the economic ladder almost invariably opens the doors of social influence and prestige. This is a universal tendency, the difference being in the speed with which economic influence gets translated into social or even political influence and power.

The degree of mobility was found to vary from one country to another, and from one social group to another in the same country. It was highest in urban centres, in the middle class, particularly in the business community, but lowest in the countryside and among the tribes. Although tribal society has few rigid formalities, and the tribesman calls the tribal chief by his first name (indeed, in Kuwait and Saudi Arabia this used to be the practice with the Ruler and the King until very recently), yet the place of the various tribes *vis-à-vis* each other is assigned in a solidified pattern, as is the place of individuals within the clan and the tribe. The rigidity reflects itself in limited marriage. But, more importantly in the present context, it reflects itself in the activities which it is considered correct for the tribe as a subsociety to undertake, and those which it is not, and further in those activities that a man may undertake and those which he may not unless he chooses to run away from social opprobrium. With these observations in mind, it can be seen that the countries with large tribal or semi-tribal groups show a low level of mobility, particularly as tribal values spill over into the villages and towns long after tribesmen settle to sedentary life.

Lebanon, Algeria, Tunisia, Egypt, Syria, Iraq, Jordan and Kuwait are all countries where mobility is assessed as very high today, leaving apart the exceptions made in the last paragraph where they apply. Morocco and Libya fall in an intermediate position, and Sudan and Saudi Arabia at the other extreme. However, two qualifications of significance have to be made. The first is that even in Saudi Arabia remarkable mobility has begun to be seen; the present Cabinet has a majority of commoners. The second qualification is that the path of mobility has two lanes; thus, those countries which have opted for a socialist transformation, and in which far-reaching circulation of élites and leaderships has been witnessed, present the paradox of removal of social and economic blocks, but imposition of political blocks. The latter can be and often are very limiting to mobility. The imposition is effected on grounds of suspicion of insufficient allegiance by certain groups or individuals, not of insufficient competence.

Four factors have been said to enhance mobility: education, universal service in the national army, development, and emancipation of women, even if partial. Again here, as in the case of the loosening of the traditional system of authority, the energetic drive for development has contributed to the speeding and easing of mobility, inasmuch as it opens numerous and vast opportunities for income and advancement, and that erodes the resistance to economic and social mobility. The values of most of the ruling groups also enhance mobility, since equality is preached incessantly, and the mass media of communication give the theme of equality continued support and diffusion.

These findings, and the causes behind them, can all be seen to serve the cause of development. But once again it has to be emphasised that the values behind mobility, or motivation for that matter, cannot be invested in the service of development unless they have a social content. In other words, mobility which merely permits self-seeking ends and interests may lead to economic growth, but not to mass-oriented development. The point hardly needs further elaboration.

4. OIL AND ARAB ECONOMIC CO-OPERATION AS DETERMINANTS

The growth of the oil and gas sector in the five major oil-producing and -exporting countries has been traced in the country chapters of Volume I. Likewise, the record and modalities of Arab economic co-operation in the thirty years 1945-75 have been critically presented and analysed in Chapter 14 of Volume I, when development was assessed within its regional framework. The role and function of oil in this framework was also assessed. What is left to be undertaken in this section — and this will be done as briefly as possible — is to specify more concretely how oil can be a determinant of development both at the country and the regional levels; how economic co-operation can also be such a determinant for each of the countries involved, and for all of them as a larger community; and how oil can contribute to the intensification and the spread of co-operation and complementarity and thus to development.

It remains to be said that we shall use the term 'oil' to mean hydrocarbons, namely oil and gas in whatever combination they abound, and the term 'co-operation' to include all forms of joint economic action purporting to enhance complementarity, co-operation proper, joint projects, programmes or institutions, and all forms of supranational activity moving in the direction of ultimate integration and Arab economic unity.[85] While the discussion of co-operation has so far seemed to take for granted that co-operation is beneficial to the parties engaged in it, in this section there will be some attempt to justify co-operation, especially as a factor for development. Finally, the reader's indulgence is requested if parts of this section sound so close to parts of Chapter 14 of Volume I that they seem repetitive. This is only on the surface. For, basically Chapter 14 examined the situation actually in existence, while here we are concerned with the course co-operation ought to take if it is to be influential in development. The normative or suggestive tone of the present section is explicit, while it was largely implicit in Chapter 14.

The discussion of oil will first turn to the manner in which this resource can and does serve the society, and how its service can be considerably extended to turn it into a very powerful determinant of far-reaching and profound development. In the second place, the discussion will draw attention to serious pitfalls into which some of the benefits of the resource can fall and get irretrievably lost, if care is not taken by the Arab countries to protect the resource and optimise its usefulness.[86]

(a) The first and ongoing aspect of service of the oil resource is as a major source of revenue to the state, whether this revenue is used at home for economic and social development, for the support of the current budget, or for transmission to the public at large through the first two uses or through other direct or indirect mechanisms. In some countries, notably Kuwait and Libya, a policy of large-scale land purchase from the public has been one such mechanism, while free or subsidised public services and welfare benefits have been another. Abroad, oil can be beneficially used to help the development of other countries, Arab, Third World, or advanced industrial, or yet to help the international economy in moments and areas of stress.

(b) All the oil countries, but in varying degrees of seriousness, determination and effectiveness have used the oil resource and the oil concessionary companies to enhance the technical skills of their nationals engaged in the sector. But what they can and should now achieve in this field is enormously more, as a result of the extension of national sovereignty over oil resources and the control and management of the sector, the maturing of the institutional framework for such control and management, the accelerated drive for training in general and in oil in particular, and the much greater need for trained manpower arising from the exercise of control and management and the vertical integration of the various industries and activities in the sector.

(c) Closely related to the area of training is another which is both a prominent aspect and a determinant of development. This is education, both in general, and of specific categories which are critical for development. Earlier investigation of education in different contexts has revealed that the oil countries have directed considerable resources to education. But now, and for many years to come, the intensification of the effort will be possible, both in horizontal extension and in vertical deepening. Obviously, financial resources are not the only constraint to such intensification; other constraints are manpower and time. Nothing much can be done to cut time requirements short in the training of teachers, foremen, physicians, engineers or economists. However, the number of men and women to be trained as trainers and as trainees can be considerably increased now.

(d) When the oil sector was being controlled and run by foreign concessionary companies, its 'example or demonstration effect' was rather limited. This was because of the alienation inside which the sector was isolated, and its very advanced and complicated technology and organisation, which placed it well beyond the reach of national establishments in the sense that it did not act as a source of inspiration and a model to emulate. This is not to say that many small businessmen, workshops and technicians did not engage in business with the oil companies, get ideas from association with them, or receive decisive encouragement by them. It is only to underline the limited nature of the example effect of the oil companies. However, the situation is now quite different on almost every level, with the sector nationalised, its management and control Arabised to a considerable extent, and its alienation removed. This does not mean that the technology of the various operations associated with oil, from prospecting all the way to the manufacture of petrochemicals, is any less complicated: indeed, with the greater recourse to refining and the petrochemicals, greater complexity in the technology and in organisation has been introduced. Yet much of the manpower involved in these many operations is national, and the sector has pulled down the Chinese Wall that used to keep out the business community around it. The oil and the non-oil sectors are now intercommunicating compartments as they never were before.

(e) This indeed means that oil can further contribute to development through closer integration with the rest of the economy. The integration is being achieved not merely indirectly through the example effect to which reference has just been made, but directly as well through the introduction of more activities related to oil and gas. These fall into two categories: first, surveys and prospecting, drilling, pipeline installation, production, export, refining, and the manufacture of petrochemicals, which are all parts of the oil sector 'family' of activities and industries, and secondly, other activities and industries to which the oil sector is related through backward or forward linkage. There is hardly any sector or major area of economic activity in the non-oil part of the economy of an oil country which is not influenced by the oil sector — from banking to education or furniture-making and transport.

(f) At the institutional level, the oil sector has created pressure for sophisticated organisation to emerge in the various oil countries. This has been necessary in order for these countries to have the mechanisms and authorities capable of handling the new, extended and complex operations involved. Whether with respect to the management of surveys and prospecting, or of export, or yet of price and volume determination, and whether in feasibility studies or research — in all these aspects the need has been great, and is still growing, for modern, efficient and large organisations. Many of these have emerged, ranging from the highly integrated and self-assured Sonatrach of Algeria, down to the newest and still hesitant restructuring and reorganisation of the Oil Ministry in Kuwait upon the nationalisation of the oil companies in March 1975. The development of organisation in the oil sector proper is an important developmental step, but this further promotes modernisation of organisation in other sectors that have to deal with oil authorities.

(g) The oil sector is becoming increasingly qualified to operate as 'the leading' sector in development, in the Rostovian sense of the term. Not only is it an engine of development, but it is destined to be a leader among the sectors in activating the process of development. The human and political factors apart (to which we attach a special significance as direct, prime movers), it is the oil sector that is the central engine of development in the oil countries. This can be clearly seen in or ascertained from the many aspects in which oil can contribute to development, as our discussion has attempted to show. No other one sector occupies such a central position and diffuses its influence as strongly and as far out.

(h) The oil sector can further contribute to long-term development by enabling the oil and other Arab countries to co-operate in the search for alternate sources of energy. This might sound paradoxical or self-defeating for the sector. Yet brief consideration of the wastefulness of burning the 'noble resource' of oil and gas as fuel, while it can be put to much more beneficial *and* remunerative use in the manufacture of fertilisers, proteins, and the many hundreds of other petrochemical products, will show that the search for alternate uses of energy is at least as urgent for the oil-producing as for the oil-consuming countries. The former will be better advised to economise in the depletion of their hydrocarbon resource in order to have it in adequate quantities when they reach a higher level of industrialisation, not just (or not mainly) as a fuel but as industrial feedstock. To export the bulk of the oil presently produced as crude is inimical to the current interests of the Arab oil producers, but almost suicidal for the long run. It must be added that the Arab contribution to the search for alternate sources of energy must not be merely financial. Arab scientists must be involved in the search, and to the extent possible, part of the research must be located in the Arab world. The relevance of this search for development is evident.

The discussion so far conducted has concentrated on the main aspects of the contribution of the hydrocarbons resource to development. No reference will be made here to the role of oil in increasing the capability of the Arab countries to defend themselves and to protect their national security and sovereignty. This aspect is related to development, in the sense that defence capability is necessary for safeguarding the national economies, including oil, in an explosive region, parts of which are under Israeli occupation. However, as the point was discussed in Chapter 14 of Volume I, no further space will be devoted to it here. As far as development proper is concerned, we need only say by way of summing up that as a determinant of development, if wisely used, oil can be useful in two major ways. It can speed the process whereby alternative sources of income can be developed that in due course will substitute for oil when it is largely depleted. And it can also speed the process of the industrialisation of hydrocarbons proper, and promote the education and training of manpower at large. This is the most significant service which oil can contribute to development; it distils all the other services that have been emphasised.

Yet oil is not an unmixed blessing; it can be abused and misused, and the policies governing its handling (whether as a physical or a financial resource) can be dangerous and detrimental to development, both in the shorter and the longer run. Indeed, a quick look at the present will be sufficient to establish the point. However, we will not examine the other side of the coin of oil which is far from bright, since we have had occasion in the last chapter, though within the framework of a general discussion, to emphasise some of the serious oversights, misconceptions, or wrong foci of Arab development. Likewise, we have referred to oil and Arab development more concretely in Chapter 14 of Volume I, where the dangers of the present use of oil were examined. All we need do here is to underline the point that oil, this most valuable national and regional resource, suffers serious dissipation and wastage, partly because of excessive production and fast depletion for the low-priority purpose of its use as a fuel; partly because of the insufficiently thought-out and prepared development plans for which oil revenues are being used; partly because of massive wasteful consumption which the volume of these revenues permits and even encourages; and partly because of the rather heedless rush to conclude contracts for machines and technical help at exorbitantly inflated prices and with insufficient consideration for the appropriateness of the technology imported. The hastiness is all the more deplorable since many of the contracts cannot be fulfilled owing to the low execution capability of the oil countries.

These negative aspects of the otherwise beneficial availability of oil and gas, important as they are, remain probably of less significance than some other aspects. At the local (national) level, these include the misconception of the notion of development whereby the process remains focused on the achievement of a high rate of growth while the direct and tangible needs of the masses remain largely unsatisfied; the insufficient devotion of resources and attention to the development of science and technology at home, so that the national capability to sustain overall development and to contribute to education and science can be substantially enhanced; and the misdirected overseas investment policies which, arguably, fall short of optimising the allocation of resources if compared with policies placing greater emphasis on investment in the Arab region at large. In addition to the insufficient allocation of investment funds for economic and social development in the non-oil countries (Arab and Third World as well), there is the fragmented, *ad hoc* approach to much of whatever investment is undertaken. There is no need to devote more space to these negative aspects, which we have described as the 'other side of the oil coin' that is largely overlooked in the generally facile self-congratulation on the large national fortune made out of oil. This fortune constitutes 'the bright side of the coin'. Instead, focus will be directed later in the section on the positive aspects and potential of oil in development. But, while emphasis has so far been on national development, later on it will be on regional development, or more precisely, on the promotive role of oil in extending and deepening regional co-operation, and how this co-operation in turn acts as a determinant of national development.

It is logical, then, to turn presently to an examination of how co-operation can itself be a determinant of national development, apart from its promotive function of regional development if the region were to achieve a true measure of concrete unity. The examination will not be undertaken in detail; as in the case of the discussion of oil some headings will be cited and enlarged upon in the briefest manner.

(a) The first such heading is the widening of the market made possible through multi-lateral trade and payments arrangements under the Council for Arab Economic Unity (CAEU) and the Arab League in general, or under bilateral arrangements. To the extent that such arrangements lead to an expansion and facilitation of trade, and to the provision of scope for new products (and services), they promote expansion in production or the initiation of new lines of production in the exporting countries.

(b) Obviously, the mere widening of the market will lead to greater competitiveness among producers. Admittedly, the exposure will hurt many establishments, but it will also strengthen others and provide a motive for cost-reduction and more efficient operation. The hard-core cases of incurability will call for a policy of reallocation of capital or gradual liquidation, as the European Community provided in its formative years. Such a policy assumes the existence of some central body to take the compensatory and other measures necessary, and the power to act in this manner. The CAEU is the authority most qualified for the task. What is of direct interest at the present moment is that the advantages to be reaped from the widening of the market should in the aggregate far exceed the damage sustained by some. No studies have been undertaken around this point; all we can venture is the deduction that the balance of the account will be distinctly positive, especially if we take into consideration that even the weak establishments will find in the expanding economies of the region a greater opportunity either to achieve healthiness, or to move into other lines of production.

(c) Co-operation will provide substantial advantages of scale. This is true of the production of goods and services as it is of the joint undertaking of research in the natural and social sciences, of the promotion of technology, and of the joint establishment of specialised institutions of higher learning and of professional and technical training. The case is all the stronger for those goods that are highly similar, whose current fragmented production raises unit costs unduly and which will therefore benefit from an enlargement of the producing entities, and of those areas of research and training relating to similar problems which had better be approached jointly. As illustrations of the latter, we may list agriculture in arid zones; training in the skills needed in the wide range of activities associated with the oil and gas sector; and financial and monetary management necessitated by the vast expansion in the volume of resources without a comparable expansion in the region's money markets.

(d) Complementarity is another important area of co-operation. This is most obvious in the development of a petrochemical industry, where there is currently a great deal of duplication. This is associated with insufficient concern with marketing once the potential of the various establishments is translated into actual production, high overhead costs of fragmented research and management, and the inflationary effect of competition for the services of the limited supply of trained manpower. The complementarity can take the form of vertical integration whereby one country can produce at one stage in the chain or process, leaving other stages to other countries, or else it can take the form of complete, integrated production of one product in one country and other products in other countries. Both forms involve deliberate division of labour, but the first is restricted to one process or product within an integrated industry, while the second involves the location of one integrated industry or activity in one country and of another in another country. The illustrations of possible complementarity go much beyond industries in the sector of hydrocarbons, to cover the metallurgical and engineering, textile, power and other industries, as well as professional and technical training. Here again there is very pressing need for the examination of the areas, modalities and benefits of specialisation and complementarity, and a strong *prima facie* case for co-operation in the service of national development.

(e) External economies on a regional level can also be achieved through co-operation. The argument for such economies at the one-economy level can be extended to the region. External economies can be realised both via the widening of the market and the resultant expansion in the scale of production, and specialisation and complementarity. Thus, many lines of production of goods and services, and of research and training which are too large and expensive for any one country can become appropriate on a regional co-operative scale. Once established on such a scale, they make possible and economical the initiation of allied or related industries and activities whose initiation would otherwise have made neither good sense nor good economics for any one country by itself. Illustrations of such possibilities abound in the sectors of power, transport, communications, agriculture, industry, science and technology – in short, in most aspects of economic life.

(f) The free or less restricted mobility of capital and manpower constitutes another beneficial fruit of co-operation. We have had occasion to see that such mobility has risen in the post-war period, but particularly in recent years. But the need for yet greater mobility is very pressing, now that the region has entered a phase of accelerated economic and educational expansion thanks to the new oil situation. A more even distribution of capital and trained manpower across national frontiers has obvious advantages to surplus and deficit countries alike.

(g) The improvement in the pattern of distribution has one aspect of particular importance. This is the absorption of a larger proportion of the financial resources of the large oil-producing and -exporting countries in the region itself, rather than the diversion of the bulk of these resources to the money markets of Western industrial countries. Such diversion carries with it some serious dangers to the national economies and to the region as a whole. Foremost among these dangers are the devaluation of the leading currencies, the depreciation of the value of the money placed in Western banks or in securities, and the growing tendency for the Arab oil countries involved to become *rentier* societies relying heavily on interest and dividends, instead of becoming partners in the development programmes and projects in the region's countries. Such a partnership can involve direct participation in production, in formulas calling for the co-operation of manpower as well as capital from the countries concerned.

(h) Finally, economic co-operation, which demonstrably leads to the interlocking of the region's economies and paves the way to integration, with what that means in benefits to all countries involved, further enhances co-operation tendencies outside the realm of economics. Thanks to the creation of a better climate of intra-regional co-operation, a larger measure of co-ordination can become possible in the cultural, social and political realms, with a reduction of the wasteful frictions and misunderstandings characterising the Arab world of today. The cause of development, with which we are primarily concerned in the present context, cannot but benefit substantially as a result.

The discussion has so far dealt, even if briefly, with the role of oil, and of co-operation, as a determinant of development. What remains to be pointed out is the role of oil in such co-operation, and the resulting promotive influence of this role in development. This sequence deserves special consideration, now that it has become manifest that the few years of increased oil revenues have led to much greater co-operation than the preceding post-war decades. The snail-like slowness of the course of co-operation before 1973 is already well-known to us, and its main causes have been outlined in Chapter 14 of Volume I. In contrast, it is currently observable that there is much greater dynamism and decisiveness in the realm of co-operation, although this co-operation mainly takes the form of jointly financed projects, more than anything else. Whether under the aegis of the Council for Arab Economic Unity or the Organization for Arab Petroleum Exporting Countries, or independently of both organisations as in the case of joint banks, an impressive number of joint Arab projects with an enormous aggregate capital have come into existence in the past few years. The Arab Fund for Economic and Social Development has also begun to be active in promoting such joint projects.

It is still too early to undertake a meaningful assessment of the effectiveness of such co-operation as a determinant of development, although obviously it is beneficial. But co-operation can be beneficial in depth, not just marginally as it still is. An honest appraisal of its impact will show that it is modest, considering the size and population of the region, and of the potential for true co-operation. Yet it is significant that some wide strides have been taken, firmly and speedily, in recent years. This in itself has promise.

However, for co-operation to be of much greater benefit to the national and the regional development, many more areas of co-operation have to be involved, and several modalities other than jointly financed projects have to be tried. Manpower participation in the joint projects has to be promoted; the flow of manpower across national frontiers has to be not just permitted but encouraged; joint educational and research undertakings have to be launched; but above all, a joint vision of development leading to the formulation of one Arab strategy and the necessary policies is essential.

The place of oil in this whole process is central. It provides the means that can be applied to the possibilities and opportunities. The flow of oil resources in the region in much greater volume will reduce disparities by helping speed development in the capital-hungry countries without retarding it in the capital-surplus countries. It will also permit a movement in the opposite direction of skilled manpower from certain capital-receiving countries such as Egypt, Lebanon or Jordan, to capital-surplus countries like Saudi Arabia, Libya or Kuwait — to say nothing of those oil countries which are not included in this study, like Abu Dhabi and Qatar. Indeed, the abundance of financial resources in Saudi Arabia, Libya and Kuwait can itself create pressures for the search for investment opportunities in the capital-deficit countries. The search now leads to investment by one country in another, as well as to projects jointly financed by two or more countries, for the benefit of one, or more than one, country. These forms of investment and variations of them have to be encouraged. But if oil and co-operation are to act as strong determinants they must lead to the emergence of many forms of joint action and to complementarity, in as many sectors as possible; likewise, emphasis must increasingly be placed on projects the beneficiary of which is not just one country but several, or the community of Arab countries as a whole.

For this idealised vision to materialise, the harnessing of oil in the service of greater co-operation, and the moulding of co-operation to involve the energies of Arabs from different countries, not just their surplus capital, must proceed from a clear vision of the benefit and necessity of co-operation and the understanding that co-operation is as beneficial to the creditor as to the recipient. It must also proceed within well-considered channels and modalities deriving from careful formulation of joint plans and policies. To say this is to emphasise the central point that for oil and co-operation to become a powerful determinant of development, there must first emerge a strong and sincere political will to co-operate. Such a will is taking its first steps now.

5. TOWARDS AN UNDERSTANDING OF THE PROCESS OF DEVELOPMENT

This is the last section of the chapter. It is also the most speculative in an already speculative chapter. The tentativeness of the discussion in the four earlier sections called for hesitation and qualification; by its nature, the present section, which sets out to draw some overall conclusions, calls in addition to a great deal of caution. The tentative conclusions — and we will have to bear in mind all along that they are thus qualified, although the qualifying adjective will not be repeated — relate to single determinants or to clusters of determinants and to all of them collectively in interaction. Likewise, the conclusions will comprise an attempt to highlight the more important individual determinants in each of the clusters. The differentiation among determinants or clusters in their operation will also be related to different phases or levels of development.

Finally, an attempt will be made to understand the process of development as it has unfolded (or as it is here thought to have unfolded) in the post-war years in the Arab world in response to the impact of the various determinants. The qualifying words 'Arab world' and 'post-war years' are not accidental to the preceding sentence. They are there to prepare the reader's mind in advance to the very final conclusion of the chapter relating to the question whether there is one general theory or system of thought which can explain the process of development for all countries and all time.

The concluding section will probably look short for a very long chapter. But this is deliberate, for two reasons. The first is the fact that the four preceding sections on clusters of determinants have all had their own conclusions, leaving little need for a renewed attempt to draw partial inferences from the discussion. The second is that precisely because the chapter is long, it has been thought advisable to word the overall conclusions as briefly as possible, in order to bring them into sharper focus.

1. The first conclusion that derives from the discussion in this chapter is that it is extremely difficult to distinguish between what determines and what is determined in the present context. There have been occasions when this point was emphasised, with the specific warning that the emergence of some of the determinants listed in the last chapter (or others of the same general nature) is itself an indication that development is taking place. We feel that this objection is unavoidable, merely because in the nature of the case the cause and effect become confused owing to the interdependence between them. This sort of complaint about factors of development, or stages of development as in the Rostovian scheme of thought, has been of long standing. It probably cannot be escaped.

Perhaps it would be wisest for students of the problem to keep reminding themselves that they are here face to face with a case of interdependence, where the determined and the determinant influence each other, and where the determined often takes the shape of the determinant, or else comes into being as the determinant comes into operation. Education, acceptance of technological change and mobility influence the course of development; yet their materialisation in itself can be said to denote development or to be accelerated by it. However, in spite of the 'chicken-and-egg' relationship obvious here, for presentation purposes development can be said to be the effect or determined, and education, acceptance of technological change and mobility to be the determinants.

To say this is not to deny the difficulty of identifying the function of each, in view of the interchangeability of functions. This very difficulty has led Irma Adelman and Cynthia Taft Morris to use the method of factor analysis in their admirable study, to which we have referred on several occasions. This method does not treat one variable (or a set of variables) as dependent, and the other as independent, but both in effect as dependent on each other or as interdependent, although in the underpinning of analysis, as in the conclusion, it is clear that development is the dependent variable, or the determined, and the other factors or indicators are the independent (or more independent) variables, or the determinants.

While emphasising the element of interdependence and interaction, we are not measuring its extent here. In fact, the methodology adopted in this study — unlike the technique of factor analysis — does not permit quantified measurement. The utmost that can be attempted is to indicate the fact of interaction and to rank the different degrees of interaction as between one determinant and another, or between clusters of determinants.

To make the point regarding interdependence and interaction which is the focus of these few paragraphs is not an end in itself. The purpose goes beyond the formalistic 'giving notice' of the awareness by the writer of the interaction between development and its determinants. In fact, it is intended here to emphasise that in the final analysis development is much more than a mere rise in national income per head in real terms. It goes beyond this over-simplified and -simplistic indicator to include many other indicators, as was particularly shown in the last chapter. The determinants examined in this chapter are among those indicators. To record this point is to lead to the confusion that has been described, inasmuch as the 'indicators', by their very nature, speed the process of development *and* constitute components of it. Were the content of development to be much simpler and narrower, the confusion would not arise.

2. The first conclusion must be stated, but we can go further. The convention is here suggested that once the interdependence between what is determined and what determines has been pointed out, it must not be referred to again. Instead, from here on development must be taken as the determined, so that the other conclusions to follow may be presented in greater clarity and without equivocation.

The second of these is that the determinants within each cluster vary widely with respect to their power to influence the course of development. The variation arises essentially from the content of each of the determinants and the manner in which they operate. There has thus been repeated insistence, occasioned by the foregoing analysis, that the determinants fall into categories, three of which can be recognised according to one possible system of categorisation. One is that of prime movers, or determinants properly speaking, in the sense that they operate on other economic (and socio-political) forces in society and bring about behaviour of a developmental nature or consequence. The second is that of supplementary or supportive determinants, which are factors or influences that come into operation after other factors of stronger impact have been active, or after direct and powerful determinants (of the type described here as prime movers) have been in action. The coming into operation of this second category depends largely on the operation of the first. The third category can be called framework or 'platform' determinants. These are generally of an institutional nature and create the climate for the operation of the prime movers and for the usability of supportive determinants.

Some illustrations can make the point clearer. The first category includes, *par excellence,* factors involving human will and the power to determine the course of things. It is trite to assert that behaviour in the present context is primarily human behaviour, and that it is men acting within institutions or frameworks of power and authority, that can take decisions of developmental significance. The determinants that answer to these specifications are primarily the developmental orientation and commitment of the political leadership (in the political-administrative cluster), entrepreneurship and management, and less so manpower in a broader sense (in the economic cluster), and motivation (in the socio-cultural cluster). The last-named determinant is not the only one that can be selected out of its cluster; some of the agents of change were found to be of special power, including the political leadership and the middle class. However, the former manifests its influence mainly through the commitment to development of the political leadership which has already been singled out for prominence, and the latter includes as a most important component the entrepreneurs and top executives — a factor which has also been singled out.

The second category of supportive determinants includes primarily capital availability and the resource base. Of paramount significance in the resource base are the hydrocarbon resources, although the notion of the resource base is wider and more comprehensive and comprises other minerals, and land and water. However, it was found in the analysis that oil is by far the most important resource, except perhaps for Morocco and Jordan (and to a lesser extent Tunisia) where phosphates have in recent years emerged as a major resource and developmental factor. In the political and administrative cluster of determinants, there is primarily the civil service and the role of the public sector. Finally, the socio-cultural cluster has four determinants of nearly equal significance, but with education standing out and social mobility and acceptance of technological change following in importance. (The role of agents of change has been commented on already.)

The third category of framework or institutional determinants includes agrarian reform, Arab economic co-operation, and other basic institutional changes of relevance and significance in the economic cluster, the planning institutions and process, as well as broad participation and political stability in the political-administrative cluster, and possible acceptance of technological change in the socio-cultural cluster. Although the last factor has been listed as a supportive determinant, it can also be viewed as a framework determinant, as it relates to a certain climate or atmosphere conducive to development.

We realise the categories are not water-tight, particularly the second and third, which are more difficult to distinguish between than the first on the one hand and the second and third on the other. But the differentiation undertaken here is rather helpful because it clarifies our views and helps us understand the priorities among the determinants with respect to their operation. These priorities will become yet clearer towards the end of the chapter.

3. Closely related to the question of categorisation and the singling out of certain determinants as being more active and more directly operative than others is the question of the relationship between the socio-economic system in force and the influence of the determinants. Thus the development orientation and commitment of the political leadership, which is an operative and strong factor in *any* system, is definitely more so in one where the public sector broadly defined plays a significant role in directing the economy and making the basic investment decisions in it, as well as other decisions relating to education and training, planning, resource development, and the like. One other aspect of the relevance of the socio-economic system is the degree of centralisation in decision-making in society and the extent of popular political participation which is possible and is actually exercised. The scope for entrepreneurial talent in particular and for the middle class to press for development in general, like the extent to which economic motivation operates as a driving force, all relate to the type of economic and social system in force.

It is definitely not implied here that under a system of socialism or state capitalism all the economic decisions are made by the government or some other central body. Nor is it implied that the economic motivation acting on entrepreneurs and manpower in general is totally absent, having been replaced by some form of social motivation expressing primarily responsiveness to the needs of the masses, not the private profit. Things are not that clear-cut or easily divisible into black and white. It is common knowledge that there is a great deal of ambivalence and overlapping of systems, and this is particularly true of the Arab countries, socialist and capitalist alike. Indeed, to cite these categories thus without qualification immediately draws protest, because neither system exists in pure form anywhere, and less so in the countries that form the focus of our study. Nevertheless, as we have attempted to show elsewhere, each of the twelve countries has predominant features or a predominantly socialist or capitalistic flavour that permits us to classify it under the one or other category. It is with this in mind that we looked at the determinants in operation to see how they related to one system as against another.

The differentiation in this context which has been suggested is one of degree or nuance, not a basic one. Thus, as indicated already, the leadership's commitment to development is of paramount significance in either system (or in the mixed system, for that matter). However, it remains to be added, by way of qualification, that the force of this determinant, or its relevance, is stronger in a system of socialism or *étatisme*. Again, motivation remains economic, and the profit motive remains highly operative, in whatever system is selected for illustration in the Arab world. But, as a qualifying observation, it can be added that this motive is tempered by some consideration of mass needs in the capitalist, private enterprise system; while the predominance of the motive of the satisfaction of mass needs in the socialist system is also tempered by some consideration of profitability.

Furthermore, in all the capitalist countries except Kuwait and Lebanon, regardless of type of system, the populace enjoys very little political participation. Even in Lebanon, the true measure of participation is being increasingly questioned owing to the gross distortion of popular will in elections. On the other hand, Algeria, which does not have a parliamentary system in the sense ordinarily understood, and Tunisia which claims to be socialist, both permit a measure of participation that is certainly not experienced in most capitalist Arab countries. The illustrations can be extended and amplified, but this is hardly necessary. We can therefore end with the conclusion that there is some nuance or differentiation between the operation of certain determinants in the framework of one social system as against another, but that the differentiation is not substantial, in view of the overlapping of systems and the absence of 'pure type' systems that conform to the textbook model in its extremism of either socialism or free-enterprise capitalism.

4. Yet another generalisation to make is that the clusters of determinants come into prominence in their operation at different moments in the growth history of countries. Expressed differently, the impact of the economic, political-administrative and socio-cultural clusters is felt more at one phase or stage of development than another. However, the range of influence is not open-ended; that is, it does not fade to zero or nearly so at the lower end or rise to infinity or nearly so at the other. Our research suggests that there is some flexibility between a lower and an upper end, but that the span is not very wide. This is to say that the development orientation of the political leadership may become less significant at a higher level of growth and development, or that capital availability may be less of a constraining factor at a lower than a higher level, but that the differentiation in impact between one phase and another is one of small degree.

It is necessary to specify here. Important as it is for all stages of phases of development, the factor of leadership commitment to development is distinctly more crucial and critical at a lower than at a higher level of development. This is probably because at the higher level many centres of economic decision-making, both in the public and the private sector, would have emerged and gained experience and confidence, thus reducing somewhat the economy's dependence on the political leadership for developmental decisions. The same applies to political stability or the civil service, or yet the role of the public sector in economic affairs. To generalise: the cluster of political-administrative determinants as a whole, though with variations among its components, is most critical and crucial at the lowest level of development or the very initial phase of its motion. The role remains crucial, as movement is registered from one phase to another beyond and higher, but at a reducing scale.

The research has also suggested that even the socio-cultural determinants, which are of great importance at the lower level of economic performance in so far as social and cultural constraints are very retarding factors then, do not occupy as critical and crucial a place as the political factors. Two explanations seem to us apposite here. The first is that the political authority is capable of providing or shaping the institutions, the incentives, the regulatory mechanisms, and above all the education and training which can on the one hand loosen the socio-cultural constraints and on the other hand promote the socio-cultural positive forces making for growth and development.

The second explanation is that political action can be undertaken more quickly and crisply, and political change in leadership and institutions can be effected more expeditiously than social action or social change. Since, additionally, the political leadership at a low level of economic performance and development enjoys unduly high prestige and great power, it can – if it is correctly oriented – bring about those changes and take those measures which are destined to influence the course of socio-cultural determinants in the direction desired. The opposite cannot be argued, since the much slower change in socio-cultural values and institutions will influence the political machinery and its decision-making capability almost imperceptibly and will therefore be unable to be the initiating force in the process of change and development. If we understand Adelman and Morris correctly in their conclusions, they reach the opposite conclusion, namely that the socio-cultural factors begin to operate effectively ahead of the political factors – or rather they act as constraints more seriously at a lower than at a higher level of development.[87] Our fieldwork, library research and observations suggest the opposite. One could subscribe to the proposition, or accept the conclusion, that the socio-cultural factors are more basic, more profoundly operative than political and administrative factors. But this is not to say that as factors operating in the process of development socio-cultural factors begin to have their effect felt ahead of their political counterparts. The opposite – it seems to us – is more understandable and tenable, and conforms much better to our research and observations.

But whatever place is assigned to the political as against the socio-cultural factors or determinants, there is no disagreement between our findings and those of Adelman and Morris with respect to economic determinants. These operate most strongly at a relatively more advanced level or phase of development. Arranged in the order of their operation with respect to phases, the clusters begin with the political-administrative, move on to the socio-cultural, and end with the economic. (In our categories, oil and Arab economic co-operation have been set apart for presentation, for reasons explained at the time. But they continue to belong to the economic cluster.)

Economic determinants become more critical as the economy's performance rises, or as certain political and socio-cultural conditions are satisfied. It is probably more conducive to clarity to talk in terms of conditions and their satisfaction. Thus, capital may be available in abundance, but if political stability and law and order are lacking, or the civil service is very corrupt and inefficient, or yet if motivation is low or seriously constrained, or training is at a minimal level, then the abundance of capital will be of little avail: much of this capital will remain sterile, or, worse still, will flee the country if it can. The same applies to the resource base, which will remain under-utilised if the political leadership or the civil service are incapable of taking the right decisions relevant to resource development and utilisation, or of applying the measures formulated for the purpose.

Illustrations can be multiplied, but will not add further strength to the point. What should be underlined, however, is that the defencelessness of economic factors, if the term may be applied, is little appreciated in the Western advanced industrial countries.

Unduly high significance is attached to the economic factors in development as having extreme potency. There is further an assumption that the economic horse pulls the political and socio-cultural carriage. What is being maintained here is that the economic horse indeed pulls the political and socio-cultural carriage, but *only after* the carriage has been got into shape to move, and has been pushed forward some distance. In other words, and in order not to belabour the metaphor, only when economic life gains some sophistication, and economic performance begins to become promising — namely when development begins to be in motion — do the economic factors begin to play their role in full. The presumption here is that by then the political and socio-cultural constraints would have been weakened or loosened and the promotive factors brought into action. As Adelman and Morris had found, the *homo economicus* does not make his entry on to the stage very early in the drama.[88] (Nevertheless, the economic forces are influential at *all* levels of development, and they help reshape the political as well as the socio-cultural forces and institutions, no less than these help reshape their economic counterparts.)

5. The attempt to determine the sequence in which each of the clusters of determinants has its turn to operate most effectively must not create the impression that any one cluster can be dispensed with for a period of time while the other clusters exert their influence. All the clusters operate all the time. They act on the economy and react to it; likewise, they act on and react to each other. In other words, there is continuous interaction among the clusters of determinants, and between them as one large group and the process of development. The interdependence and interaction between the factors or determinants and development is a point that has received some attention already. For instance, we are well aware that social mobility influences development, as development in turn influences the speed and directions of mobility. Likewise, education and training speed the course of development, and development enriches the quality of education and shapes its institutions and relocates its directions.

In the economic sphere, the infrastructure, like the resource base, is an important supportive determinant that provides the underpinning and some of the inputs called for by development, while development promotes the expansion of the resource base. Furthermore, the political management of the economy has a direct and strong influence on the exploitation of the resource base and on economic performance in general and the base and performance in turn can help the enlightenment and the rationality of the political management. Likewise, development and the structure of the market (especially its dualistic aspect) interact in a distinct manner, though the action of the former on the latter is stronger than that of the latter on the former. (The reader will recall that the monopolistic, like the dualistic structure, has a negative effect on development.) Finally, in the political field, participation and the broadening of the base of political decision-making serve the cause of development by widening interest in it and creating greater commitment to it, inasmuch as participation leads to commitment; yet at the same time development smooths the ground for greater participation and adds rationality to the process of decision-making. And so on for the other determinants.

However, it is not as widely recognised that the determinants influence and help each other. To start with, it must be indicated that no one determinant, no matter how important, is sufficient by itself to greatly influence the intensity and course of development. Furthermore, there is no one determinant among those we have examined, and probably many others which we have had to leave out of the analysis, that is not necessary for development. It can probably be accepted more readily that none is sufficient by itself, than that none is unnecessary. First thought might suggest that some determinants are of little or no import at one phase or another of development — say mobility, or Arab economic co-operation, or the civil service or planning. Yet a second look will show that while it is true that the degree of significance or decisiveness of one or more determinants might be low, it is never zero. And, what is more telling, none is irrelevant.

Yet as this is said, it ought also to be emphasised that the relevance might not be very obvious, or direct, or high at all times. But at one time or another, at one phase of development or another, each of the determinants is not only relevant but critical and highly influential. One determinant might seem to cause trouble in the present context: the agents of change. It was actually found during the field-work that some components were hardly influential in some of the countries. Yet, in every single country, at one or another phase of development, one or more of these agents was or had been in operation. It is with respect to the composite group that the assertion just made regarding relevance applies.

6. Oil and Arab economic co-operation deserve separate mention among our conclusions. Our analysis provided evidence that the oil resources have been a major instrument in the development of the oil countries themselves. It also provided evidence that until very recently, Arab co-operation has been of very little significance for the development of the individual Arab countries. However, these conclusions have to be adjusted to suit the situation of the early seventies. The adjustment will take two main directions.

First, oil has now come to be an important factor in the development of non-oil Arab countries. Though it is true that for several of these, capital transfers from oil countries still constitute a modest proportion of total resources directed to development, for a few others they constitute a large proportion. And, even for the first group, the capital transfer from oil countries is rising and expected to rise much higher. (The transfer is effected bilaterally or through joint Arab action. The latter is effected through the Arab Fund for Economic and Social Development, the Organization of Arab Petroleum Exporting Countries, the Council of Arab Economic Unity, or through other arrangements and mechanisms.)

Secondly, Arab economic co-operation has come to take a new reality, to become much more intensive, and to move along many new channels. Until the mid- or late 1960s, emphasis was mainly on the facilitation of trade among the members of the League of Arab States, and as a second thought on the easing of balance of payments problems. In neither area was the success striking, or even passable. The causes were numerous, and the more important among them were presented in Chapter 14 of Volume I. Indeed, the failure of Arab efforts at co-operation — the very slow and half-hearted trade facilitation measures, the many still-born projects that did not go beyond the stage of formation, if they left the drafting stage at all — was made more painful by the exaggeratedly ambitious modalities of co-operation adopted that — on paper — got well beyond co-operation. The arch-example of such incongruity was the Agreement of Arab Economic Unity. Total unity in effect was involved under the AAEU, yet in actual practice a shipment of tomatoes or house slippers could not be assured safe passage across Arab frontiers, and an Arab traveller could not be certain of not having to wait for hours at the frontier of a sister Arab country.

These and other inconsistencies still exist. But, there is alongside a much larger measure of true co-operation. This co-operation has gone beyond the facilitation of the movement of goods to include other forms. In fact, intra-regional trade is and will continue to remain for years to come a very small proportion of the region's trade with the rest of the world. Instead, the emphasis today is on complementarity, or the integration of many aspects of individual Arab economies inside a widening web of relations. The predominant form the process is taking is the joint project. Such a project may be a bank; an association of metallurgical industries; the integrated development of the agricultural sector in a major agricultural country like the Sudan; a housing scheme; a hotel industry; a pipeline; a corporation dealing in oil services, investment, tankerage or dry-docking; a training endeavour; a development fund, or finally an Arab Monetary Fund. This is by no means an exhaustive list of actual institutions. Even as an inventory of areas of co-operation, it is definitely incomplete, and is being made somewhat obsolete as it is being prepared.

One other prominent area that deserves mention is the growing volume of manpower crossing national frontiers to work in Arab countries not its own. Admittedly, visa, work and residence permits still consume an inordinately long time, but the demand and supply pressures are so strong that in spite of the delays, the number of Arab expatriates in the work-force of a number of oil countries is substantial. On the other hand, Arab capital is moving in much larger volume, and with fewer handicaps than ever before.

These new trends are of some significance for development in the oil and non-oil countries. It must be emphasised here that it is the newly increased oil revenues that have accelerated the move to greater complementarity. The conjuncture of oil and co-operation — the former widening and strengthening the latter — is beginning to become a powerful engine of development and has tremendous promise for the future if the trend of the past two or three years is maintained. If it is, then the region will witness close complementarity and a large measure of economic integration which all the solemn agreements and declarations of the past failed even to launch. But the propitious conjuncture of rising oil revenues and the drive for economic complementarity require a deliberate regional vision of and approach to development for the best results to ensue, rather than the fragmented, accidental and haphazard approach still characteristic of the region's behaviour.

7. Before we move on to the presentation of the final, overall lessons learnt from the study, we would like to make one more generalisation which is not restricted to any one cluster of determinants or phase of development, but rather to all of them together, and to the study as a whole. This is that the emerging picture is very complex, and that this complexity is the product of many factors. Thus, to begin with, the categories of determinants act with different rates of speed as we have indicated, with the socio-cultural determinants being on the whole the stickiest and slowest to act. Furthermore, within each category, the determinants also differ in the speed of their operation.

In the second place, these inherent different rates of speed and of effectiveness are superimposed on different levels of development. We have observed during the study that no one determinant maintains its rate of speed and effectiveness between one level of development and another. This superimposition of inherently different rates of speed of action on different levels of development produces a yet more complicated situation if the analysis moves from the short to the long run. Thus, one determinant may not seem to be operative within a short span of time, only to prove to be very powerful within a long enough period.

A third cause for complexity is the existence of different pulls by closely related determinants within the same cluster. The fact that certain determinants are political, socio-cultural or economic does not mean that they all move in the same direction or with the same force, or at the same time. Thus, planning may not exert a promotive influence before entry into a later stage of development, although the political category of determinants *on the whole* exerts its influence earlier on. Another illustration will make the point clearer. The fact that the emergence of effective mass media communication is important for political development, and that the media usually become effective only at a relatively high level of economic development (a point which Adelman and Morris make in their conclusions),[89] does not invalidate the finding we have reached in this study, namely that the political determinants operate at an early stage to put development in motion. The seeming contradiction can be explained in that what should be looked for is the *net effect* of various political determinants pulling at different points of time and with different degrees of force. If this net effect is focused on, it would be seen that the inference relating to the political category of determinants as a whole is borne out.

Having emphasised the complexity of the picture and the overlapping of its lines, it remains for us to say that what in the short run seems to be complex and confused is very likely to become clearer in the longer run, when the determinants are allowed more adequate time to operate. Furthermore, in the longer run and with development proceeding at a positive rate, intermingling and diffuseness between economic and social institutions and forces makes way for greater specialisation, and therefore for greater clarity and distinctness in roles and functions. This is another way of saying that as development proceeds, the economic forces acquire greater relevance and operate more forcibly, and the constraining effects of the socio-cultural and political factors become weaker. This in itself, but more so added to the greater resultant differentiation between the economic and non-economic forces and institutions, would permit a clearer reading of the functions and the impact of the different determinants.

8. An attempt has been made in this long chapter to see the determinants selected in the last chapter in operation. They were examined first as clusters placed in broad categories. In the present section we have undertaken to draw the most salient conclusions of the chapter, whether these related to single clusters, to the categories, or yet to the whole range.

In this very last part of the section, we will try to see what lessons can be learnt from the study in its two volumes, but particularly from the present volume (Volume II), with respect to an understanding of the process of development as it has unfolded, or as it is expected to unfold, in the Arab world. As far as possible, the lessons will be sought through the intricate interaction among determinants as a body on the one hand, and development on the other. To start with, references to development will on the whole relate to economic development, that is, they will not be underlain by insistence on the much more comprehensive and profound aspects and content of development as set out in the conceptual part of the last chapter. However, later on, the exploration of the unfolding of development in the full sense of the term will be undertaken. The lessons that will be sought will be tentative, even more so than the observations on and inferences from the manner in which the determinants were thought to operate. What are those lessons?

In fact, the individual or particular lessons that our study warrants are all woven into one comprehensive lesson, which sums up our perception of how development has proceeded in the twelve countries examined in the period 1945-75. This perception does not apply with equal strength or appropriateness to all the countries, although at a distance it will seem to do so. (Those differentiations which are considered significant and meaningful will be brought into relief during the discussion.) Nor does the perception apply to all phases of development in any one country's experience. Indeed, these spatial and temporal differences are themselves part of the lesson we have learnt during the conduct of the study. We had started with the expectation that they existed, but this was an initial proposition, strictly speaking. The field-work confirmed the proposition. Finally, a word regarding the tone of the presentation to follow. It will sound assertive, and perhaps a different use of verb tenses would have better supplied the touch of tentativeness and modesty underlying our findings and our perception. However, now that the reader is warned, we feel that the format and tone need not constitute any further block to a true understanding of what this presentation sets out to say.

The first urge that stirs for achieving development is dissatisfaction with present conditions resulting in tension and some restlessness. But this tension, if it is to open the way to development-promoting behaviour, is to be positive in orientation. We could perhaps call it 'creative tension', as against destructive tension, which leads in the opposite direction. Creative tension cannot be effective unless it is felt by a large part of the stratum of political leadership (which includes government circles, the army, or a strong political party which supports the government), and/or a political party in opposition, provided it is powerful enough to influence the leadership; and finally some articulate and influential part of the general public like the press, university professors, or the labour unions. For this creative tension to be effective, particularly when it emanates from sources outside the political leadership, it has to be intense, to involve strong pressure groups, and to be sustained.

The political leadership must be responsive to the pressure, and must have a genuine development orientation which will turn into strong commitment in due course. A superficial interest, particularly one which is feigned merely in order to soothe public feeling or to tide over an acute crisis, only to be dropped afterwards, will not start the sequence of events leading to development. Furthermore, the political leadership must evolve and elaborate a vision of development which is as comprehensive as possible, and must channel its development commitment through avenues that can serve the purpose. These channels will include some form of planning, even if merely indicative; the collection of statistical data that serve as inputs in planning, programming and project formulation; the establishment or else strengthening of institutions set for the service of investment and research; and the provision of resources called for by investment requirements. Finally, the commitment must be associated with civil service adequacy, political stability and law and order for it to express itself effectively as a powerful determinant.

The commitment and the policies and measures will be insufficient unless there is a large measure of motivation directed to economic advancement and sensitive to economic incentives, and unless the motivation is supplemented by strong economic and social mobility. The motivation and mobility will be all the more action-promoting the more widely they are felt in the business community and among other groups constituting the middle class, among the labour unions, and among the civil servants and particularly the technocrats. The type of socio-economic system is not of crucial significance here, inasmuch as a high level of economic motivation among the population at large will only be slightly dampened under state capitalism or socialism, if social motivation remains high in the public sector. Thus, if economic motivation is sharply restrained, some other forms must continue to be allowed if the inherently high motivation is not to be deflated and wasted.

Related to motivation is the strength of the entrepreneurial spirit. This factor must exist to supplement motivation and to give it expression in the actual formation of business establishments. The entrepreneurial resources may be quite limited at the outset. But if given scope, and if the economic climate is favourable, the resources will grow with the accrual of rewards and the confidence thus gained. The point calls for three qualifications. First, a reasonable measure of political stability of the voluntary, creative type must be available, within a milieu of national unity and purpose. Second, economic policy within which entrepreneurship will function must have a reasonable degree of soundness, consistency and constancy. Otherwise, entrepreneurial expectations will become subject to inhibiting fluctuations and will then falter and drop below the critical line of action. Third, if the entrepreneurial resources in the private sector are minimal, or if they are of reasonable volume but the socio-economic system is inhibiting, then the public sector must provide scope for public entrepreneurship to emerge and to operate, or for joint entrepreneurship in mixed-sector activities. Otherwise the chain of events will break at this point.

Four determinants become highly relevant here, of the types we described earlier as supportive and framework or environmental. These are the presence of some resource base that is of commercial value and that promises reasonable returns to entrepreneurial effort; a social and economic infrastructure above a critical, minimal level, which permits certain basic functions to be performed (in transport and communication, public utilities and urban facilities, housing, irrigation, and health and education); capital availability to make possible some net investment that moves the economy beyond stagnation; and manpower with some skills and the readiness to enter gainful employment at the going rates of pay. Some substitution is possible among these four determinants, with abundance in one compensating for serious shortage in another, but all have to be present in some quantity and to be of quality that is not so poor as to inhibit the developmental effort. Special emphasis must be placed on education in the present context.

Where the resource base is concerned, and land more particularly, another condition has to be satisfied. This is that a specific framework or institutional determinant has to be present and in operation, namely agrarian reform. This determinant is of particular significance when the structure of land ownership and of tenure in general is highly exploitative, and where the pattern of land holdings is extremely skewed. In these and related instances it would be crucial for agrarian reform to be initiated and for the structure to be so altered as to provide incentives to the very small landowners, the share-tenants, and the landless agricultural labourers, while providing room for large-scale operations through co-operative or collective arrangements.

The sequence which is being depicted is not hard and fast. Variations can take place, and have taken place, in the context of the Arab economies and societies. This is particularly true once the development process has been set in motion. In other words, the initial steps seem to us to be inevitable, but the process might proceed in slightly different avenues from there onwards. However, one of the determinants which by now must have been very operative, and without whose operation the provision of infrastructure and, more so, the agrarian reform, cannot be undertaken effectively is a development-oriented civil service. Obviously, it is not warranted to expect the public administration to be highly trained, motivated, qualified and disciplined. These attributes go parallel with an advanced level of development. But if the process of development is to begin to unfold, and if it is to have a chance of moving satisfactorily and of being sustained, then the civil service has to have the attributes listed in some measure.

The quality of the political leadership is of direct relevance and great significance for the type of public administration that will emerge: the rules of recruitment, allocation of duties, in-training, promotion, upgrading and sanctions are extremely crucial to the quality and effectiveness of the civil service. Likewise, the degree of success in the inculcation of loyalty to the state rather than to particularist interests, of integrity, and of the notion of public service will determine whether the administration will be a promotive or an inhibitive factor for development.

Parallel with the shaping of the civil service, the system of education and of training will have to be expanded to serve as many youths of school age as the resources and teaching force permit, as the quality of education and training becomes a matter of concern. The connection between the public administration and education and training is direct and close. Since the main reference here is to the public system of education, it is obvious, first, that the teaching force is a major component of civil servants, and secondly, that the ministry of education has to be adequately equipped to undertake the many and complex assignments of curricula preparation; the planning, design and provision of facilities; the training of teachers and trainers; the preparation of textbooks; the setting and administration of examinations; and the more sophisticated functions of retraining of teachers, deepening of the teaching process and its extension to reach all three cycles, the promotion of research, and the advancement of science and technology.

Before the economy can move to a distinctly higher level of performance, not only the factors to which reference has been made will have become operative, but society will have shown clear signs of acceptance of technological change and the readiness to adopt more advanced methods of production and distribution of goods and services, and more efficient organisation of establishments. The means of transport and the media of communication, as well as education, will have prepared the ground for the acceptance of improved technology and organisation.

Reference was made in the last chapter and in the introductory part of the present section to the question which has occupied a number of development economists, as to whether or not a development theory exists. The literature includes many works whose titles include such phrases as 'the theory of growth' or 'the theory of development'. Leaving the works that are described as presenting a theory of growth aside, for they mostly use the term 'theory' in a restricted sense which is suitable to the limited concept of economic growth, we find that only a few other works pretend to present an integrated theory of development. Such integrated theory sets out to concern itself with development in a broad sense, involving economic and non-economic elements and components, to explain the process of such development with a large measure of generality or wide applicability, and to predict or assess the developmental potential of societies. The few claims made for the existence of such a theory were thought in the last chapter to be rather ambitious and insufficiently substantiated.

The research behind, and the conclusions deriving from the present study have confirmed the initial position taken in the last chapter. Although in the present section we have suggested a sequence of likely events or a process which development is thought to have taken in the Arab world, the suggestion is indicative and very tentative and purports merely to speculate on the operation of the major determinants in a fashion conducive to development. No rigorous system of thought was attempted. What is more important is this writer's belief that multi-sided and comprehensive development as here defined does not lend itself to rigorous theorising and cannot be made to fit into the structure of a theory in the strict sense of the term — namely one of general applicability as far as past experience is concerned, and of predictive power as far as future expectations are concerned.

At best, all that can be said is that this study can enable us to formulate a loose intellectual and analytical framework of some explanatory and predictive value for the Arab world — and hopefully, though to a more limited extent, for the Third World at large. Within this framework, individual countries can and do show some substantial variation. This is not a negative or sterile conclusion, considering the complexity of development and the intricate interaction of the economic with the political and socio-cultural aspects of development, and further considering the play of many forces and institutions, and above all of human will and decisions, in the weaving of the fabric of development.

If one were to be cynical, one could say that the most salient generalisation flowing from the study is that no one overall generalisation can be made for the Arab region as a whole. But a more positive approach would lead to the realisation that development in the three post-war decades has indeed followed a course that can be identified and mapped, though this course has been wide and its banks hazy enough to accommodate individual country variations within. It is reasonable to expect movement along this course to continue for those countries whose progress over the past three decades has been slow, but to expect some adjustment in the course of those other countries whose performance has been relatively good.

If the process of development moves more or less as suggested, then the conditions will have been rendered suitable for the speeding of development. But speed will not be achieved unless two basic prerequisites have been met. The first is that of social education, involving the sharpening of awareness of the imperativeness of development, coupled with large-scale mobilisation of the nation's will and its forces behind the development effort. For the awareness and the mobilisation to be sharpened and effected, respectively, there must be large-scale participation by the adult population not only in the development effort, but prior to that in the conception of the needs and objectives which development is to serve, and in the decision-making process in the social and political spheres.

The second prerequisite is that development should be mass-oriented and should provide some distributive justice. In other words, the fullest and best effort of society cannot be counted upon to be forthcoming unless the contributors to the effort were to feel that they are the main beneficiaries of the fruits of this effort. To benefit, they will have to realise that the content of development and its criteria and indicators are not mere statistical landmarks like abstract rates of growth, or glamorous showpieces that do not get directly translated into the day-by-day needs of the masses in terms of food, clothing, housing, jobs and schools for the children. If development continues to be expressed in aggregates that remain beyond the five senses of the masses, like a rise in exports, an easing of balance-of-payments stringencies, or a rise in the income of a favoured minority then it will fail to get popular support and commitment. This is not to say that the aggregates, or the rate of growth, are not relevant to the needs of the masses. Far from it. Yet the masses cannot 'feel' the beneficial value of these indicators unless they see them with their own eyes in the form of jobs and food and houses and schools. For the political leadership, and for the entre-preneurial class, to attend adequately to the masses' needs, is to include a distinct social content in their perception of development. The policies and mechanisms which express this social content, like transfer policies, direct taxes, social welfare, insurance, and the like, are the concern of the decision-makers in government and the private sector. But their concrete expression for the bulk of the population involves the satisfaction of such basic needs as those that have been enumerated, and their quantitative and qualitative improve-ment at a sustained rate.

The Arab countries have mostly moved along the development course in its first phase, namely in readying the economies for improved performance and, in some instances, in actually achieving such performance. It is the latter phase that is still lagging behind – the phase which relates to the satisfaction of mass needs. We say this in spite of the progress-ive taxation introduced in most countries, the social insurance schemes instituted, or the expansion of education. But there is much more yet to be done before the typical remote farmer or the urban *bidonville* dweller can be said to live a life of some human dignity. It is this target which is the true yardstick, and the compelling challenge, of development. In our reasoned judgement, based on extensive observation and study, the challenge is still far from adequately met. What is more serious is that only in a small number of Arab countries is it already a matter of grave concern for policy- and decision-makers. As to the private sector, by and large it has not yet acquired anything like a reasonable sense of social responsibility. We can only conclude, therefore, that the determinants in operation have succeeded in starting the process of economic development moving, but the process of comprehensive and profound development is still to be set on its course.

NOTES

1. The determinants listed and discussed are presented in the order in which they appeared in section 3 of Chapter 1, Volume II (this volume).

2. Whenever reference is made to the individual Arab economies, as in the present discussion, this draws, and is based on, material in the country Chapters 2 – 13 of Volume I. Only when some new material is at issue, or some new observations are made that call for bibliographical notation, will new references be made in the notes.

3. The relationship between the performance base (or the technology prevailing) and the resource base occupied writers in the nineteenth and early twentieth century, when technological progress was making relatively wide strides. See, for instance, John Stuart Mill, *Principles of Political Economy* (D. Appleton and Company, New York, 1909), Vol. I, Book I, Chs. VII and VIII, in contrast with the general tone of T. R. Malthus in *An Essay on Population* (Everyman's Library Edition, 1914), especially Vol. II, Book III. (Edwin Cannan's *A History of the Theories of Production and Distribution from 1776 to 1848*, London, 1917, contains a useful summary and discussion of classical views on the broad subject under reference here.)

4. J. H. Boeke, *Economics and Economic Policy of Dual Societies* (New York, 1953). We have simplified the concept of dualism here considerably, as the reference is not meant to provide an adequate discussion of it. See Benjamin Higgins, *Economic Development: Problems, Principles, and Policies* (New York, 1959), especially Chs. 10, 11 and 12, for a presentation and critique of dualism.

5. About 10 per cent on the average for the twelve countries surveyed.

6. See David H. Finnie, *Desert Enterprise* (Cambridge, Mass., 1958) for an examination of the Middle East oil industry 'in its local environment'. See also different issues of the *Aramco Handbook*, published by the Arabian American Oil Company.

7. Deep insights can be gained in this connection from Clark Kerr, John T. Dunlop, Frederick Harbison and Charles A. Myers, *Industrialism and Industrial Man: The Problems of Labor and Management in Economic Growth* (Cambridge, Mass., 1960), and Dunlop, Harbison, Kerr and Myers, *Industrialism and Industrial Man Revisited* (Princeton, 1975). For the relationship between the degree of industrialisation and the level of national income, see Simon Kuznets, 'Quantitative Aspects of the Economic Growth of Nations', especially II: 'Industrial Distribution of National Product and Labor Force', in *Economic Development and Cultural Change*, Vol. 5,

July 1957, Supplement, pp. 3-111. See also H. B. Chenery, 'Patterns of Industrial Growth', *American Economic Review*, Vol. 50, September 1960.

8. The reader is referred to the many country sources of relevance which were noted in country Chapters 2 to 13 of Volume I. In addition, see the country papers submitted to the 'Interregional Seminar on Selected Aspects of Industrial Policy' held at United Nations Economic and Social Office in Beirut, UNESOB, from 4 to 15 January 1971. An earlier assessment appeared in United Nations, *Industrial Development in the Arab Countries* (New York, 1967) containing selected documents presented to the 'Symposium on Industrial Development in the Arab Countries' held in Kuwait, 1-10 March 1966.

9. Syria, Iraq and Tunisia are cases in point. See Dr A. Sallouta, *Industrial Development and Policies* (Monograph, mimeographed; undated but believed to relate to 1974); Ferhang Jalal, *The Role of Government in the Industrialization of Iraq 1950-1965* (London, 1967); and Philippe Aydalot, *Essai sur les problèmes de la stratégie de l'industrialization en économie sous-développée: L'exemple tunisien*, (Série Economique No. 2 of *Cahiers du C.E.R.E.S.* (Centre d'Etudes et de Recherches Economiques et Sociales, Tunis, April 1968).

10. The country chapters in Volume I referred to industrial financing institutions; see also the papers of the Second Industrial Development Seminar held in 1971, to which reference has been made. For a comparative analysis, see 'Financing of Industrial Development in Various Countries of the Middle East', in UNESOB, *Studies on Development Problems in Selected Countries of the Middle East, 1973* (New York, 1974).

11. See Yusif A. Sayigh, 'The Place of Agriculture in Economic Development', *Land Economics*, Vol. XXXV, No. 4, November 1959, for a discussion of the relationship between agriculture and development. For a list of references on the subject, see F. F. Johnston and J. W. Mellor, 'The Role of Agriculture in Economic Development', in *American Economic Review*, Vol. 51, September 1961. See also United Nations, *Land Reform, Defects in Agrarian Structure as Obstacles to Economic Development* (New York, 1951), and Peter Dorner, *Land Reform and Economic Development* (Penguin Modern Economics Texts, 1972). References specific to the Arab countries appear in country chapters of Volume I.

12. Reference is made here to the 'barrage issue' which was mentioned in Ch. 13 of Volume I. The issue centred around the complaint that the choice of location of several dams or barrages had little economic or tech-

nical justification, but had instead been made on politico-social grounds. See a series of articles in *Al-'Alam* (a Rabat daily; Arabic) in June 1972.

13. This statement is based on the perusal of the local Arabic press in Egypt over the last two or three years (and also in Kuwait, quoting Egyptian sources). No official documentation is available in support of the accusations made.

14. To a great extent, the differentiation made here is essentially one between economic development narrowly defined, and comprehensive development as understood and presented in the first chapter of this volume.

15. The question of capital availability covers a wide area of interest. Not only does it raise basic issues relating to domestic savings and capital inflows from the rest of the world, but also to the degree of development of financial institutions and their ability to attract domestic savings and foreign capital and to allocate the funds available optimally from the point of view of development. The literature of relevance is very extensive.

16. The present writer has examined the question of this capability (or capital absorptive capacity) in 'The Financing of Development in Developing Countries', in *Financial Resources and Development in Lebanon* (published by the Association of Development Studies, Beirut, Lebanon, 1967; Arabic), pp. 29-92. In this connection, see Francis X. Colaço, Development Centre Studies, OECD, *Economic and Political Considerations and the Flow of Official Resources to Developing Countries* (Paris, 1973); see also the whole series of OECD annual publications (Development Assistance Committee) relating to the flow of aid. The question of aid has received considerable attention; the following works have been consulted in the present context: (a) F. Benham, *Economic Aid to Underdeveloped Countries* (OUP, 1960); (b) I. M. D. Little and J. M. Clifford, *International Aid* (London, 1965); (c) H. J. P. Arnold, *Aid for Development: A Political and Economic Study* (London, 1966); (d) Raymond F. Mikesell, *Public International Lending for Development* (New York, 1966); (e) E. K. Hawkins, *The Principles of Development Aid* (Penguin Modern Economics, 1970; (f) Jagdish Bhagwati and Richard S. Eckaus (eds.), *Foreign Aid* (Penguin Modern Economics, 1970); for a critique of foreign lending, (g) Cheryl Payer, *The Debt Trap: The IMF and the Third World* (Penguin, 1974); and (h) T. Mende, *From Aid to Recolonization: Lessons of A Failure* (London, 1973).

17. It is interesting to see how sensitive Adam Smith himself was to the importance of these non-economic factors; other classical economists also reflected similar concern. The concern is no less real for being sometimes subsumed.

18. The development plans, examined in Chs. 2-13 of Volume I, show this clearly.

19. The Arab Fund for Economic and Social Development has entered into an agreement with the UNDP on the one hand, and the 20 Arab states, members of AFESD, on the other. The agreement aims at the identification and preparation of such regional projects. The AFESD is the executing agency of this agreement.

20. The literature on manpower and development is extensive; obviously, only a limited number of studies have been consulted in the preparation of this section on

manpower – notably the following: (a) Theodore W. Schultz, *Investment in Human Capital: The Role of Education and Research* (New York, 1971); (b) Schultz, 'Investment in Human Capital', *American Economic Review,* Vol. 51, March 1961; (c) Frederick Harbison and Charles A. Myers, *Education, Manpower and Economic Growth: Strategies of Human Resource Development* (New York, 1964); (d) Harbison and Myers, *Management in the Industrial World* (New York, 1959); (e) Harbison and Myers, *Manpower and Education* (New York, 1965); (f) J. Douglas Brown and Frederick Harbison, *High-Talent Manpower for Science and Industry* (Princeton, 1957); (g) UNESCO, *Economic and Social Aspects of Education Policy* (Paris, 1964); (h) Frederick Harbison, *Education Planning and Human Resource Development* (Paris, 1969); (i) Harbison, *Human Resources as the Wealth of Nations* (Oxford University Press, 1973); (j) Walter Galenson and Graham Pyatt, *The Quality of Labour and Economic Development in Certain Countries* (Geneva, 1964); and (k) Eli Ginzberg, *Manpower for Development* (New York, 1971). For a substantial, though now old, bibliography, see Industrial Relations Section, Princeton University, *Manpower Problems in Economic Development: A Selected Bibliography* (Princeton, 1958), prepared by Keith Simpson and Hazel C. Benjamin. The Final Report of the Inter-University Study of Labor Problems in Economic Development (later designated as the Inter-University Study of Human Resources in National Development), entitled *Industrialism and Industrial Man Revisited* (Princeton, 1975), Appendix I, contains a list of many books and articles of interest and direct relevance.

21. This statement is based partly on interviews, partly on published reports. The latter will be referred to specifically further down.

22. This was experienced concretely in three instances: (a) The 'Survey of Qualified Persons' (Hasr-ul-Kifayat) undertaken by the American University of Cairo in the early sixties (and reported on in a publication with the same title, 1963; Arabic); (b) the survey of the supply of and demand for economists undertaken by the Economic Research Institute of the American University of Beirut in 1964 (undertaken and reported on by Yusif A. Sayigh in *Economics and Economists in the Arab World,* a monograph, 1965); and (c) a survey of the training facilities for the service of the oil sector in the Arab member countries of the Organization of Arab Petroleum Exporting Countries, reported on in a monograph entitled *The File of the Centers and Institutes of Training Related to Oil in Member Countries* (a monograph for internal use, 1975; Arabic).

23. For a discussion of the main methods used in the assessment of manpower requirements, see Harbison. op. cit., item (h) in note 20 above, and UNESCO, op. cit. See also: (a) Eugene Staley, *Planning Occupational Education and Training for Development* (New Delhi, 1970); (b) Russel C. Davis, *Planning Human Resource Development: Educational Models and Schemata* (Chicago, 1966); (c) International Institute for Educational Planning, Fundamentals of Educational Planning Series, No. 1, Philip H. Coombs, *What is Educational Planning?* (Paris, 1970); (d) IIEP, Fundamentals of Educational Planning Series, No. 3, Frederick Harbison,

Educational Planning and Human Resource Development (Paris, 1969), referred to in note 20, item (h), above; and (e) National Science Foundation, *The Long-Range Demand for Scientific and Technical Personnel, a Methodological Study* (Washington, D.C., 1961).

24. 'Note on Some Demographic Characteristics of Selected Countries in the Middle East', in UNESOB, *Studies on Development Problems in Selected Countries of the Middle East, 1969* (New York, 1970). The essay relates to 5 out of the 12 countries covered in this book, but these are sufficiently representative. See also UNESOB, *Studies . . . 1970*, 'Demographic Characteristics of Youth in the Arab Countries of the Middle East: Present Situation and Growth Prospects, 1970-1990', Table 3, p. 77.

25. UNESOB, *Studies . . . 1969*, essay quoted in note 24 above; Tables 11A and 11B, pp. 57 and 58 served as basis for the calculations in the text here, adjusted and generalised for the Arab region.

26. UNESOB, *Studies . . . 1968*, 'Some Aspects of the Development of Human Resources in Various Countries of the Middle East', p. 37.

27. See in this connection: (a) Committee on International Migration of Talent (of Education and World Affairs, Inc.), *The International Migration of High-Level Manpower* (New York, 1970); (b) CIMT, *Modernization and the Migration of Talent* (New York, 1970); and (c) A. B. Zahlan, 'The Brain Drain', *Middle East Studies Association Bulletin*, Vol. 6, No. 3, October, 1972. Zahlan has examined the question of the brain drain more intensively than any other scholar in the Arab world.

28. The study undertaken by OAPEC, to which reference has been made in note 22 above, approaches the question of technical manpower for the oil sector from a regional standpoint.

29. In Joseph A. Schumpeter, *The Theory of Economic Development* (Cambridge, Mass., 1947, originally published in German in 1909; translated by Redvers Opie). A. J. Meyer should be given credit for being the first writer to draw attention to entrepreneurship and its dearth in the Arab world, in his article entitled 'Entrepreneurship: The Missing Link in the Arab East?' in *Middle East Economic Papers, 1954* (Beirut, 1954). He followed this with an essay on entrepreneurship in his book *Middle Eastern Capitalism: Nine Essays* (Cambridge, Mass., 1959).

30. David C. McClelland, in *The Achieving Society* (Princeton, 1961), and Everett E. Hagen, in *On The Theory of Social Change* (Homewood, Ill., 1962), but also in other writings – mainly journal articles.

31. For an examination of entrepreneurship in the various institutional sectors, see Yusif A. Sayigh, *Entrepreneurship and Development: Private, Public, and Joint Enterprise in Underdeveloped Countries* (doctoral dissertation at the Johns Hopkins University, 1957). Much of the conceptual discussion that follows is based on this work. See also, by the same author, *Entrepreneurs of Lebanon: The Role of the Business Leader in A Developing Economy* (Cambridge, Mass., 1962), especially Ch. 2.

32. This is partly why trade has not been examined as a determinant of development, in spite of the prominence given to its role in development by several econo-

mists, foremost among whom is probably Jacob Viner in *International Trade and Economic Development* (Glencoe, Ill., 1952). Another reason for the disregard of trade is that, where it relates to exports, its developmental role is essentially a reflection of the impetus the production of exportable goods gives to development, but trade is not *in itself* the motive force in the process; and where imports are concerned, its developmental role is restricted to the example or demonstration effect that imports have on the production of substitutes, and is not an original driving force in development as we understand it in this study. (Gerald M. Meier in *International Trade and Development* (New York, 1963), briefly surveys the major writings on the impact of an export-oriented sector on development. For a justification of the use of trade as a developmental factor in a context similar to the present one, see Irma Adelman and Cynthia Taft Morris, *Society, Politics and Development: A Quantitative Approach* (Baltimore, 1967), pp. 126-8.)

33. Sayigh, *Entrepreneurs of Lebanon . . .*, op. cit.

34. This statement should by no means belittle the notable entrepreneurial role and contribution of national Egyptians in the inter-war years. However, in the present discussion we focus basically on the post-war period, especially 1952-75.

35. Reference here is to Frank H. Knight, *Risk, Uncertainty and Profit* (Boston and New York, 1921), who attributes entrepreneurial profit to the element of uncertainty. His differentiation is based on the insurability of risk and the non-insurability of uncertainty.

36. It is quite natural and understandable for political scientists to have devoted greater attention than economists to the political factors and indicators of development. A list of the major writings by political scientists would be too long for our purposes. But, for relevant material and many useful references, see G. A. Almond and J. S. Coleman (eds.), *The Politics of the Developing Areas* (Princeton, 1960); M. F. Millikan and D. L. Blackmer (eds.), *The Emerging Nations* (Boston, 1961); Joseph LaPalombara (ed.), *Bureaucracy and Political Development* (Princeton, 1963); J. R. Pennock (ed.), *Self-Government in Modernizing Nations* (Englewood Cliffs, N. J., 1964); David E. Apter, *The Politics of Modernization* (Chicago and London, 1965); Samuel P. Huntington, *Political Order in Changing Societies* (New Haven and London, 1968); and W. W. Rostow, *Politics and the Stages of Growth* (Cambridge, 1971).

Additionally, the following references are of special interest: S. M. Lipset, 'Some Social Requisites of Democracy: Economic Development and Political Legitimacy', *American Political Science Review*, March 1953; Morroe Berger, 'Arab Ideologies, National and International' in Programme in Near Eastern Studies, Princeton University, March 1960 (mimeographed); Leon Carl Brown (ed.), *State and Society in Independent North Africa* (Washington, D.C., 1966), relevant essays; and Charles A. Micaud, with Leon Carl Brown and Clement Henry Moore, *Tunisia: The Politics of Modernization* (London, 1964), the relevant parts.

37. The term 'visible hand' is in reference to state action, as in Yusif A. Sayigh, 'Development: The Visible or the Invisible Hand?', *World Politics*, July 1961.

38. Particularly Almond and Coleman, Pye, and the few other writers cited in note 36 above. Adelman and

Morris, op. cit., fit into the same category in so far as they attribute scores to individual countries on the basis of certain political indicators.

39. Summaries of, or important clauses in, the constitutions appear in Europa Publications, *The Middle East and North Africa,* in the annual issues consulted (particularly those for 1971-2 to 1974-5.

40. There is no dearth of official published material containing royal or presidential pronouncements. In addition, the press of Lebanon, which has been perused, is very news-conscious and has been in the habit of printing such pronouncements whenever they have been made over the past two or three decades.

41. The literature on planning and development is immense, and the works consulted can only be a small fraction of what is available. Some of these have been, or will be referred to elsewhere, mainly in Volume I. But see also L. J. Walinsky, *The Planning and Execution of Economic Development* (New York, 1963), and A. Waterston, *Development Planning: Lessons of Experience* (Baltimore, 1965).

42. Adelman and Morris have found that leadership commitment to development is a very strong factor — indeed one of the strongest if not the very strongest among all the political factors or indicators. See pp. 78-81 and the relevant parts of Chs. 4 to 7 of their book (already cited).

43. The writer obtained extensive literature from the Secretariat-General of the ruling party — speeches by the President, party conference proceedings, position papers, and the like — which has served as basis for part of what has been reported on Tunisia.

44. Perusal of the weekly editions of the authoritative *Middle East Economic Survey* (published in Beirut) confirms these statements most strongly, whether in reporting on numerous ventures entered into with TNCs, or in interviews with prominent members of government.

45. See Yusif A. Sayigh, 'The Experience of the Arab Countries with Planning', paper given at a conference on the theme of planning in the Arab world held by the Federation of Arab Economists in Kuwait, March 1973, for a much fuller evaluation of this experience. Other papers evaluated the experience of a number of individual countries, notably Iraq, Jordan, Syria, Egypt, and the Maghreb countries. (The *Proceedings* are in the press as this is being written.) It is worth stating that the present writer was less critical of the planning experience of the Arab world in the 1973 paper than he is now.

46. In addition to the works cited in note 36 above, the reader is referred to Everett E. Hagen, 'A Framework for Analyzing Economic and Political Change' in Robert E. Asher *et al., Development of the Emerging Nations* (Washington, D.C., 1962), and Manfred Halpern, *The Politics of Social Change in the Middle East and North Africa* (Princeton, 1963).

47. See the various essays in LaPalombara, op. cit. For other general references, see: (a) Manfred Halpern, op. cit.; (b) League of Arab States, The Arab Organization for Administrative Sciences, *Laws and Regulations of the Civil Service in the Arab States and Countries* (Cairo, 1971; Arabic), Vols. I and II; (c) League of Arab States, The Arab Organization for Administrative Sciences, *Laws of Local Administration in the Arab States and Countries*

(Cairo, 1971; Arabic), Vols. I and II; (d) W. Hardy Wickwar, *Modernization of Administration in the Arab East* (Beirut, 1963); and (e) Hassan Ahmad Tawfiq, *Public Administration* (Cairo, 1972; Arabic), dealing mainly with the situation in Egypt within a general conceptual framework.

48. Reference here is essentially to the concept of the 'big push' associated most with P. N. Rosenstein-Rodan, 'Problems of Industrialization of Eastern and South-Eastern Europe', *Economic Journal* (June-September 1953), and reprinted since in some volumes of readings.

49. In this connection, see U. K. Hicks, *Development Finance: Planning and Control* (New York, 1965); E. M. Bernstein, W. W. Heller *et al., Savings in the Modern Economy* (Minneapolis, 1953); United Nations, *Domestic Financing of Economic Development* (New York, 1950); and Edward Nevin, *Capital Funds in Underdeveloped Countries: The Role of Financial Institutions* (New York, 1961).

50. Many of the works cited in connection with manpower are relevant in the present context. (See note 20 above.)

51. Published material on many of these points is extremely scanty or non-existent. However, we came across the following specific works during research and field-work: (a) Khalil al-Ghalayini, *Civil Service in Saudi Arabia: Study and Analysis* (Riyadh, 1382, i.e., 1962); (b) Mo'tassim Bashir, *Administration and Development: The Role of the Civil Servant in Sudan* (Ph.D. dissertation, University of California, Los Angeles, 1967); (c) Gerard Timsit, 'Le statut général de la fonction publique algérienne', *Revue Algérienne des Sciences Juridiques, Politiques et Economiques,* June 1967, No. 2; (d) Various issues of *The Sudan Journal for Administration and Development,* a periodical published by the Institute of Public Administration, Khartoum; bilingual, English and Arabic), especially Vol. III, 1967, special issue on 'Civil Service in A Changing Society'; and Vol. VI, 1970; (e) Mohammad Tawfiq Sadiq, *The Evolution of Government and Administration in the Kingdom of Saudi Arabia* (Riyadh, 1965; Arabic); (f) Various issues of *Public Administration,* a periodical published by the Institute of Public Administration of Saudi Arabia (Riyadh; Arabic), especially those of April 1968, September 1968 and December 1970; (g) Sbih Missoum, 'Le statut de la fonction publique', in *Revue Algérienne* ..., March 1967, No.1; (h) Said Ben Bachir, *L'administration locale du Maroc* (Casablanca, 1969); (i) Michel Rousset, *L'administration marocaine* (Institut d'Administration Publique, Paris, 1971); (j) Ch. Debbasch, J. Leca, A. Remili, O. Marais, J. Waterbury, A. Khatibi, M. Rousset, L. Ben Salem, A. Zghal and R. E. Germann, *Pouvoir et administration au Maghreb: Etudes sur les élites maghrébines* (Centre National de la Recherche Scientifique, Paris, 1970); (k) Ahmed Mahiou, 'Le contentieux administratif en Algérie', *Revue Algérienne* ..., September 1972, Vol. IX, No. 3; (l) Ismail Sabri Abdallah, *Organization of the Public Sector* (Cairo, 1969), with special reference to Egypt. For an older study on Egyptian bureaucracy, see Morroe Berger, *Bureaucracy and Society in Modern Egypt* (Princeton, 1957); (m) Safa' Hafez, *The Public Sector and the Horizons of Socialist Evolution in Iraq* (Beirut, 1965; Arabic); (n) Mohammad Jamal, *Evaluation of the*

Performance of the Mixed Enterprises in Kuwait (M. A. thesis, American University of Beirut, 1971); (o) A. H. Hanson, *Public Enterprise and Economic Development* (London, 1965); (p) Adnan Iskandar, *Bureaucracy in Lebanon* (Beirut, 1964); (q) George Grassmuck and Kamal Salibi, *Reformed Administration in Lebanon* (Beirut, 1964); (r) Iskandar Bahir, *Planned Administrative Reform in Lebanon* (Beirut, 1965; and (s) Michael C. Hudson, *The Precarious Republic: Modernization in Lebanon* (New York, 1968).

52. See several essays in B. F. Hoselitz and W. E. Moore (eds.), *Industrialization and Society* (Glencoe, Ill., 1958); Clifford Geertz (ed.), *Old Societies and New States* (New York, 1963); Huntington, op. cit., especially Chs. 1, 2, 3, 6 and 7; and E. A. Shils, *Political Development in the New States* (The Hague, 1962). Earlier notes on political determinants have some relevant parts as well. For references specific to the Arab region see, in particular, Halpern, op. cit., and Berger, op. cit.

53. This statement was written before the flare-up of the large-scale, destructive civil war which began to devastate Lebanon in the spring and summer of 1975.

54. Reference here is to the Islamic tradition of *Shoura* (consultation, taking counsel or advice), and to tribal councils where all tribesmen had, and still have in tribal subsocieties, the right to express their opinion on issues under discussion.

55. See note 73 further down for references on this subject. The citations were delayed on the grounds that the bulk of the discussion of the role of the military would come later on.

56. Yusif A. Sayigh, *Entrepreneurship and Development . . .,* op. cit.

57. For a condemnation of the retarding effect of ideology, see Joseph J. Spengler, 'Theory, Ideology, Non-Economic Values, and Politico-Economic Development', in Ralph Braibanti and Joseph J. Spengler (eds.), *Tradition, Values, and Socio-Economic Development* (Durham, N.C., 1961), especially pp. 28 ff; and for an examination of ideology as a framework of development, see Wilbert E. Moore, 'The Social Framework of Economic Development', in ibid., especially pp. 61 and 62. See also Debbasch *et al.,* op. cit., on élites in the Maghreb; John Waterbury, *The Commander of the Faithful: The Moroccan Political Elite – A Study of Segmented Politics* (London, 1970); Abdelkebir Khatibi, 'Etat et classes sociales',, in *Etudes Sociologiques sur le Maroc* (published by the *Bulletin Economique et Social du Maroc:* Sociologie, Tangiers, 1971); Georges Ketman, 'The Egyptian Intelligentsia', in Walter Z. Laqueur (ed.), *The Middle East in Transition* (London, 1958); and Wilfred Cantwell Smith, 'The Intellectuals in the Modern Development of the Islamic World', in Sydney Nettleton Fisher (ed.), *Social Forces in the Middle East* (Ithaca, N.Y., 1955),

58. Moore, loc. cit., pp. 57 ff.

59. Ibid.

60. The following works were largely consulted in connection with the socio-cultural determinants, in addition to works of relevance that are cited in other contexts as well: Lucius Battle, 'Cultural Contributions to Development', in William R. Polk (ed.), *The Developmental Revolution: North Africa, The Middle East and South Asia* (Washington, D.C., 1963); relevant parts of Fisher (ed.), op. cit.; Grigori Lazarev, 'Changement

social et développement des campagnes marocaines', in *Etudes Sociologiques sur le Maroc* (already cited); relevant parts of Leon Carl Brown (ed.), *State and Society in Independent North Africa* (Washington, D.C., 1966); and of Micaud, op. cit.; and Fredj Stambouli, 'Tradition et modernité à travers les processus d'urbanisation en Tunisie', in *Revue Tunisienne de Sciences Sociales,* Vol. 8, No. 26, September 1971. In addition, there have been several references to works or essays as in Hoselitz, Moore, Shils, Smelser, Lerner, Halpern, Berger and Okun and Richardson (either already cited or to be cited further down) that are of direct relevance.

61. The scholars named are a select sample. The writings in question include: Talcott Parsons, *The Social System* (Glencoe, Ill., 1951); Neil J. Smelser, *The Sociology of Economic Life* (Englewood Cliffs, N.J., 1963); Talcott Parsons and Neil J. Smelser, *Economy and Society* (New York, 1965); Wilbert E. Moore, *Social Change* (Englewood Cliffs, N. J., 1963); B. F. Hoselitz, *Sociological Aspects of Economic Growth* (Glencoe, Ill., 1960); and B. F. Hoselitz and W. E. Moore (eds.), *Industrialization and Society* (Paris, 1963).

62. The schema is Parson's. For Hoselitz's different view, see Ch. 2 of his book, *Sociological Aspects.*

63. A small number of Arab economists constitute the spearhead of rebellion against the unquestioning acceptance of the notion of the superiority of modernisation and Westernisation, and of Western models as being suitable for Third World conditions without drastic adjustment. This group also insists on the condition that development, in its full sense, ought to be mass-oriented and to be felt by the poor peasants and urban workers. Economists of this orientation cluster mainly in the Third World Forum and the Third World Economists Association.

64. See Samir Khalaf and Emile Shwayri, 'Family Firms and Industrial Development: The Lebanese Case', *Economic Development and Cultural Change,* Vol. 15, No. 1 (December 1966). Khalaf has made other contributions to the understanding of social forces, social change and modernisation in the Arab world, but the writings in question do not fit into the present context. See also A. Demeerseman, *La famille tunisienne et les temps modernes* (Tunis, 1967).

65. See Henry Bienen's *Violence and Social Change: A Review of Current Literature* (Chicago, 1968). While this small volume does not deal directly with violence as a mode of change for development, it nevertheless examines the expression of violence in the pursuit of social change.

66. Rostow's schema in *The Stages of Economic Growth* emphasise this notion of a continuum; indeed, the notion can be encountered in the writings of many economists who equate development and modernisation. A very explicit expression of this is to be found in D. Lerner's *The Passing of Traditional Society* (New York, 1958).

67. In addition to the educational aspects of manpower to which reference was made earlier, the reader's attention is drawn to the following works which have been consulted for the examination of the points on hand: (a) Hans Singer, *Children in the Strategy of Development* (New York, 1972); (b) Kurt Danziger, *Socialization* (Penguin Science of Behaviour, 1971);

(c) M. Blaug (ed.), *Economics of Education* (Penguin Modern Economics, 1968); (d) OECD, Study Group in the Economics of Education, *Organizational Problems in Planning Educational Development* (Paris, 1966); (e) OECD, Study Group in the Economics of Education, *Financing of Education for Economic Growth* (Paris, 1966), (f) OECD, Study Group in the Economics of Education, *The Residual Factor and Economic Growth* (Paris, 1964); (g) William G. Bowen, *Economic Aspects of Education: Three Essays* (Princeton, 1964); (h) Daniel Houet, *La formation professionnelle par ses propres moyens* (Centre d'Etudes du Développement Economique et Social, Rabat, 1961); (i) Herbert S. Parnes, *Forecasting Educational Needs for Economic and Social Development* (OECD, Mediterranean Regional Project, Paris, 1962); (j) *The Educational Policy in the Saudi Arabian Kingdom* (1970; bilingual: Arabic and English; publisher, author, and place of publication not indicated, but it is presumed here that this is a government publication printed in Riyadh); (k) *Revue de Planification de l'Education dans les Pays Arabes* (published by the Regional Center for Educational Planning and Administration, Beirut; Arabic but with titles in French also), especially Vol. 5, No. 13 (February 1967), Vol. 6, No. 18 (September-December 1968), Vol. 9, No. 27 (September-December 1971), and Vol. 10, No. 28 (January-April 1972) for studies on manpower and education, the cost burden of education, the new strategy of the Regional Center in the service of educational planning in the Arab countries, and new techniques in education and their applicability to the Arab world; (l) Abdul Qadir Yusif, *The Formation [Training] of the Arab Educator* (The Regional Center . . ., Beirut, October 1974; Arabic; mimeographed). This monograph has a most useful reading list including studies on the interrelationship of education, manpower and development for almost all the Arab countries; (m) Suad Khalil Ismail, Mohammad Ahmad Ghannam, and Mustapha Ahmad Zaatary, *The Present Situation with Respect to the Planning and Administration of the Evolution of Curricula in the Arab Countries: A Survey* (The Regional Center . . ., Beirut, 1975; Arabic; stencilled); (n) Mohammad Ghannam, *Education in the Arab Countries: Sequel to the Marrakesh Conference (1970)* (The Regional Center . . ., Beirut, 1975; Arabic); (o) David C. Kinsey, 'L'éducation en masse et ses implications socio-économiques en Tunisie' in *Revue Tunisienne de Sciences Sociales*, Vol. 8, No. 24, March 1971; (p) Khalil Zamiti, 'Problématique de la Contradiction survenue entre formation professionnelle et emploi en Tunisie', and Mme Alya Chomikha Baffoum, 'L'adéquation formation-emploi: étude socio-professionnelle', both in *Revue Tunisienne* . . ., Vol. 8, No. 25, May 1971; (q) The Arab Planning Institute, Kuwait, in co-operation with the Government of Bahrain, Proceedings of *Seminar on Human Resource Development in the Arabian Gulf States*, held in Bahrain, 15-18 February 1975 (Kuwait, 1975); (r) Several studies on education in Iraq, dealing with educational problems in several areas. Summary notation will be made of these: (i) Baghdad University, Center for Educational and Psychological Research, Abdul-Jalil al Zawba'i and Mohammad A. Ghannam, *The Future of the Graduates of Secondary Schools in Iraq* (Baghdad, 1968; Arabic); Musari' al-Rawi, Mohammad A. Ghannam, and Salih A. Sirriyya, *Industrial [Vocational] Education in Iraq: Its Status, Problems, and Growth Requirements* (Baghdad, 1968; Arabic); Ahmad Abu al-Abbas and Musari' al-Rawi, *Waste in Elementary Education in Iraq* (Baghdad, 1972; Arabic); (ii) Ministry of Education, *Resolutions and Recommendations of the Third Study Seminar on Planning for General Education, 1966,* 4-13 May (Baghdad, 1971; Arabic); (iii) Baghdad University, Abdul-Jalil Zawba'i and Mohammad A. Ghannam, *Higher Education in Iraq: Trends of Its Growth and Its Problems* (Baghdad, 1968; Arabic); Mohammad A. Ghannam and Mohammad Saif il-Din Fahmi, *The Future of Secondary Education in Iraq and Its Requirements of Instructors 1965-1975* (Baghdad, 1966; Arabic); and (iv) Ministry of Higher Education and Scientific Research, *Report of Seminar on the Planning of Higher Education in Iraq,* held in Beirut 8-14 November 1970 (Baghdad, 1971; Arabic).

68. The statements made here draw not only on extensive interviewing in the field, but also with members of the Regional Center in Beirut. (For the most recent presentation of comparative educational statistics, see *A Statistical Panorama of Education in the Arab Countries,* prepared by Ingvar Werdelin, Bernic Lindgren Hooker and Jane Susu-Jonkhadar and published by the Regional Center, 1972; English and Arabic.)

69. This point is discussed at some length in Sayigh, *Entrepreneurs of Lebanon* . . ., Ch. 1.

70. The re-examination of curricula is discussed in some of the items in note 67 above. It was also covered during the interviews, mostly in Egypt, Iraq and the Maghreb countries.

71. The literature relating to the role of science and technology in development is extensive. Ample proof is provided by the two-volume bibliography covering several hundred pages, under the title *Science, Technology and Public Policy: A Selected and Annotated Bibliography,* editor Lynton K. Caldwell, assisted by William B. DeVille and Gertrud W. Lindesmith (Department of Government, Indiana University, Bloomington, Ind., 1969). We will restrict ourselves here to the citation of one reference specific to the region: UNESOB, *Regional Plan of Action for the Application of Science and Technology to Development in the Middle East* (New York, 1974). This study is operational and specific. (See also Jerome Wiesner, 'Science in Development', in Polk (ed.), op. cit.)

72. Many of these agents of change receive consideration in the literature on the Arab world; note 73 below lists several works that include discussion on one or another of the agents. But perhaps the one work that includes between its covers the largest array is Fisher (ed.), *Social Forces* . . ., which has already been cited. This book includes essays centring, *inter alia,* around cultural factors in social dynamics, the nomads, the villager, the industrial worker, the bazaar merchant, the entrepreneurial class, the economic planners, the army officer and the intellectuals.

73. There was a period in the fifties and sixties when writings on the role of the military and of power élites in development abounded; since then they have been quite scanty. In addition to references to this role in Halpern, Berger, Braibanti and Spengler (eds.), Millikan and Blackmer (eds.) and Polk (ed.), which have already been cited, see: (a) J. J. Johnson, *The Role of the Military in the Underdeveloped Countries* (Princeton, 1962);(b)

C. Wright Mills, *The Power Elite* (Oxford University Press, 1965); (c) Sir John Bagot Glubb, 'The Role of the Army in the Traditional Arab State', in J. H. Thompson and R. D. Reischauer (eds.), *Modernization of the Arab World* (D. Van Nostrand Company, Inc., 1966); (d) Morroe Berger, *Military Elite and Social Change: Egypt Since Napoleon* (Princeton, 1960); and (e) Sydney Nettleton Fisher (ed.), *The Military in the Middle East: Problems in Society and Government* (Columbus, Ohio, 1963).

74. The middle class and minority groups, as well as other social forces acting as agents of change, are discussed in the works cited in notes 72 and 73 above. In addition, see: (a) Charles Issawi, 'Social Structure and Ideology in Iraq, Lebanon, Syria and UAR', in Reischauer (ed.), op. cit.; (b) Gordon H. Torrey and John F. Devlin, 'Arab Socialism', in ibid.; (c) Manfred Halpern, 'The Character and Scope of the Social Revolution in the Middle East', in Polk (ed.), op. cit.; (d) D. E. Novak and R. Lekachman (eds.), *Development and Society: The Dynamics of Economic Change* (New York, 1964); (e) Morroe Berger, 'The Middle Class in the Arab World', in Laqueur (ed.), op. cit.; (f) Charles Issawi, 'Economic and Social Foundations of Democracy in the Middle East', in ibid.; and (g) Sa'id B. Himadeh, 'Social Awakening and Economic Development in the Middle East', in ibid.

75. See note 32 above explaining why trade was not considered as a determinant of development. Very much the same reasons prompted this writer not to include merchants in the study on entrepreneurship in Lebanon. See Sayigh, *Entrepreneurs of Lebanon . . .*, Chs. 2 and 3.

76. Everett E. Hagen, in an earlier mimeographed paper, and in conversations with the author, emphasised the role of minorities, 'deviants' and 'outsiders'. See also his book *The Economics of Development* (Homewood, Ill., 1968), pp. 221-3.

77. See Ithiel de Sola Pool, 'Communication and Development', in Myron Weiner (ed.), *Modernization: The Dynamics of Growth* (New York, 1966); David E. Apter, *The Politics of Modernization* (Chicago, 1965), especially Chs. 11 and 17; and Lucian W. Pye, *Communications and Political Development* (Princeton, 1963).

78. Vilfredo Pareto, *The Mind and Society* (4 vols., London, Jonathan Cape, 1935). T. B. Bottomore discusses the notion in *Elites and Society* (Penguin, 1964), Ch. III.

79. McClelland, op. cit. (and his associates) coined and contributed most to the elaboration of the concept. Hagen (*On The Theory of Social Change*, already cited), adopted the concept and wove it into his work on development and how it is initiated.

80. Sayigh, *Entrepreneurs of Lebanon . . .*, Chs. 2 and 4.

81. See W. W. Rostow, 'The Nationalization of Take-off', in Polk (ed.), op. cit., pp. 54 and 55. This paper was originally given as an address at a conference held in Washington, D.C., in May 1963. The verbal presentation was more dramatically worded than the essay in the volume cited.

82. The relationship between religion and progress occupied a seminar held for the purpose in June 1963 in Manila. The papers and proceedings have been published in Robert N. Bellah (ed.), *Religion and Progress in Modern Asia* (New York, 1965).

83. Several works have been consulted in connection with these items, but all have so far been cited in one context or another. However, three works that proved of special value ought to be mentioned here: Weiner's *Modernization . . .*, Apter's *The Politics of Modernization*, and Braibanti and Spengler's *Tradition, Values, and Socio-Economic Development*. (See also Part Seven in Bernard Okun and Richard W. Richardson (eds.), *Studies in Economic Development*, New York, 1961.) For a few rare references on motivation specific to the region, see Noureddine Belgaid Hassine, 'Motivation et aspirations ouvrières', in *Etudes de Sociologies Tunisiennes* (Bureau de Recherches Sociologiques), Vol. 1, 1968 (with respect to Tunisia); Aliyya Hassan, 'Social Adaptation in the Inayyis Area', 'Change in Values', and 'Social Values and Development', all papers in Arabic, mimeographed, available to the writer but without further identification except that they were given at the First Arab Psychology Conference in May 1971.

84. This was imparted in interviews, but also corroborated in some published material. The present writer read a series of four articles in a daily of Riyadh (May 1964), in the first three of which the author, a prominent man, had set out to prove that the earth was flat and not spherical. However, these 'convictions' ought not to be given unduly great significance, with education making headway and the findings of science becoming more firmly established in the minds of many older men.

85. Two conferences of the Federation of Arab Economists between 1970 and 1975 have centred on Arab economic co-operation and complementarity, in addition to a few seminars bringing together smaller groups.

86. The present writer has discussed these questions on more than one occasion. Fuller attention is given to them in 'Oil in Arab Developmental and Political Strategy: an Arab View', John Duke Anthony (ed.), *The Middle East: Oil, Politics and Development* (Washington, D. C., 1975). See also 'The Role of Oil in Development', paper prepared for a training programme on the 'Basic Aspects of the Oil Industry', organised by the Organization of Arab Petroleum Exporting Countries, Kuwait, for the period 4 January – 4 March 1976. The papers were all to be delivered as lectures and later incorporated in a volume.

87. Adelman and Morris, op. cit., Chs. IV-VII.

88. Ibid., p. 172.

89. Ibid., p. 261.

3 The Outlook for Development

The first volume of this study consisted of a critical survey of the performance of the twelve Arab countries covered, in terms of economic development, over the post-war period 1945-75. The appraisal was conducted on the basis of certain standards or criteria which had been briefly set out in the introductory chapter. The final chapter of Volume I (the companion volume) carried the appraisal from the one-country to the regional level, containing an examination of development in its regional framework.

The present volume (Volume II) has been mainly concerned with the identification of the major economic, political and socio-cultural determinants of development, and the manner and intensity with which they operate. In a sense, Volume I and the first two chapters of the present volume have dealt with the recent past and carried the discussion to the present. This chapter, with which the whole study is concluded, addresses itself to the foreseeable future. Leaning heavily on the lessons of the past thirty years, and on the examination of the determinants in operation, we venture now to assess the prospects for development in the Arab region over the last quarter of the twentieth century.

The territory whose outlook for development will be scanned covers the twelve Arab countries from Morocco furthest west, to Iraq furthest east. However, as the exploration will reveal, many of the expectations expressed and the predictions ventured apply to the region as a whole. It will also be realised that in conducting the exploration we will bear in mind the determinants to whose operation we devoted the last chapter, although some will be accorded more emphasis than others.

The evaluation of the outlook for development will be made in very general terms, mainly because detail and precision can thus be avoided. The avoidance is deliberate, given the nature of the exercise. Prediction carries with it heavy risk under the best of circumstances; in the present context it is almost reckless, considering the number of countries and of variables involved, the speed with which some of the economic and other parameters change, the interplay of international factors that have a profound impact on the life of the region, and the tentativeness of many of the conclusions and judgements made with respect to the post-war period which constitutes the launching pad or base for the assessment of the future. Finally, in order to bring all our concluding observations and predictions into relief, and to avoid confusion through diffusion, we will be as brief as possible.

The assessment starts with Iraq, and will move westward as the country chapter arrangement had done before. It will also end with the Arab region as a whole, in an attempt to make some predictions relating to Arab economic co-operation and Arab efforts to achieve complementarity and conduct significant economic endeavour jointly. Oil will occupy a significant place in the context of this regional approach.

Iraq's prospects seem to be very good, judging by its physical resources, capital availability, recent performance, and the commitment of its leadership to development. Yet the country has to attend to a number of shortcomings and weaknesses if it is to make good the *prima facie* promise. Foremost among these in the political sphere is the achievement of a greater measure of national unity and political stability, popular participation, activation of the civil service, and adjustment of the socio-economic system in a manner which permits a more productive balance between the public and the private sector and allows greater scope for motivation. Action with respect to the more important economic and socio-cultural factors is also called for, but it would seem less critical than in the political and administrative sphere. Thus, the land, water and oil resources are being managed quite efficiently, although the agrarian reform measures have only in the last few years begun to become conducive to greater production and to the first steps of the rejuvenation of the countryside. Education and training are being attended to energetically, and serious concern is shown for the development of manpower. One significant aspect of manpower, namely entrepreneurship, which is in short supply, can be promoted if the allocation of emphasis between the private and the public sector is readjusted and corrected in a manner that permits greater motivation and provides scope for entrepreneurial drive. Finally, industrialisation is gaining momentum: more adequate resources are directed to it, better training is attempted to supply it with the manpower it needs, pre-investment and feasibility studies are improving in quality, and the formulation of policy and of the system of priorities draws less complaint now than it did some years ago.

It was observed in the country chapter for Iraq that the political 'management' of the economy was the most retarding factor in many of the post-war years. This management has improved considerably. Yet, in our view, there is need for more substantial improvement. Such improvement has to take three directions. The first is greater delegation of authority in the whole pyramid of power: at the higher rungs and in the public administration alike. The second is greater professionalisation of the civil service, a condition which implies heavier emphasis on competence than on party loyalty. The last is greater accountability of civil servants and decision-makers to the public, a condition which can only be satisfied if there is a wider and truer measure of political participation and freer expression of opinion. We venture to say that if these conditions are satisfied, the other economic and social factors will look after themselves, so to speak. Yet on balance, we can conclude that with Algeria, Iraq constitutes the brightest spot in the outlook for development which is being forecast here.

Kuwait presents a contrast in more than one way. It is much poorer in natural resources, except for hydrocarbons, and this discrepancy is likely to continue to handicap the country. The small size of the population, the generally low level of motivation manifested, and the generous welfare benefits are likely, in combination, to keep the developmental effort of Kuwaiti manpower depressed. On the other hand, the political management of the economy, which showed intelligence and continuity in the past two decades is likely to continue. The scope for industrialisation remains small and shows little promise of considerable expansion. The government's management of its financial reserves is excellent, but this can provide only little compensation for the shortage of real resources, and little solace for those Kuwaitis who are concerned about the speed with which they are turning into a *rentier* society. The abundance of financial resources has led in the past several years to some loose budgeting and spending, and threatens to do so to a further extent in the years to come, as the forces leading to this phenomenon — vested interests, excessive unchecked dependence on government, permissiveness in pricing — are gaining momentum in what looks like an irreversible course.

Given the constraints of manpower, natural resources and size, the outlook for development in Kuwait lies, or should lie, mainly outside its national frontiers. Like other capital-surplus Arab countries with a small population, the high *per capita* purchasing power is no sufficient substitute for the deficiencies and constraints from which the economy suffers. Nor can the scope for development essentially lie in holding massive bank deposits or substantial stocks and bonds in the industrial world, if the society is not to live mainly on 'unearned income'. Part of the answer to this burden of fortune is for Kuwait to invest heavily in the Arab economies and to be directly involved, and participate, in the production processes towards which capital is thus directed. The other part is to design and pursue policies at home aimed at reorienting the Kuwaiti work-force so that it may show greater sensitivity to industrial and other productive prospects inside the country at the level of entrepreneurs, and greater sensitivity to financial motivation reflected in training for, and taking, many of the professional and vocational jobs now filled by expatriates, at the level of labour. Only through a judicious mixture of sound investment and work in the country; investment and direct involvement in the many opportunities offered by the Arab world, whether in bilateral or joint projects; and a modest investment (financial and real) in the industrial countries, can Kuwait compensate for the handicaps its small economy faces.

The country has an intelligent top leadership, and can rightly expect this leadership to provide continuity. Yet its commercial community is very strong and rather excessively self-centred. One danger in the years ahead lies in the joining of forces between this community and certain elements in the political leadership with a view to maximising personal vested interests, in a manner that can only accidentally serve the public interest. Given the fact that petroleum is a wasting resource, and the speed with which public expenditure is rising, the country's main hope lies in the formulation of sound economic policies by a wise leadership focusing on large-scale investment in the Arab and other Third World countries, and forestalling while it can too solid an alliance between individual or group vested interests and some loci of power — an alliance that overlooks the whole country's long-term interest while focusing on short-term particularist interest. As of now, the outlook can be said to be cautiously hopeful that sound economics and national interest would prevail in the years to come.

Probably nowhere else as in Saudi Arabia does the future seem to promise quick material transformation along with a lagging social transformation, with as much waste of resources in the process. The immense hydrocarbon resources are depleted fast in absolute terms, though in relative terms where production is expressed as a proportion of reserves the depletion seems to be quite slow. The economy, and more so the society, is unable to absorb all the financial resources deriving from the production and export of oil.

Saudi Arabia will have to widen the major bottlenecks in the several years to come, if it is to make sound economic use of its financial resources, and not see them flow out in large volume to settle in Western banks and stock markets, only to dwindle in real value at a fast rate. These bottlenecks are essentially skilled and educated manpower, motivation at the level of labour, large-scale acceptance of technological change, rejuvenation of the countryside, the building of institutions in the economic and political spheres capable of coping with the demands of an economy that is set on a course of fast development, and greater participation by the population (or at least that component of the population whose education and experience permit it to contribute to the process of policy-making and implementation via participation).

Judging by the experience of the kingdom over the past decade and a half of more determined development work, and by the world of ideas and the system of priorities that move the economy and society, the outlook seems to suggest contradictory pulls for many years to come. These pulls may not be apparent on the surface, but this does not make them any less real. Thus, there is likely to be an immense drive for investment in imported machinery; in the building of roads, ports, airports and telecommunications; in the expansion and improvement of public utilities and services; and in the capital of various financial institutions. This investment will continue to outdistance the capability of Saudi manpower – both in numbers and in education and skills – and will necessitate the 'importation' of hundreds of thousands of foreign labourers. If these are non-Arab, so chosen in order to minimise communication between them and the population, then the demonstration and technological transfer benefits will be minimal. Were they to be Arab, the 'danger' of the more socially open ideas they would certainly introduce would be maximal.

The socio-cultural question apart, purely in economic and technical terms, the population will be unable to absorb the huge investments, the techniques, the processes, and generally all the 'newness' involved in as short a span of time as that which is planned and expected. The speed will also carry with it the continued waste of resources, and the permissiveness in pricing and contracting with foreign firms, that have been marked over the past few years. Given the socio-economic system prevailing, private fortunes will be accumulated at a very high rate and in staggering magnitudes. Yet considerations of social justice cannot be kept outside the picture, even within the double context of a system of private enterprise and an insulated society.

The pace of social transformation stands in contrast with that of economic transformation. Considerable as the effort exerted to spread education is, it still comprises a rather small part of the total population of school age. The outlook here is for substantial numerical improvement in the years to come. But the content and methodology of education are not likely to be put in serious questioning, and they will probably continue to constitute a slowing factor, being heavily tradition-bound and extremely cautious with respect to the world of ideas and interaction with outside cultural forces. In society at large, the encouragement of the acceptance of new techniques and gadgetry will probably remain insufficiently matched by encouragement to accept new social ideas. The implications for development of economic exposure coupled with social insulation are imbalance-creating and retarding. Furthermore, the question can legitimately be posed whether the free or subsidised services offered, and the high rates of growth achieved, can long provide satisfaction to a population which will increasingly realise how much below average national income that of most of its individuals is, and what staggering fortunes are amassed by the relatively few. The outlook for development cannot be assessed in isolation from such questions.

While Saudi Arabia is likely for the foreseeable future to remain a capital-exporting country, Jordan is likely to remain a net importer of capital. Yet apart from this difference, or perhaps because of it, Jordan's leadership promises to continue to combine its commitment to development with the capability to formulate relatively sound strategies and policies.

That Jordan is a capital importer is only partly attributable to the scarcity of its natural resources. This scarcity, though real in the absolute sense (except for phosphates), has become more oppressing as a result first of the influx of a large Palestinian refugee population in 1948 (and again in 1967), and then of the loss of the West Bank, or the Palestinian part of the kingdom, during the 1967 Arab-Israeli war. Yet given the meagreness of resources, the heavy demographic pressure, and the continued considerable dependence on foreign aid, it remains true that Jordan has managed the foreign aid rather efficiently and shows every sign of continuing to do so. (That a large part of the aid is diverted to the military establishment qualifies the judgement; nevertheless efficiency cannot be assessed in isolation from the country's view of security and its imperatives.)

The crucial questions for the Jordanian economy for the many years to come — abstracting from a radical change in the region's political situation — will remain what they had been for many years. These are: how to absorb the large mass of the unemployed (and underemployed) into gainful employment; and how so to develop the economy as to considerably reduce (or preferably altogether abolish) the excessive dependence on foreign aid. Our examination of the determinants in operation on the whole accorded Jordan a satisfactory score on most counts. Thus its education and training policies are adequate. Motivation and entrepreneurship are not in seriously short supply. The degree of acceptance of technological change is not unsatisfactory. And the economic system is not inhibiting but on balance promotive to development. These favourable factors promise to continue in the foreseeable future. Yet their conjuncture will remain insufficient to remove (or substantially reduce) unemployment and dependence on foreign aid.

The achievement of these desiderata, along with those of a satisfactory economic performance and high rate of growth, can only come about if heavy investment is undertaken for many more years, and a structural shift takes place permitting the emergence of many export-oriented, labour-intensive industries and agricultural crops. Furthermore, the supportive policies and factors have to remain as favourable as they have been, or to become even more so. However, as far as massive investment is concerned, this can only be effected if the country resorts yet more to intensified foreign aid. The outlook for development therefore revolves essentially around the country's capability to attract massive foreign aid for many years, in order ultimately to achieve virtual independence from such aid. In conclusion, our estimate is that such independence will not be totally achieved in the next decade; nevertheless, development will proceed satisfactorily, with a commendable drop in the size of unemployment. The structural shift to which we alluded will not be possible on a scale that can permit the achievement of the desiderata indicated, though these will be appreciably approached.

If Jordan is a country of near chronic imbalance (between the domestic and the external sectors), Syria is one of nearly continuous and inherent balance. It stands somewhere in the middle between those countries with meagre natural resources and poorly educated and trained manpower, and those with very rich resources and a relatively substantial reservoir of qualified manpower.

The basic features of the economy are likely not only to continue to be development-promoting, in the sense of remaining favourable and conducive to development, but to become more so. In other words, the exploitation of the natural resources (land, water, petroleum, phosphates), the development of the rural sector, and the industrialisation process are likely to proceed further and more efficiently. This is based on the expectation that the leadership will continue to be strongly committed to development and capable of translating this commitment into sound economic policies and measures, inside an economic system which is acquiring greater balance between its public and private sectors, after being rather rigid inside a doctrinaire strait-jacket.

The bright outlook forecast here is also predicated on the continued expansion of education and training, fast technological transformation, the provision of greater scope for private entrepreneurship and the loosening of bureaucratic constraints on public entrepreneurship, the improvement of conditions in the countryside, and capital availability. The last factor calls for special explanation. Thus Syria, normally, and given its oil exports of recent years, could find the bulk of its investment requirements domestically. However, with the military budget being as large as it is and calling for substantial external payments of hard-earned foreign exchange, the country will have to depend on a large volume of foreign aid to close the gap in its external sector. This gap is not inherent but largely incidental. It is very likely that the country's needs in foreign capital for a number of years to come (assuming the problem of Palestine to continue unsolved for the duration) will be forthcoming, essentially from other Arab countries.

Development policies and the execution of related programmes and projects, while not ideal today, are on the whole satisfactory, and promise to improve. Taking the whole situation into account, therefore, the outlook for Syria's development is good. Furthermore, this estimate is not restricted to the purely economic aspect of development, but to its social aspect as well. Syria is one of those few countries where the social content of development is not neglected. In brief, by and large, the various factors making for future development are favourable, not brilliantly so but quite satisfactorily. Likewise, the performance expected, though not outstanding, is good.

As indicated earlier in the context of the examination of the recent economic history of Lebanon, and of the operation of the determinants of development in it, this country is atypical and differs in many respects from the remaining Arab countries. The assessment of the prospects of future development are shaped and coloured by the special factors in operation in this country's case.

These prospects depend heavily on the manner in which the economic system will allow order and some regulatory and corrective forces to operate while retaining its main distinguishing features of liberalism, freedom of enterprise, and scope for the highly motivated entrepreneurs and manpower in general. They also depend on the manner in which the establishment will forestall the basic and large-scale contradiction between the relatively few who have power and affluence and the relatively many who believe themselves to be underprivileged on both scores. That the latter are better off than their counterparts in virtually all other Arab countries, and that they have a greater scope for economic and social mobility, does not make the contradiction any less explosive or more palatable. Their reference group is their own much more privileged neighbours, not their distant less privileged counterparts in other countries.

The economic and social determinants are generally favourable to the process of development. Were this process to depend solely on them, and were development to be mainly understood in its economic context, the prospects would be distinctly cheerful. However, the political cluster of factors is emphatically less favourable. The commitment to development by the leadership is, and threatens to remain, weak and oscillating. The institutions and forces that channel, or give expression to, this political cluster are so designed or so constituted as to be self-perpetuating. The alliance between political and economic interests in the hands of the few provides these with enormous power which it would not be possible to challenge in the normal course of events. Hence the explosiveness of the situation and the serious qualification necessary to the outlook for development. This outlook, which is distinctly good on almost every other count, is fraught with danger on the socio-political count.

Yet this rather critical and grim evaluation must not be left unqualified. The resilience of the Lebanese and their ability to adjust when the odds turn against their course of action promises redress and correction in the future. It is true that those seeking redress are not those who can administer it. But our qualifying note of optimism derives from the strong expectation that the tight circle of monopolised power will have to break somewhere; once there is a breakthrough, correction becomes possible.

Egypt presents a sad array of sharp contrasts: a large population with an impressive reservoir of manpower comprising many who are educated and trained by regional standards, with relatively meagre resources, notwithstanding the Nile, petroleum and iron ore. As the foremost among the Arab countries and their leader, Egypt suffers from economic deficiencies (both in liquid finance and in capital assets in the public utilities and means of transport and communication) that force it to seek aid from its smaller sisters. Its political position places on it responsibilities which its means cannot support. The fast growth of its population and the rise of consumption expectations are far from matched by the national product and the rate of its growth.

All this constitutes a characterisation of the present. Yet to evaluate the prospects of the future one has to take the recent past and the present into account. The basic factors can be seen to pull in different directions, and to continue to do so for many years to come. This is expected even under a more purposeful and less ambivalent political-economic leadership. Thus, the fast expansion in education and training will persist in contributing its rather large share to unemployment and underemployment, both of which are substantial. The liberalisation of the economy and the opening up of more opportunities for private entrepreneurship are declared or practised in the teeth of opposition and resistance by a generation brought up on the notions of socialism and egalitarianism under Nasser. The spread of technology in many sectors in the urban economy will continue to occur against a background of a massive peasantry which is as traditional in its outlook as in its tools, and which does not have the disposable income even for a decent basic level of living, let alone modernising its tools of production. The country will probably continue to enjoy political stability and a large measure of national unity, but less genuine political participation. The agrarian reform has been drained of any further substantial promise, with agriculture already at a high plateau of productivity; yet the peasantry is only slightly less miserable than it had been a generation ago, and expects nothing better than a marginal improvement in conditions in the several years to come. The industrialisation process has lost its momentum; yet there are few signs that the years to come will provide the badly needed respite during which the economy will absorb the many industries that have been installed, and the industry will be cured of its many ills and deficiencies. The oil reserves are a very stingy ally; they yield little for a great deal of effort.

That still leaves out of consideration capital availability. The account here is confusing, probably because it is confused. The student of the economy is at a loss in attempting to assess the volume of foreign aid, in recent years, or further back. The attempt to predict future prospects is that much more difficult to undertake. But even if the declared grants and loans proved all to have been received, and an even somewhat larger volume were to be expected for several years, the Egyptian economy in its present damaged shape — tired, dilapidated, considerably purposeless, very hungry for a wide array of capital goods and public services — will only be able to show moderate signs of health. An important political consideration attaches to the inflow of foreign aid, Arab and American alike. This is that the economy must be further liberalised and become more 'open', a polite way of saying it must shed any remaining Nasserist-socialist garb. This will probably not be unpalatable to the *dirigeants,* but it can stir considerable unrest and discontentment. In the final analysis, the prospects of development in the years to come will probably depend on the clarity of direction given to the country, the steadfastness of purpose that the leadership will be able to command, and the achievement of mutual accommodation and harmony between conflicting interests and schools of thought. As of now, it would seem that the conjuncture of these three factors has a slim chance of materialising. Consequently the prospects do not seem to be large. In no other case does the writer hope as much that his judgement be proven wrong.

The outlook for development in Sudan depends heavily on massive foreign aid, like that of Egypt, and equally on an appropriate political alignment. But the other factors and conditions differ widely. Thus Sudan suffers from a high frequency of political unrest, the sparseness of population in a vast country which has immense land and water resources, the serious modesty of the reservoir of educated and trained manpower, the narrow spread of technological advance and its acceptance, the very small industrial base, the very inadequate means of transport and storage, and the great disparity between potential and actual achievement in agriculture and livestock-raising. The country has to be brought forward from a state of near primitiveness in many respects to one of satisfactory performance, with short capital and skills, with institutions making their first shy steps, political instability, and a low and narrow economic base; what it can claim to its credit is essentially its soil and water.

It is no wonder that the outlook is not sanguine. Yet this statement has to be explained and qualified. What is really meant is that the prospects are basically excellent, but that the time horizon required for materialisation is very far, and the supporting factors and conditions are very hard to find and meet. For the several years to come, it would be difficult to have a legitimate expectation of much more than marginal improvement. The outlook for substantial development therefore remains a matter involving a much longer run than for most other Arab countries.

The time dimension could however be reduced, were the country to enjoy a long spell of political stability, national unity, and a measure of political participation to which it seems to attach a premium. The socio-cultural constraints would no doubt act as a strong retarding factor, but the promotive political factors would in the event help to loosen the constraints and provide greater scope for motivation, education and other socio-cultural factors. In our estimate, the prospects of such redress coming from the direction of political factors are slim, although the commitment of the leadership to development is a strong positive factor. Good intentions are no substitute for concrete action.

Libya, though a large oil producer with a small population like Kuwait, has a broader economic base, more favourable land resources amenable to agricultural production, and a landscape and coastline capable of providing the requisites for a flourishing tourist industry, were the other facilities and conditions to be made available and satisfied.

However, an assessment of the prospects for development has to take into account several other factors. Two of these are in abundance and serve to favour marked development. These are the presence of large reserves of oil which can be put into valuable commercial and industrial use, and abundance of investment capital. The commitment of the political leadership promises to remain high and sincere, and the translation of this commitment into appropriate policies and measures promises to continue. Yet orientation towards development, the flow of related legislation and policies, and sensible planning are not sufficient in themselves, though of primary importance. There is need for continuity of policy, concentration on the drive for development, voluntary, creative political stability, orderly political life with minimum oscillation, an acceptable degree of popular participation, and a motivated and secure civil service. These factors all fall in the political field. Our estimate is that it will take several years for the maturing and seasoning processes of time to have their beneficial impact on a young leadership. It is also our estimate that the country is heading in the right direction with respect to the factors enumerated, but slowly.

Other factors in the socio-economic field have also to be made operative. Foremost among these are the broadening of training and the inculcation of high motivation in the work-force; the expansion of entrepreneurial resources and the provision of scope for their drive within a system that is restrictive and inhibiting to a certain and not inconsiderable extent; the attraction of farmers back to the land in cases of emigration to the cities, and the promotion of agricultural activity in general; the steady and rational industrialisation of the country; and the development of tourism.

The outlook in all these areas of action is mixed, but generally favourable. Education and training are proceeding fast; it is the question of motivation that bedevils the government's efforts. The likelihood is that the movement of large numbers of the country's youth towards vocational training will remain rather slow, and that for years to come there will still be a marked preference for government jobs or urban employment in shops and companies over work in carpentry, soldering or plumbing. Again, the motivation of potential entrepreneurs will be activated and satisfied only slowly and partially, as the outlook is that the government sector will remain predominant and will provide only a small scope for entrepreneurial ambitions in the private sector. Agriculture is already the recipient of significant funds and attention, and promises to continue to be so. On the other hand, tourism cannot flourish until the whole social atmosphere becomes more relaxed, and certain amenities and facilities which the tourist insists on having are made available.

Taking all these items in the double-entry account into consideration, it would seem that the prospects of broad-based development are moderate; that extremely heavy dependence on the oil sector will continue; that the appropriate political climate and manpower training and motivation will remain the main bottlenecks; and that the government will direct a large part of its financial reserves towards investment in the Arab world only to an extremely limited extent. On the other hand, the social content of development receives and will continue to receive the attention it merits. To conclude: the hope for faster development lies essentially in the hands of the leadership and its readiness and ability to satisfy those internal conditions of stability and participation to which we alluded earlier, and its readiness to treat the Arab world as its strategic economic depth for the investment of surplus resources. Our prediction is that these conditions will be satisfied only slowly.

Tunisia, Libya's western neighbour, provides a sharp contrast. Indeed, the contrast is so much a case of dovetailing that the two economies seem to have a large degree of complementarity, if only co-operation between neighbour states were to follow the dictates of logic and rationality.

As our earlier discussion of Tunisia has revealed, the country enjoys considerable stability by regional standards, and has enjoyed political continuity that is remarkable by any standard. Its leadership has maturity and is generally not impulsive in its decisions. The social climate, like the amenities and facilities, is inviting to holidaying and tourism. Motivation is high, and the opportunities for entrepreneurial talent and drive are large and open. Education and training are moving ahead satisfactorily. Agricultural and industrial development is proceeding as fast as the resources permit, the constraint being mainly economic. But against these factors, investment capital is short, and phosphate resources, though impressive, are far from compensating for the modesty of oil reserves.

This concentrated account, while ending on a note of reserve and some gloom, leads us to justified optimism for the future. It seems highly probable that the economy will overcome the problem of capital shortage through the receipt of foreign aid, mainly from Arab countries. This aid will probably be used judiciously and effectively, and bring about satisfactory growth in an economy whose record in this respect has been commendable. However, it would take some time before Tunisia's growth could become self-sustaining, unless oil exports were to be increased in volume at the current remunerative real prices, and unless phosphates maintained their present level of production, exports and prices. In this favourable eventuality, growth could become self-sustaining (that is, self-financing) in the medium rather than the long term.

One dark cloud hovers over this generally cheerful prediction, and that is the possible fall of the country into serious political unrest and confusion after the disappearance of the remarkable President Bourguiba from the scene. The danger of unrest and the loss of political stability and orderliness is real. Yet, if we are to venture a prediction, it is that the nation would soon settle back to stability and orderliness, even if it was to be initially overtaken by a sense of loss of direction.

The country chapter on Algeria in Volume I, and again the references to this country during the examination of the determinants in operation in the last chapter, have generally emphasised the country's determined and rewarding drive for development over the decade 1965-75, and the great promise of the future. Indeed, there is very little to add in the present context. Though handicapped in several respects, Algeria has picked up the challenge with great determination and skill and succeeded, in a very short period of time and against formidable odds, to turn this challenge into an opportunity, and to move from potential into materialisation. These generalisations are as true of the oil sector as of industry, agrarian reform, or transport and communication, and as true of manpower, education and training, as of technological transformation and political commitment to development. In all these respects, it seems legitimate to expect the country to achieve remarkable advances in the years to come.

Yet the bright picture depicted and projected is not free of blemish. Some qualifications are called for. Foremost among these is the concern that the greater concentration of real power may turn the beginnings of popular participation into an arid hope, and that the country might be run with a certain degree of dourness while it deserves some relaxation after its hard years of war and economic sacrifices. Another qualification relates to the economic system. This system is essentially *étatiste,* with most productive assets (with the notable exception of land and private housing) in public hands. There is real danger that in the context of a public sector of such dimensions any nascent or potential private entre-preneurship might be stifled, without it necessarily being channelled towards the public sector. Next, there is the growing bureaucratisation. Although professionalisation of the public administration is proceeding fast, there is a suspicion that bureaucratisation is proceeding faster. As revolutionary zeal recedes, the heavy hand of 'establishmentarianism' presses increasingly to slow work down, intensify formalism, and create new particularist loyalties. Finally, there is the burden of massive unemployment which the country has failed to shake off to any noticeable extent.

However, this assessment must be closed on a note of marked optimism. The prospects of Algeria seem to us to be very bright — indeed the brightest in the Arab world if we are to consider not merely economic development, but likewise the development of education and technology, the intensified concrete concern for the masses, genuine self-reliance, and the drive towards self-sustained growth in the full sense of the term. The country closest to Algeria in the race for comprehensive development is Iraq, as already indicated.

Morocco is the last of the twelve countries to be considered. Judged on the basis of its economic endowments, the economic infrastructure, the ability to obtain capital aid to close the gap from which it chronically suffers, and the rate of growth achieved over part of the post-independence period, the outlook for the future seems promising. Yet this would be an over-simplification.

The assessment of the prospects is complicated by the conflict between a number of the factors in operation. Thus, some of the favourable economic factors are counter-weighed by some unfavourable socio-cultural factors, like poor motivation, a degree of tribalism, and dualism in the society and economy. But more significantly, the commitment by the leadership to development, avowed and convincing on the whole, is counteracted and rendered less meaningful by the inordinately large slice of the rewards and benefits of development that goes to a rather small alliance of privileged élites. The relative freedom of speech, the press and the trade unions, which is in itself a promotive factor to the extent that it provides an outlet for mass demands, is deflated by the high concentration of real power and decision-making in very few hands. Popular participation, and the opportunity to espouse progressive ideas, which are given some scope through elections and the formation of parties and of trade unions, are counteracted by a powerful leadership which is intent on asserting its own will in the light of its own ideas and convictions.

Questions like the very large volume of unemployment and the shortage of investment capital apart, the country suffers from a noticeable degree of indifference, because of the contradictions just described. This makes the outlook for development less bright than it could be, were the causes of the indifference to be removed. Apathy is not conducive to massive mobilisation behind the drive for development, particularly where the more articulate segments of the population are concerned.

The prospects for development therefore depend heavily on the achievement of a truer measure of voluntary, creative stability, removal of the contradictions enumerated, greater and more effective concern with the interests and the needs of the masses in the content of development, and the achievement of widespread support and mobilisation for the development effort. Thus the outlook revolves essentially on the resolution of certain political problems. If these are satisfactorily resolved, then the country's endowments (including its rich reserves of phosphates, and its marked touristic appeal) coupled with its proven ability to obtain capital aid from Arab and non-Arab sources alike, and with the then released capabilities of its labour unions, students, and intellectuals, promise to permit a commendable developmental performance. Alternatively, the situation may continue to be marked by alienation and disaffection, and the current efforts to bring about development will only succeed in sustaining a rate of growth whose level, though satisfactory in itself, is not very meaningful for the bulk of the population. A satisfactory rate of growth is no substitute for comprehensive development that is mass-supported and mass-oriented.

Only in a restricted sense is the development of the Arab region, actual or potential, the sum total of that of the individual countries which constitute it. The narrowness of such a view lies in its oversight of the dynamics of co-operation and complementarity. The added benefit and impact arising from joint, regional action arises from the gains it transmits back to the individual countries in various forms, such as increased trade, reduced costs, external economies, or better distribution of human and material resources. These gains can have a multiplier or accelerator effect, as the case may be, on the individual countries, or yet optimise the distribution of resources across national frontiers. In addition, joint action makes possible the launching of totally new industries or activities, of a complexity, size or capital which no one country alone would be capable or desirous of coping with. This broadens the range of goods and services produced in the region.

Most of the bigger undertakings launched in recent years are of this latter type, including the companies established by the Organization of Arab Petroleum Exporting Countries, the large programme designed by the Arab Fund for Economic and Social Development for the integrated development of agriculture in Sudan, the programme for the identification and preparation of regional projects organised by the Arab Fund jointly with the UNDP, or indeed the Arab Fund itself. A variant of this form of co-operation is the body of institutions set up under the wing of the League of Arab States for the co-ordination and general promotion of the metallurgical, engineering, and a few other major industries. The Industrial Development Center of the Arab States, IDCAS, the Arab Food and Agriculture Organization, AFAO, the Arab Labour Organization, ALO, and the several like organisations which were listed in Chapter 14 all fall in the same general category. They enjoy a large measure of autonomy, although this is being subjected to attempts at curtailment by the Secretariat of the League.

The forms and modalities of co-operation and complementarity experienced so far do not exhaust the possibilities, either in type or number. In recapitulating the nature of their usefulness we are merely suggesting what may be expected in the years to come. We believe that Arab co-operation or complementarity will move along five avenues in the future. The first relates to trade and payments, and it involves the further facilitation of intraregional trade and the undertaking of more serious steps to smooth the balance of payment difficulties encountered by some of the countries. This avenue is the oldest and, as far as trade is concerned, the most familiar.

The second is mainly concerned with development financing and its mechanism is the national, one-country fund operating in several other countries. There are four such funds now in existence, and it is expected that they will expand their operations. Though important, their lending has not been crucial, that is, if their credits are related to total investments in the borrower countries. Yet looked at individually, some of the loans have been crucial for the sectors into which they have gone. The Kuwait Fund for Arab Economic Development will continue to be the leader in the field — in resources available, experience and mastery of the art.

Thirdly, there is the joint financing and launching of projects by individual countries getting together under some formula or arrangement to establish a project or programme in and for one country. The Potash Company of Jordan, the proposed programme for the integrated development of agriculture in Sudan, and SUMED, the Suez-Mediterranean Pipeline, are illustrations. We expect many more of this type of undertaking. But another form which is related constitutes the fourth avenue of action. This is the participation of several countries in a large undertaking which is to serve them all. The four companies set up by the oil Ministers under the aegis of the OAPEC are examples, as is the Arab Fund. This avenue of action is one in which a great deal of hope can rightly be invested, as it provides for the multiplicity both of beneficiaries and of participants in capital and operation.

The fifth and last avenue to be discussed is the setting up of bodies that do not have a share capital and whose function is not to invest directly, but to co-ordinate, regulate, supervise, or generally liaise between the various Arab countries for the promotion and/or better operation of certain industries or activities. Such is the Council for Arab Economic Unity itself, IDCAS, the AFAO, the ALO, OAPEC, the unions of the metallurgical and other industries — and the many other like organisations under the League of Arab States. All these institutions, though in widely varying degrees, exercise functions of great value without themselves having capital funds to dispose of. The worthiest service of some of them is the conception of ideas and their translation into concrete programmes and projects, some others are mainly of service in the conduct of studies, training, co-ordination, planning and design, and technical assistance. A few combine all these services.

Each of these avenues is of significance in its own right, but some provide scope for the dynamics of complementarity and co-operation much more than others. In the years to come, it is our estimate that the last four modalities of action, but particularly the last two, will come into much greater prominence and extend their area of service and usefulness. The national funds for development, though likely to become of paramount importance for the region's individual countries, will probably not become major agents in regional development via joint projects. They will instead extend their participation substantially in such projects as they are conceived and formed by other institutions. Before we close this paragraph, it is necessary to emphasise two points with respect to the many co-ordinating and technical institutions now loosely under the League of Arab States. The first is that the autonomy of these institutions has proved valuable for efficiency, and that it will be guarded jealously in the future. The second is that most of these institutions enjoy enlightened, devoted, and capable leadership. This leadership, in turn, is attracting associates of similar qualities. The process promises to continue and become stronger.

Oil occupies a central position in this whole scenario, although it has been mentioned only incidentally in the last several paragraphs relating to the outlook for regional development. Indeed, it will influence each of the approaches to Arab economic co-operation, mostly directly. Thus, even expanded trade will in no small part reflect the vastly increased revenue and financial resources, directly as far as the oil countries are concerned, and indirectly through the investment and spending undertaken by these in non-oil countries. The activity of the funds is all dependent on oil revenues. The formation of joint projects, whether of the third or fourth category described, will owe a great deal to greater capital availability, thanks to oil exports. Even in the case of capital participation by non-oil countries, the connection is evident; it should not be forgotten that much of the promotive drive usually comes from the oil countries. (It is to Kuwait's credit that it has usually taken the lead.) Needless to say, the joint projects formed under OAPEC owe their existence totally to oil. Finally, the fifth category of institutions, whose role does not derive from capital availability but from delegation of authority or competence by the individual member countries, has benefited from the increased significance of oil in the region. This is manifest in the possibility of obtaining larger operational budgets, the greater ease with which capable personnel can be recruited or capital can be obtained for such projects as are launched through the conception and initiative of these institutions.

This estimate should not be closed before the other, grim, side of the coin is presented. Thus, future economic co-operation is likely to remain slow, though definitely mounting and expanding in scale and reach. The slowness will be particularly noticeable in projects involving official capital participation. Furthermore, the present hesitation to develop inter-country resources (like rivers, hydroelectric potential, or mineral reserves in shared or disputed territory), or inter-country facilities (like roads, railroads, navigation lines, airlines, or telecommunications) will probably continue to mark the several years to come. Another disturbing prospect is the insufficiency of co-ordination in the establishment of similar industries and activities, or of ones which would be much more efficient if designed on the basis of regional complementarity and integration, whether vertical or horizontal. Oil refining, tankerage and petrochemicals are a major case in point. In these and other instances, the benefits of streamlining, co-ordination or integration will largely be forgone because of the indifferent attitude to co-operation in this field which still largely characterises official behaviour. Yet other areas of possible action which will be slow to materialise include the joint formulation and implementation of large-scale education, training and research policies of regional reach, or of policies involving the regulation and intensification of movement of manpower from surplus to deficit fields and countries. Even more in the distant future are such matters as the standardisation of regulations regarding travel, residence, work and ownership of assets by nationals of one country in another. Equally distant are standardised fiscal, monetary and other economic policies. Arab economic unity itself, which has been solemnly agreed to by several counries, is a dream for the unforeseeable future.

One broad generalisation deserves to be made here. This is that the region's countries have recently started to learn how to invest and work together, and only very recently have they started to have the means to do so. The learning process is proceeding and promises to lead to much fuller co-operation. But the co-operative steps will on the whole remain slow and hesitant. For the foreseeable future they will fall short of true economic integration or unity. But it is our view that there will be a transition in the near future from co-operation in its minimal forms, to complementarity. Oil will be both a catalytic agent and a major input in this transition.

Yet on another plane, the outlook for the region's utilisation of its oil is not very reassuring. On a number of occasions references have been made to the other, unsatisfactory side of the oil coin. This related to some of the policies and practices of the oil countries with respect to the volume of production and export of crude, and to their use of a part of the revenues, as the situation took shape in the aftermath of the Arab-Israeli war of October 1973. The present estimate looks ahead into the years to come.

There are reasons to believe that the rate of depletion will be insufficiently connected to the oil countries' own future needs, decades to come, for oil both as a fuel and as an industrial input. The sensitivity and response to the appeal of higher prices are too strong, if the long-term interests of the producers are to be primarily considered. While the producers have to take into account the interests and needs of the importers in determining the volume of production, it is legitimate for them to insist that the use of oil as a fuel ought to submit to firm discipline, so that waste of this most important resource may be brought down to a minimum. In our view, such discipline is not likely to be demanded, except marginally and feebly. The enchantment with the oil revenues is too strong for that.

These revenues are not an unmixed blessing. There are first the pertinent social considerations relating to over-dependence on the interest and dividends deriving from the portfolio and bank investments of those revenues not spent or invested in directly productive projects. In addition, there is in most of the oil-producing countries such a permissiveness towards maldistribution of wealth and income that the accumulation of private fortunes is proceeding at a rate that is downright shameful, in a mood of complete callousness towards poverty and social need. Furthermore, the maldistribution is coupled with many instances of grossly lavish and ostentatious consumption.

Finally, an inordinately large proportion of the unused revenues find their way not to needy development projects, but to bank accounts and stock markets in the industrial world, where they experience a serious loss in value, as inflation continues to erode the worth of money. And another proportion goes into arms, most of which will become scrap in a few years' time as the technology of weaponry advances fast, probably without ever being put to the use for which, professedly, they had been imported in the first place. (These statements take into account the whole region. But it is only fair to exclude Algeria, Iraq and Libya — in that order — from most of the harsh statements made here. The first two use their revenues fully, while all three avoid the maldistribution to which reference has been made.)

What of the future? The answer does not seem to be noticeably encouraging. There is every indication that the same process will continue, yet with more misspending and over-spending, even where the funds are used for development work. The longer the oil countries get used to their newly achieved level of revenue, the more attached to it they will become, and therefore the less ready to impose a strict self-discipline relating not only to the use of oil revenues, but also to the volume of production. And, although we expect investments in the Arab capital-needy countries to rise in absolute terms, the rise will probably be slow and modest for years to come.

We are ready now for some broad concluding observations relating to the outlook for development in the region. These go beyond the confines of the twelve countries formally included in the study, and beyond economic development, with its indicators and deter-minants. Yet they flow directly from the observations with which the last chapter was concluded.

The outlook for the region's real economic growth is bright, although the rates of growth expected in the next decade or so will probably vary widely, say between 5 and 10 per cent. Parallel with this growth, the rates of population increase are likely to reach a plateau and flatten, or even begin to drop slightly. Modernisation will spread, with its shining new gadgetry, its factories, aeroplanes, TV antennae and Wimpy snack bars alongside its technical institutes and liberal arts colleges. The statisticians and many of the economists will sit back in comfort, watching the mounting curves and rejoicing over the achievements registered. So will the politicians, except that they will also make flamboyant speeches, mostly of self-congratulation.

Yet the rejoicing will be only partially shared by most of the scores of Arab millions, along with those few grumpy economists who are reckless enough to insist on injecting a heavy dose of social concern into their economic criteria. The reserve of those who will share only partially in the acclaim is not a matter of temperament or confusion. It is rather the product of social concern coupled with strictly economic reasons.

Five reasons for the reserve deserve singling out. The first is that the rates of real econ-omic growth forecast, no matter how satisfactory and commendable, will be unable to conceal the high rates of unemployment and the much higher rates of underemployment that threaten to persist for many years to come. The improved conditions of most members of the labour supply, assuming this were to materialise concretely, would still be no solace for the millions of unemployed. The sufferers will become even more disenchanted and less easy to reassure, the better off their colleagues become.

The second reason is closely related. It is the tendency of schools, clinics, hospitals, housing schemes, social centres and basic amenities, like public transport, piped water and electricity, to become available much more slowly to the far parts of a country than to the capital and other cities and towns. The radiation or ripple effect has a tendency to consume itself within a short distance of the centre. Yet even when and where these facilities and services reach much further away from the large urban communities, they become poorer in quality, and less adequately manned, in the process. This is a feature which the statistics recording the expansion in facilities and manning often succeed in concealing, but which cannot but drastically qualify the quality of the development claimed. The feature derives from the fact that development is not yet adequately mass- and need-oriented, although professions to the contrary are loud and frequent.

The third reason for concern is the narrowness of the concept of 'self-sustained growth' in use. Most often it is taken to mean the ability of the economy to finance further growth from its domestic savings. But the concept ought to be enlarged to include the capability to innovate domestically and to develop education, science and technology (and the capital goods appropriate for domestic needs) from within. No growth can become truly self-sustained unless it is internally motivated, triggered and propelled — in addition to being internally financed.

In the fourth place, reserve is called for by the gap between the socio-economic democracy achieved — modest as it is — and the much more modest political democracy achieved. The curtailment of political democracy has usually been rationalised by the need first to establish socio-economic democracy, involving equalisation of status and opportunities, and higher and more secure incomes: that political democracy (whatever its form) cannot be genuine and genuinely lived, unless a foundation of socio-economic democracy has been laid. The sad truth is that political democracy, even in its more modest participatory forms, has been postponed in most countries, and even rationed in reduced dosage. The improvement felt by many in terms of social and economic conditions, even if marginal, has acted as a sedative. It has led to the acceptance of the postponement or even curtailment of participation, and created the soporific hope that political democracy would soon be allowed in large dosage. The intellectuals are most to blame for silence and a certain extent of self-deception in this connection. The fear of sanctions has muzzled protest and the pride of conviction for many.

Lastly, the drive for development, even if narrowly defined, will remain restricted unless it acquires a truly regional dimension alongside its one-country dimension. Arab economic co-operation and complementarity must be built into the concept, the strategies and the policies of national development, if this is to be optimised. Arab co-operation makes even better economics than politics.

The five causes for concern which justify the reserve with regard to the outlook for development in the Arab world in the several years to come flow from the broad notion of development adopted in this study. It must have become obvious that such a notion can be viewed as a form of socio-economic liberation for a society genuinely and deeply seeking development. Such liberation will essentially embrace four forces: that making for increased production which places at the disposal of society distinctly more goods and services of the type its masses truly need and want; that making for improved distribution which truly and effectively answers to the needs of the vast majority who qualify to being the legitimate beneficiaries of the country's economic performance, inasmuch as they are equally the main contributors to this performance; that making for improved economic, scientific and technological capability without which development will remain inordinately dependent on external help, and will fail to become self-sufficient in the full sense of the term; and that making for the increased dignity of the citizen and his ability to participate in all political and economic decisions relating to his work and life-style.

Finally, the process of comprehensive development will remain constrained unless the problem of Palestine and the Palestinians meets with a just and speedy solution. This consideration is of as great relevance to the development of the region as a whole as to that of the individual countries within it. So long as the problem remains unresolved, large resources will continue to be diverted to the military establishment everywhere in the region, but particularly so in the countries closest to Palestine. But what is more serious is the diversion of effort and the diffusion of focus involved. Whether the resources, the effort, and the focus are considered at the one-country or the regional level, they will lead more speedily and satisfactorily to comprehensive development only if the claim on them which Palestine makes ceases to be pressing. The exigencies of true development for society, socio-economic liberation for the citizen, and justice for the Palestinians thus converge on one focal point.

How can this point of convergence be reached? On many occasions in this study heavy emphasis has been placed, within the context of each country, on the political factor of commitment to development by the leadership in an atmosphere of creative stability, national purposefulness and popular participation. Likewise, emphasis has been placed, within the regional context, on the desire and the will of individual countries to co-operate, and on the conceptualisation of strategies and policies conducive to the fruition of this desire. Yet these assertions pose more questions than they answer.

A few such questions stand out with particular prominence: How can development orientation by an authoritarian government in the present context of Arab politics be reconciled with popular participation and a reasonable measure of true democracy? How can the Arab countries' exaggerated sense of national sovereignty be reconciled with true and meaningful co-operation and complementarity? What are the dynamics of change which, on the one hand, can permit and lead to genuine democracy, and, on the other hand, permit and lead to active inter-Arab co-operation? Finally, how can the vicious iron circle which now stifles hope be broken, in order to provide access to comprehensive and deep development, the individual's political and socio-economic dignity, and the region's fruitful co-operation?

These questions remain unanswered in this study, though fundamental and pressing. The answers ought to be sought elsewhere. Nevertheless, it must be pointed out here that some countries have avoided the issues and pretended that there were no questions to answer. Some others, recognising the issues and the questions, have sought a political short cut to the answers through military take-overs and authoritarian government. Neither approach has provided satisfactory answers. All that we can venture to suggest in these concluding remarks is that there is no short cut to the point of convergence. It has to be approached the long and hard way — that of popular participation, societal sacrifice, and struggle for human dignity. There will no doubt be resistance by many governments to true popular participation, which is the first step to take. But there is no alternative to the necessity of breaking the iron circle if the objectives are to be seriously sought.

Index

10°   40°   5° West of Greenwich 0° East of Greenwich 5°   20°   25

Middle East & North Africa

YUGOSLAVIA Sofia BULGA Skopje Plov

Barcelona Ajaccio CORSICA Rome ITALY Tiranë Thessal
Naples Bari GREECE

Valencia SARDINIA Tyrrhenian Ionian Sea Piraeus

C. St. Vincent PORTUGAL SPAIN Granada Cartagena Balearic Is. Cagliari Sea Palermo SICILY

Tangier Gibraltar (Br.) Ceuta (Sp.) Melilla (Sp.) Algiers Tizi Ouzou Constantine Annaba Bizerta Tunis Pantelleria (It.) MALTA

Mina Hassan Tani Rabat Fez Meknès Oran Mostaganem Médéa Setif Batna Sousse Sfax MEDITERRANEAN

Casablanca Middle Atlas High Plateaus Saharan Atlas Aurès Mts. Chott Djerid G. of Gabès Djerba I. Tripoli Homs Beida

Marrakesh High Atlas Anti-Atlas Béchar Touggourt Ghardaia Ouargla Misurata G. of Sidra Benghazi Jel Akhdar Tobruk

Sidi Ifni Hamada of Dra Beni Abbès Great Western Erg Great Eastern Erg Gadames WESTERN PROVINCE Mersa Brega EASTERN PROVINCE

MAURITANIA ALGERIA Tademait Hamada Tinrhert Hamada El Homra Sebha LIBYA Umm el Abid Zella Jalo Oasis Serir of Kalanshu

Ain Salah Ft. Flatters Soda Mts. Jofra Oasis Hon Marada Kufra El Jauf

Reganne Tanezrouf Tassili-n-Ajjer Djanet Gat SOUTHERN PROVINCE El Gatrun Murzuch Zuila Wau el Kebir Birel Harash Ed Dacar Oases Rebiana Libyan Desert

In Eker TAHAT 9,840 Tamanrasset Tibesti Serir

MALI Adrar of the Iforas Tassili Duan-Ahaggar SAHARA Hoggar NIGER Aozu Djado Tibesti EMI KOUSSI 11,201 10,709 10,335 Faya Mourdi Depression Ennedi CHAD DARFUR

Timbuctu L. Faguibine Niger L. Haogoundou TAMGAK MTS 8,900 Agadès Azbine or Air Tazilizlet Bodelé Depression Oum Hadjer Geneina El Fasher MARRA MTS 10,130

UPPER VOLTA Ouagadougou White Volta Niamey Sokoto Maradi Zinder L. Chad (Tchad) Abéché Batha Azoum Mogororo

GHANA Tamale Black Volta TOGO BENIN Kainji Res. Kano Kaduna Bauchi Maiduguri N'Djamena CENTRAL

ASHANZI Kumasi Akosombo Dam NIGERIA Jos Plateau Benue Gombe Sarh AFRICAN EMPIRE BAHR

Oyo Ibadan Abeokuta Makurdi Bangui

Lagos Porto Novo Enugu Calabar Buea CAMEROON N'Gaoundéré Ft. Crampel Bangui

Gulf of Guinea Bight of Bonny Macias Nguema (Eq. Guinea) Victoria Douala Yaoundé CONGO (P.R.) ZA

EQUATORIAL GUINEA Bight of Benin

0° East of Greenwich 5°   10°   15°   20°   25°

Conical Orthomorphic Projection
Origin 27½° N; Standard parallels 16° N. & 38° N.